"Nobody works harder at making the Internet
a better and safer place for kids than Parry Aftab."
—Robin Raskin, *Family PC*

"*The Parent's Guide to Protecting Your Children in Cyberspace* is
the quintessential roadmap for smart parents who want to supervise
their kids' outings on the information super highway."
—Barbara J. Feldman, Syndicated Columnist, *Surfing the Net with Kids*

"A great source for parents to get 'up to speed' on safe Internet use and on the
controversial issues surrounding the Internet today. Parry Aftab's sound,
balanced approach to children's online safety will give parents the knowledge to
establish their own rules and guidelines for their kids."
—Ernie Allen, President, National Center for Missing & Exploited Children

"Parents who aren't Internet-savvy have a friend in Parry Aftab.
Just as with her first book, Parry has once again deciphered—and
de-mystified—the cyberworld. What's great about this new tome
is its ability to both inform and *empower* adults without overwhelming
them. I highly recommend it to all. It's must reading for the
responsible parent with cyber-active kids."
—Len Pagano, President, Safe America Foundation

"As a new parent who's online a lot, I wonder what cyberspace
will be like when my kids start crawling through the Net. I think
about how they can benefit from the wonderful aspects of the Net, without
being threatened by the less friendly. It's comforting
that a sincere authority like Parry Aftab has brought her mind
and soul to bear on these issues. I think she's just in time."
—Joshua Blackman, Publisher, *The Internet Lawyer*

"Parry Aftab's new book should be given a 'Platinum Status' rating
for not only empowering parents with the tools and knowledge to
supervise their children's Internet activities (even for those who
have NEVER been online) but also because it is full of humor,
great advice, recommendations, and all in plain English!"
—Michael J. Madonna, President,
New Jersey State Policemen's Association

"If you want to know about children and the Internet, there's
only one person to ask . . . Parry Aftab. Parry understands what
parents need and want to know, and gives it to them in this entertaining
and easy-to-read guidebook. As a parent, I am grateful for this book!"
—Dr. Stoyan Ganev, President, United Nations General Assembly, 87th Session

The Parent's Guide to Protecting Your Children in Cyberspace

Parry Aftab

McGraw-Hill

New York San Francisco Washington, D.C. Auckland Bogotá
Caracas Lisbon London Madrid Mexico City Milan
Montreal New Delhi San Juan Singapore
Sydney Tokyo Toronto

McGraw-Hill

A Division of The McGraw·Hill Companies

1 2 3 4 5 6 7 8 9 0 AGM/AGM 9 0 9 8 7 6 5 4 3 2 1 0 9

ISBN 0-07-135752-1

The sponsoring editor for this book was Susan Barry,
and the production supervisor was Tina Cameron.
It was set in New Century Schoolbook and Optima.
Printed and bound by Quebecor / Martinsburg.

McGraw-Hill books are available at special quantity discounts to use as
premiums and sales promotions, or for use in corporate training programs.
For more information, please write to the Director of Special Sales, McGraw-
Hill, 11 West 19th Street, New York, NY 10011. Or contact your local
bookstore.

This publication is designed to provide accurate and authoritative information in regard to the subject matter covered. It is sold with the understanding that neither the author nor the publisher is engaged in rendering
legal, accounting, or other professional service. If legal advice or other expert
assistance is required, the services of a competent professional person should
be sought.
*From a Declaration of Principles jointly adopted by a Committee of the
American Bar Association and a Committee of Publishers.*

To my children, Michael and Taylor Caprio, who have
always surpassed my furthest hopes and dreams and continue
to astound me in their intelligence, caring, and creativity . . .
and who love and believe in me as much as I love and
believe in them. They are my greatest accomplishments!

To the memories of my father, Mansur T. Aftab,
my brother, Richard Aftab, and my grandfather,
Raymond H. Hathaway. I think about them every day,
and wish they were here to share this with me.

To all my Cyberangels and other caring volunteers who strive
every day to make sure no child is left behind in this wonderful
technological journey, and everyone can enjoy the Internet safely.

Contents

Acknowledgments   xv

Preface   xix

Chapter 1: Bringing You Up to Speed   1
A Snapshot of Children on the Internet   1
Clueless? You'll Feel Right at Home!   2
Isn't Parenting Hard Enough Already?   2
Repeat After Me: "I Am Still the Parent!"   3
Keeping It in Perspective   4
   How Serious Is the Problem?   4
Please Don't Blame the Internet   6
   The Internet Is an "Equal Opportunity Offender" 6
   Everything Has an Internet Connection These Days 7
A Road Map to This Book   7
What Parents Ask Me Most Often About Online Safety   10
What Does the Internet Have to Offer for Families and Kids?   14
   Current Events   14
   Sports Information, Scores, and Sporting Events 15
   Games   15
   Johnny Can Write (and Research!)   15
   Special Families . . . Special Kids   17
In a Nutshell—What Are the Risks?   18

Chapter 2: The Good, the Bad, and Being Cautious   19
Learning About the Flip Side   19
When We Take Off the Training Wheels   20
Understanding the Basics   20
Stumbling into the Dark Side   21
    Searching for Trouble   21
    Bait 'n Switch   22
    Spelling Counts!   24
    Masquerading as a Famous Site: That "Dot Com" Thing   25
When the Dark Side Comes to Them . . .   27
    Spam—It's Not Just Luncheon Meat Anymore   27
Stranger Danger: How Does This Work When You're
        Supposed to Talk to Strangers Online?   33
    Chatrooms   34
    E-mail   39
    ICQ and Other Instant Messaging Services   44
    Buddy Lists   47
    Pen Pal Programs   48
The World's Biggest Billboard   50
    Online Profiles—Advertising for Trouble   51
    Filling Out Forms Online—Giving Away
        Personal Information   52
    Kids' Personal Websites   53
    Hello, Information? I'd Like to Know What
        Information You Have About My Child   53
    The Wild Wild West: IRC, FTP, Usenet, and Newsgroups   55

Chapter 3: The Dark Side   59
Are We Being Cautious Parents . . . or Paranoid Wrecks?   59
    All Risks and Dangers Are Not Equal in Cyberspace   60
Information Doesn't Hurt Children—People Hurt Children   60
What Kinds of Risks Are We Talking About?   61
    Risks to Our Children   61
Stuff You Might Prefer Your Children Not See   63
    Sexually Explicit Content—Adult Pornography   63
    Hatred, Intolerance, and Bigotry   65
    Violence and Gore   67
    Misinformation and Hype   68
    Cyber Hoaxes, Rumors, and Urban Legends   70
The Riskier Stuff: When Kids Do Dangerous Things and Buy
        Illegal or Dangerous Products Online   72

Mom . . . How Do You Build a Bomb?   72
Drugs, Alcohol, Tobacco, Guns, and Poisons   75
Are We Raising Future Riverboat Gamblers in Cyberspace?   77
Flaming, Harassment, and Cyberstalking   78
Flaming   78
Harassment and Cyberstalking   79
Cyberpredators   80
The Big Three   81
Protecting Your Computer in Cyberspace: Hackers and Viruses   82
What's a Virus?   82
Risks Your Kids Pose to Others—Including You   83
"Because I Can"—When Kids Act Out Violent
   Fantasies Online   84
"Dear Jennifer, I am going to kill you."   85
When Kids Hack and Commit Computer Crimes   86
Sticks and Stones—Defaming Others Online   89
Hey! That's My Intellectual Property!   89
Risks to You from Your Kids and Their Friends   90
Pranks That Can Cost You Your Internet Account   91
When Kids Use Our Credit Cards to Buy Things Online
   Without Our Okay   92
Protecting Your Job: Don't Use Your Business
   Account for Family Computing   92

Chapter 4: And Now for the Really Serious Stuff   95
Protecting Our Kids' Privacy and Our Privacy   95
Looking Over Their Shoulders   95
The Internet and Online Data Collection Are Different   96
How Big a Problem Is This?   97
What Are They Collecting and How Are They Using It?   98
How Do They Collect Information?   99
Using Technology to Collection Information   100
Do They Need Everything They Collect, or Are
   They Just Being Pigs?   103
The FTC to the Rescue!   104
Whom Do You Trust?   105
Protecting Ourselves from Cyberscams and
   Unfair Marketing Online   106
Targeting Cybertots: Advertising to Children Online   106
How Is the Advertising Industry Policing Itself?   108
Spending Money—What Kids and Teens Do Best   109

Shopping Online   112
What You Need to Know About Online Auctions   114
People Hurting Children: Cyberstalkers and
    Cyberpredators—The Real Bad Guys in Cyberspace   117
"Leave My Kid Alone!"—Cyberstalking and Harassment   117
The Anatomy of a Cyberpredator: Protecting Your
    Children from Molesters in Cyberspace   121

Chapter 5: And Now for the Really Boring Stuff: The Law   135
Global Access Means Finding a Global Solution   135
    What's the UN Doing to Help?   137
It's Not Totally Lawless—It Just Feels That Way   137
    Our Founding Fathers, and the Law   138
    What Do You Know About Free Speech, Really?   138
    Child Pornography—It's Not Only Disgusting,
        It's Very Illegal!   139
    Laws That Protect Your Child from Sexual Predators
        in Cyberspace   140
    Cyberstalking Kids   141
    What About Sites That Advocate or Promote Sexual
        Abuse of Children?   142
Laws Against the Sale of Drugs, Alcohol, Guns, and Tobacco   142
My Legal Disclaimer   144
Cybercops: Who Enforces the Law in Cyberspace?   144
    How Do They Find and Track People Online?   146
    Where Do You Report Trouble and Cybercrimes?   147
How You Can Make a Difference   149
    Report What You Find   149
    Volunteer Your Time   150
Help Me! What to Do if the Unspeakable Happens   151
    What to Do if Your Child Is Missing and You Suspect a
        Cyberpredator Is Involved   151
    The Community Response   152

Chapter 6: Kids Online in Schools   155
Schools Online   155
    How Do Schools Use the Internet?   156
    Does the Internet Improve Educational Levels, or Is
        It Just Another Toy?   156
    How the Internet Can Help in Creating Innovative and
        Effective Projects for Teaching Troubled Kids   157

Cats in India   159
Internet Problem Issues for Schools   161
  Children's Pictures and Personal Information   161
  Children's Creative Works   163
  Plagiarism   163
  Off-School Websites   164
  Linking to Off-School Sites   165
  Death Threats/Bomb Threats   165
  Restricting Noncurriculum Speech   167
  Pen Pal Programs   167
  Resource Credibility: Teaching Our Children Critical
    Thinking and Media Literacy Skills   167
Safe Internet Use in Schools   170
  Getting Parents Up to Speed and on Board   170
How Can Parents Get Involved?   177
  The Best Parent Is an Informed Parent   177
  Build a Solid Team of Parents, Friends, Librarians,
    and Schools   178
  Team-Building Tips   179
Stay Tuned for the Following Editorial Message . . .   180

Chapter 7: Teach . . . Your Children Well   183
Who's Teaching Whom?   183
  Let Your Children Teach You: Learning to Listen   183
Educate Your Children About the Dangers in Cyberspace   184
  The Same Old Thing—in a New and Improved Package   185
Prepare Your Children for the Unexpected . . . and People Who
    May Not Have Their Best Interests at Heart   188
Meeting Online Friends in Real Life   189
Clues We Give Away—Shannon, Now Known as "Tiffany"   195
Using an Alias: Are We Teaching Our Children to Protect
    Themselves or to Lie?   200
Kids Will Be Kids: Teaching Them Accountability   200
  What Kids Tell Us About Pretending to Be Someone Else   201
  No One Can Find Me Online . . .   202
  Avoiding Witch Hunts   204
  Is Tattling Allowed?   205
Defensive Parenting: Avoiding Problems Before They Happen 207
  Forewarned Is Forearmed: The Parent's Creed   207
The Basic Rules—Quick and Simple   211
Get to Know Your Kids, and Create a Workable "Safe-

Surfing Contract" for Them   212
How Much Do You Really Know About Your Kids?   212
Points to Consider in Setting Your Own Rules and
    Drafting Your Own Safe-Surfing Contract   214
Formalizing the Rules   215
Netiquette: Teaching Your Children How to Behave
    Properly in Cyberspace   215
Origins of Netiquette   215
Ms. Parry's Rules for Correct Internet Behavior   216
Emoticons: Laughter in Cyberspace   218
Balance: When Do You Know If They've Had Enough?   218
When Is Your Child Old Enough to Use a Computer?   219

Chapter 8: Making and Implementing Your Choices   223
Finding a Fit That's Right for You and Your Kids   223
What Are Other Families Doing?   223
What Are the Choices?   226
Yes, Virginia . . . There Is a Good Side to the Internet!   227
Finding Kid-Friendly Content   228
Approved-Site Lists   230
Relying on Tried-and-True Brand Names   232
Special Safe-Harbor Sites   233
Special Online Services for Kids and Teens   235
One from Column A, Two from Column B   236
Using Technology to Help Implement and
    Enforce Your Choices   236
Filtering, Blocking, and Monitoring—Oh, My!!   241
How They Work   242
Server-Level Blocking   249
Parental Controls from Your Online Services   250
A Little About Some Special Products   251
The Fly on the Wall: Monitoring Software   254
The 800-Pound Gorillas: The Big Four
    Multifeatured Products   254
Choosing Your Comfort Level   259

**Chapter 9: And Now a Word from the Real Experts—
The Teens and Kids**   261
"The Rules Don't Apply to Me"   262
The People Behind the Survey   262
The *Seventeen Magazine* Survey   263

They Could Write This Book for Me . . .   269
   Alyssa's, Lauren's, and Maggie's Safety Tips
     (in their own [uncensored] words)   269
   Maggie's Advice   270
"Dear Mr. President"   273
The Teenangels   277
   From the Mouths of Teens (the Real Experts) . . .
     Teenangels' Tips for Parents, Teens, and Kids   279
In Conclusion   288

**Appendix 1: Baltimore County Public Schools
   Telecommunications Acceptable Use Policy for Students**   291

Appendix 2: Trevor Day School's Acceptable Use Policy   295

Appendix 3: The Safe-Surfing Contract   301

Appendix 4: AOL's Parental Controls   305

**Appendix 5: Directory of Certain ISPs, Online Services,
   and Products Mentioned in the Book**   307

Glossary   311

Index   317

Acknowledgments

I would like to thank Lanell Sauer for being my best friend all these years, and for taking my phone calls all hours of the day and night and believing in me and my harebrained schemes, and for teaching me about life, loyalty, and God.

I would like to thank my law partner and in-house editor, Nancy L. Savitt. Nancy is the "Savitt" in Aftab & Savitt, P.C., our cyberspace law firm. Tirelessly she would search for special sites and review laws I needed to check for the book. Painstakingly, she organized all the free speech and censorship material, only to have me shorten the section to leave most of it on the proverbial cutting room floor. Yet, when I asked for more help, she was there without a complaint. Most important, she kept the law firm running during my literal and figurative absence over the last few months. She filled in for me in court, handed me the research I needed for television appearances as I arrived at the set, and tried to placate our clients while I was involved with this project. She believes in me. Nancy is one of the best lawyers I have ever known and a dear friend ever since we met on our first day of law school. She was the only one I would trust with editing my book. I was amazed how wonderful I sounded once she cleaned up my writing. I remember calling her from Washington, D.C., where I had gone to testify for FTC hearings, having stayed up all night trying to get sections of the book to work, ready to give up. She sat here in my home for days trying to help make it work. She typed in changes while I made them, gently encouraging me. I owe her everything. I also owe her parents thanks and my love for all they have done for us, and for making me feel like I'm part of their family. They are the best parents in the world, and Nancy and her sister, Susan, are extraordinarily lucky!

I would like to thank my mother, The Honorable Shirley Hammond, and sister, KidDoc, Deanna Aftab Guy, for being so terrific and endorsing my book, and Deanna's husband, Dr. Jeff Guy, who got my modem connected seven years ago and got me started online.

I would like to thank Kelley Beatty, my deputy executive director of Cyberangels, for keeping things together while I wrote this book, and through all my traveling. She is a caring and wonderful woman who gives so much of her time to others. I also want to thank Laura, Jean, Trish, Shannon, Mike C., Janice, Cougar, Toby, and all the others who make Cyberangels the most incredible program on Earth . . . who devote time they don't have to make the Internet safer for others. Their devotion, endless energy, and extraordinary talent have created a truly special program. I am honored to lead this group; they have taught me so much more than I ever could have taught them.

I would like to thank Curtis Sliwa for his vision in creating Cyberangels in 1995, before anyone else had a sense of what could be done by caring volunteers online, and Mary Galda for adding some glamour to what we do.

I would like to thank my original Teenangels, Brittany, Kathy, Jennifer, Stephanie, and Susan; and also Alyssa, Lauren, and Maggie, my little angels in training, for writing the kids' safety tips and sharing their thoughts.

I would like to thank my researcher, Sagar S. Mungekar. Sagar was valedictorian of his high school class and is a stellar student at Cornell. He has been working with me for a few years, during every school break, helping us code our website and understand new technology. Sagar was my guide into the depths of the Internet where I had never ventured before in my first book. This time he made sure all our charts worked, and made phone call after phone call to help us gather much needed information. Although I know he'll find the cure for cancer someday, I wish I could keep him around a bit longer helping us.

I would like to thank the man I love. He knows who he is.

I would like to thank all the families and friends who helped me by sharing their stories with me, and all the friends I met online who helped me get through this, especially Robin Raskin, my editor Susan Barry, Art Wolinsky, Della Curtis, and Sherry Glover for their patience, guidance and help. (I think that a quote from *Wayne's World* is in order here. "I'm not worthy . . . I'm not worthy. . . .")

I would like to thank Audrey Smith, the designer and publisher of my first book, a longtime friend and confidante, without whose talents my first book, and, therefore, this book, would have never seen the light of day.

I would like to thank my friends in law enforcement, especially the FBI, U.S. Customs, the N.J. State Police, the Royal Canadian Mounted Police, Scotland Yard (Metropolitan Police), and Interpol, who put their lives on the line, every day, to keep our families safe.

I would also like to thank our law firm administrator, Chrissy (Patricia) Peters. She is also our mother-reviewer/reader in charge of making sure we cover the topic without boring our readers. (If you're bored, don't blame me . . . blame Chrissy.) After long hours of managing our firm, she would take home sections of the book to read through what I had written. Then she was faced with the thankless task of telling me what I should change. (After all, I still sign the paychecks.)

I would like to thank Eileen Scanlon, my friend and legal assistant, for keeping my life organized and on track during all of this, and for reading through all the survey responses to pick the ones that belonged in this book.

And to Fay, my webmaster and guide, my deepest thanks for her creativity and generosity.

I would like to thank all the people who by simple acts of encouragement and caring made a difference.

And I thank God, without whom none of this would matter.

Preface

I was pulled, kicking and screaming, into my role as protector of children online. There I was, minding my own business as a cyberspace lawyer, when I received my calling. In those days I was proud of the fact that I was an e-commerce lawyer, and didn't "do" kids work. Now that's all we do. When your destiny calls . . . you have to listen.

My involvement with online safety all started a few years ago, when CNN asked me to appear to discuss free speech online, the Communications Decency Act and filtering software. Although I could easily cover the legal topics (I had hosted AOL's Legal Discussion boards and formed Court TV Law Center's Legal Helpline), I knew nothing about filtering software. My children were older, and I was an Internet lawyer for businesses. I understood corporate security, not child protection. But, when CNN calls, you learn about whatever they want you to cover . . . fast!

Following the program (where I was horribly boring, but my hair looked great) parents and teachers called, faxed, e-mailed and wrote me asking how they can keep their children safe online. I explained that I didn't "do" kids. I was an e-commerce lawyer. But the flood of responses didn't stop, no matter how loudly I protested.

I called my sister, a pediatrician, who by definition only "did" kids. I asked her to point me to a book I could recommend to these parents that would teach them about online safety for their children. After searching, she told me that there wasn't one, and suggested I write my own. On May Day in Moscow, bored in my hotel room with a bowl of borsht and a new laptop, I began my first book—*A Parents' Guide to the*

Internet. I began visiting schools and helping parents with online safety issues. I was invited by Net Nanny and Microsoft to fly out to Seattle and teach a community online safety program for them. I even chatted with Mr. Toad for Disney, teaching him (and any listening kids) how to stay out of trouble online. My law practice suffered, but I was doing what I wanted to do—making sure that ALL children, even those who couldn't afford a home computer, could learn how to use the Internet, safely. I also wanted to make sure that teachers and librarians got the help they needed and the credit they deserved. And, most importantly, I wanted to empower parents to make sure their children could navigate the Internet, finding the good things and avoiding the bad ones. I traveled around the country, speaking at all of MCI's Safe Surfing panels and at the White House Summit on Online Child Content, as well as to school and community groups.

Meanwhile, in mid-1998, Curtis Sliwa, the founder of Guardian Angels (the famous subway and street patrollers with red berets) asked me for help. He had formed Cyberangels, a program of Guardian Angels, three years earlier in response to concerns about emerging on-line safety issues. He wanted me to run the program. I agreed to run it for only a few weeks while he sought out a new executive director. But when someone sent me a tip about a child pornography site, my whole life changed. I saw a little girl being molested, and couldn't turn my back on the problem. I agreed to run the place, cyberangels.org, which is staffed entirely by volunteers.

Since then, Cyberangels was awarded the 1998 President's Service Award and has expanded its programs from a cyber-neighborhood watch on serious crimes, such as child pornography, cyberstalking and child sexual exploitation online, to broader coverage as a leading online safety education resource and help group with more than a thousand active volunteers. Our programs cover online safety education for children, parents and teachers. We review family-friendly websites and filtering software products and services. Children can even take a quiz and earn a safe surfing permit.

When UNESCO (the United Nation's Education Scientific and Cultural Organization) launched its program against child pornography and pedophilia online (called Innocence in Danger) in 1999, I was asked by the head of the worldwide program, Homayra Sellier (an international child advocate), and UNESCO's general director to head up its U.S. initiative, Innocence in Danger-U.S. Innocence in Danger-U.S. will unite advocacy groups' efforts to combat online child sexual exploitation, coordinate with law enforcement agencies and educate families about these issues. It's the first truly worldwide effort to tackle the dangerous aspects of the Internet.

Innocence in Danger-U.S. will be part of a larger initiative I head up called Wired Kids, whose goal is to make sure that *all* children are given access to the Internet (and none are left behind in this technological revolution), every teacher is given the help they need to make sure that the Internet is a safe learning tool and that the power of the Internet is used to provide information and assistance to children, and families of children, in need. That's the mission of WiredKids.org—equity, safety and education. An important part of this mission is educating parents about the Internet, so they have the tools they need to help their children navigate this wonderful resource safely.

That's what this book is all about. Remember, although we need to know where the dangers are, and how to avoid them . . . the greatest risk our children face in connection with the Internet is being denied access to this essential tool.

After all . . . it's all about the kids.

CHAPTER 1

Bringing You Up to Speed

A Snapshot of Children on the Internet

The Internet is an extraordinary resource. It lets us communicate, educate, and entertain, all at the same time. More than 50 percent of children in the United States use the Internet at school, home, or community access centers. Since 1996 the number of children online in the United States has grown from 4 million to over 19 million (roughly half girls and half boys). The percentage of schools with Internet access has increased from 35 percent in 1994 to over 89 percent in 1998. At this rate, in a few years every man, woman, child, and family pet will be online.

But many families are still holding out. They have read about dangers online and watched news reports and television specials highlight the darker side of the Internet. To these parents, there's only one option—a simple one: Keep their children off the Internet entirely.

What a shame! There are so many ways parents can make sure their children are armed against the darker side of the Internet without having to unplug them completely. Unplugging them is like throwing the baby out with the bathwater. Our children need to become Internet literate in order to hold jobs, succeed in school, or attend college. Denying them access is denying them the tools they need to succeed.

The Internet isn't optional anymore—it's *essential* to our children's futures. That's also one of the reasons we need to make sure that *all* children, no matter how much money they have or what race or ethnic background they come from or language their parents speak, have access to this technology.

1

Instead of worrying unnecessarily, we need to do something about it. We need to become cyber-savvy to guide our children online with the skill we use in guiding them through life offline. That doesn't mean we have to become techies, it just means that we should understand what the risks are, and how to manage them—our own way. (Pocket protectors are optional.)

Clueless? You'll Feel Right at Home!

Don't let a fear of technology or computers stop you—it's really easier than you think.

First, remember that you are not alone. Most of us are scared to death—we just don't let it show. Computers can be intimidating to anyone. And the people who understand them speak in Net and tech jargon none of us can decipher (or wants to).

Our computers rarely do what we ask them to, and the tried-and-true remedy for most finicky home appliances (a good swift kick!) generally doesn't work. (Although, trust me, I've tried!)

Too many of us are scared off, thinking that we have to understand computer technology to get online. We don't.

All of us can use VCRs, although few of us understand how they work. If we can pop in a videotape and push the power key and play button, we can watch movies. (And for those of us annoyed by the constant blinking "12:00" on our VCR clocks, we can even apply the nontechy solution—a thick layer of black electrical tape!)

Using computers is no different. If you can turn it on, double-click your mouse, and type in your name and password, you're surfing!

Isn't Parenting Hard Enough Already?

I can still hear your lament (okay, maybe it's closer to a whine than a lament): "Isn't parenting tough enough without having to worry about protecting and guiding our children in cyberspace? How can we warn them about the dangers if we don't know what they are? How can we help them or answer their questions when we don't even know how to turn on the computer? How are we supposed to become computer geniuses when we can't even program our VCRs?" (Didn't we just go through this in detail?)

When your eight-year-old knows more than you do about computers, I agree that it's hard to keep an upper hand. (And don't think they don't know it!) But with some simple coaching, you can learn all you need to know to keep your kids out of trouble and make sure they get the most out of their surfing experiences. (Heck, you might actually enjoy yourself and learn to use the Internet, too.)

I've included in this book everything I thought you might need to know. And if you have a question I haven't answered, drop me an e-mail at parry@aftab.com or drop by the www.familyguidebook.com site. There's also a special section of the familyguidebook.com site I've set up for readers of this book. It'll say "For readers of *The Parent's Guide to Protecting Your Children in Cyberspace*" (cute, huh?), and the password is "empowered."

We're all in this together! I have written this book to empower you! So why do you look so worried?

Repeat After Me: "I Am Still the Parent!"

Whenever I talk to groups of parents about online safety, I hear the same thing from at least one parent: "I don't worry. I trust my kids." (That's usually when you can also hear me sigh audibly.)

Trusting your children is wonderful. But it's irrelevant when it comes to online safety, because the ones you really need to be able to trust are all the *other* people using the Internet. But those other Internet users shouldn't be trusted to look out for our children's safety. That's our job.

While many of us may trust our children not to access inappropriate (however *your* family defines "inappropriate") sites, it's not that simple. Lots of "trusted" kids are getting into trouble by meeting strangers face-to-face offline because we fail to teach them the danger of these things. In addition, innocent websurfing may expose our "trusted" children to unwelcome surprises. Adult website names may be deceptively similar to common popular site names using commonly misspelled site names. A simple typing slipup is an easy mistake—one that we'd make ourselves and one that our "trusted" kids make every day.

Parents have to remember that whether or not we understand how the Web works, or even how to turn on a computer, we are still the parents. We are *still* in charge. We *still* have the better judgment. We can't cop out by saying we "trust" our children. We have to make sure that we teach them to be trustworthy, and how to avoid dangers posed by others.

As parents, we each teach our children how to make responsible decisions. We need to recognize that their tech skills far outdistance their judgment. It's our job, as parents, to fill this gap with *our* greater experience and judgment. (No one ever said parenting was easy.)

Bottom line: It's not your kids you have to distrust, it's the millions of others online. We have to arm our children with the skills they need to stay safe in this environment, while still enjoying it.

Remember: You're still the parent. The Internet hasn't changed that.

Keeping It in Perspective

As much as I wish I could, I can't write this book without focusing on the dangers in cyberspace. You can't avoid them unless you understand what dangers exist. But it is my goal to help you learn how to help your children surf safely, not to scare you away from the Internet altogether.

Although no one can dispute that there are some really nasty things on the Internet, the amount of bad content is vastly exaggerated. It just gets more attention than the good stuff.

I'm always asked when I testify before governmental agencies or talk to the press to "put it in perspective." Everyone wants to know how serious the problem is. I always use the 90 percent/10 percent rule (but you should know that I make it up). I always tell them that 90 percent of the Internet is terrific, educational, creative, and safe. The remaining 10 percent isn't. But that 10 percent often gets more traffic and attention than the rest of the Internet combined.

How Serious Is the Problem?

Everyone wants to know how many predators are online and how likely it is that their kids will be victimized. People who aren't online think that the problem is bigger than it really is, and many experienced Internet users usually think it is smaller than it really is. While we do have some statistics about actual investigations and arrests, they aren't an accurate measurement of the real problem. No matter how hard we try to quantify the problem, we fall short because so few of the incidents with cyberpredators are ever reported to law enforcement.

Based upon discussions with the cyber–law enforcement agencies I work with, here's what we do know: In the first year since its launch in March 1998, the National Center for Missing & Exploited Children's CyberTipline took in more than 7,500 complaints relating to child sexual exploitation and the Internet. Of these, a vast majority were related to child pornography (roughly 5,700) and roughly 1,000 involved online enticement of children by adults for offline sexual purposes.

But, while the National Center's is certainly the biggest of all tiplines, it is not the only tipline. The FBI has its own tipline, as does the U.S. Customs Cybersmuggling Unit (which itself receives more than fifty direct tips a day about online child pornography). The U.S. Customs Cybersmuggling Unit reports about 230 arrests of child pornographers in 1998, and has received about two thousand tips of child pornography per quarter from the National Center's Cyber-Tipline. (I'll discuss these at length in the section titled "Cybercops: Who Enforces the Law in Cyberspace?" in Chapter 5.)

Many watchdog groups have their own tiplines, as well. At the Cyberangels tipline, we receive many tips relating to child sexual exploitation and the Internet. Most are of child pornography sites. Perhaps only one case a week involves an allegation of online child enticement, and only a handful of cases involve children who had already met the pedophile and had returned home, were still missing, or had sent sexually explicit photos of themselves to the pedophile as a prelude to the face-to-face meeting. Cyberangels turns these over to law-enforcement agencies. Several of the child-enticement tips we have received have led to arrests of cyberpredators.

Other tiplines, such as SOC-UM's (Safeguarding Our Children—United Mothers, www.soc-um.org) and Ethical Hackers Against Pedophilia (www.ehap.org), receive numerous tips as well. These are reviewed by their specially trained volunteers and turned over to law-enforcement agencies.

State and local law-enforcement agencies are getting very involved in this area, too. The New York Attorney General is an expert on cyber-crimes, as are the New Jersey State Police, the District Attorney's Offices of Suffolk and Westchester Counties in New York, and many local vice squads, such as the Seattle Police and the Bergen County (New Jersey) Prosecutor's Sex Crimes Unit. (I'll introduce some of them in the "Cybercops" section.)

Thousands of local law-enforcement agencies are being trained by their police academies and national and private groups on cyberforensics. (I have even set up a new program to train law-enforcement officers via the Internet, and we will include information about this program at the new Cyber Law Enforcement page: www.cyberlawenforcement.com.)

Given what I've learned from local, state, and federal law-enforcement agencies, in 1998 the number of cases in the United States where someone was arrested for an online enticement crime was probably fewer than five hundred. (Although, the FBI Innocent Images Unit had already opened seven hundred new investigations from January to July 1999, almost double the number for the same time period the year before.)

You will be happy to know that almost all arrests lead to people going to jail. The FBI and U.S. Customs prosecutions in this area have approximately a 99 percent success rate!

However, if something bad happens to your child, the statistics are meaningless. Even if it happens to only one child in the world, if it's *your* child, that's one child too many.

Please Don't Blame the Internet

Even when something bad does happen, though, it's not the Internet's fault. It's the fault of certain bad actors who abuse it. Yet the Internet itself gets blamed for anything and everything negative that happens online.

Whenever something hits the news that is in any way related to the Internet, the talk shows are filled with people blaming the Net. (I know—I'm usually one of those asked to be on the show to offer solutions.)

Understandably, parents are frightened by all the hype, and many vow that their children will never be allowed online.

But *that* is the real tragedy. It's like never taking your children to a Broadway show, the Empire State Building, the Statue of Liberty, or the Museum of Natural History, because some areas of New York City might be more dangerous than others.

The "wrong side" of town shouldn't keep you out of the town all together.

The Internet Is an "Equal Opportunity Offender"

A woman (and cybercelebrity) I admire, Robin Raskin, the publisher of *Family PC* magazine and known as the "Internet Mom," put it best. She wrote an article for the *Family PC* website (www.familypc.com) following the Heaven's Gate mass suicide, titled "Blaming the Net. A Parent Laments: Why Did It Have to Be the Internet?" Years later, her article still echoes in my ears, and I'd like to share part of it with you.

[W]hen I heard that the Heaven's Gate cult used the Internet to espouse its beliefs and recruit members it was as troubling to me as if they'd used a home in my own neighborhood. After all, I'd been advocating Internet use for families and I knew now that the medium would take lots of the blame for the tragedy. I wondered: Why blame the Internet? If it had been a TV cult that used late night infomercials to recruit new members, no one would be questioning the value of television.

I agree (although I'm not a big fan of infomercials). It's become a kneejerk reaction to blame the Internet.

Everything Has an Internet Connection These Days

We all cringe when a tragedy hits the news—we just wait for the Internet shoe to drop. As more and more people are getting online, there always seems to be an Internet connection. Either the perpetrator had a website, or the victims do, or someone has e-mail. There's always a tie-in.

A friend of mine often complains about how unfair this is. He points out that you never read a sidebar to a kidnapping story detailing the dangers of the telephone, just because the kidnappers called in their ransom demands. I think that's because we all understand how telephones work. (We teach our children not to talk to strangers on the phone and never to tell anyone they are home alone, right?) The Internet is different, because so few of us understand how to use it—that's why it's scary. We are understandably afraid of what we don't understand.

In addition, to be honest, the Internet rarely disappoints anyone seeking to sensationalize the story. Criminal copycats show up online almost immediately. (Trenchcoat Mafia wanna-bes were online in a matter of hours after Littleton.) People claim to be accomplices, and Internet service providers chase down false leads and run into dead ends. And all of these make meaty human-interest stories.

But we shouldn't blame the Internet. We should be blaming the people who misuse it.

A Road Map to This Book

I speak to parent groups all over the world about online safety. After a while you learn that there are certain things most parents know about the Internet (whether or not they use it), and lots and lots of misconceptions. The more people use the Internet, though, the more they understand what the risks are. But even an experienced Internet user may not be able to spot all the risks to kids, or know how to avoid them.

I compare Internet activities and areas online to traffic-light categories: Red light (don't go there unless you're prepared for what it holds, and are old enough to be able to make that decision), green light (appropriate for everyone, no matter how old), and the vast majority of the Internet, which is yellow light (proceed, but use caution).

Unfortunately, I've found that many parents tell their kids that everything's a "green light," without preparing them for the inevitable collision when others don't play by the same traffic rules. Others, the parents who are waiting in the wings for the magic Internet safety bullet to arrive, see everything as a "red light," and keep their kids offline entirely, or so restricted they might as well keep them offline.

I want parents to realize that the vast majority of the content and services online fall into the "yellow-light" category, which means that we have to use critical thinking in deciding whether to trust it, and be careful that we protect our privacy and avoid both unethical marketing tactics and activities that might put children in touch with malintentioned strangers. And we need to teach our children to proceed with the same level of caution. They must be taught to look both ways when crossing the information superhighway.

That's why I explain in this book where many of the hidden online risks are. Great things we can do online are often abused, which makes them "yellow-light" activities. Certain areas online hold a greater level of risk than others—and there our children need to proceed with caution once they are mature enough to be able to handle themselves and what they might encounter.

That's how I've organized this book: The activity, how it's supposed to work, how it's abused, and what you can do about it. The riskier areas and how to spot them and stay clear of them. How to educate your children and make your own choices about what your children should be doing online, and how to implement and enforce those choices. I've even discussed how schools are using the Internet, and how you can get involved to help.

The book is divided into nine chapters:

- Chapter 1, "Bringing You Up to Speed," gives you the basic information on what kids are doing online, how to keep the risks in perspective, and, most important, how not to panic.

- Chapter 2, "The Good, the Bad, and Being Cautious," tells you how the Internet works and what can go wrong. Even the most experienced Internet users may not know how some activities online are abused. This chapter shows parents how innocent surfing might lead to the darker side, and tells them what they can do about it.

- Chapter 3, "The Dark Side," describes risks to your children online, deals with content that parents might consider inappropriate for their children, and discusses more serious risks, like cyberstalking and cyberpredators. This chapter also has sections dealing with risks to your computer from viruses and hackers, and risks to you and others caused by your children and their friends.

- Chapter 4, "And Now for the Really Serious Stuff," deals with the commercial risks when you and your children shop online, data collection from your children, and privacy issues. It also gives detailed help on cyberstalking and cyberpredators, including real cases showing how cyberpredators have lured children online.

- Chapter 5, "And Now for the Really Boring Stuff: The Law," describes how the law works online, who enforces it, and where to report cybercrimes and get help online. It also tells you how you can make a difference by volunteering to help others online, or in your community or schools.

- Chapter 6, "Kids Online in Schools," explains the online safety issues as they impact schools. It also describes some special programs that demonstrate how integrating the Internet into the classrooms can help students to learn.

- Chapter 7, "Teach . . . Your Children Well," shows you how to talk to your children about these matters and how to teach them to avoid online risks, and sets out some simple tips you can follow to help your children stay safe online. It also explains Netiquette and gives you "Ms. Parry's Rules for Correct Internet Behavior."

- Chapter 8, "Making and Implementing Your Choices," tells you what your choices are and what other parents are doing, and gives you some terrific kids-safe sites and services. It also describes the technological tools available, such as filtering and blocking software, and compares the top programs head-to-head, feature-by-feature. We even tested them and found out which ones work best.

- Chapter 9, "And Now a Word from the Real Experts—the Teens and Kids," is largely written by teens and kids. It presents the results of a survey conducted with teenage girls, thoughts from students at an inner-city school, and the safety tips written by our younger angels in training and our Teenangels (a special group of teenagers who have been trained in online safety and act as online safety ambassadors to students around the world).

You can read this book in several different ways. The preferred method is to start at the beginning, paying particular attention to the dedications and acknowledgments, and then read through without putting it down until you reach the end. (I thought I'd try to get at least *one* person to do this.)

You can also skip to the end, but since this isn't a murder mystery, it won't help to know how it ends. Or you can read whatever interests you, in any order you want. The chapters and sections are independent.

Chapters that will put some of you to sleep are included as a resource for those of you who need to know all the details. So you can skip around, and still understand the subject. If you're curious about technology and facts about the Internet, I've included some of that information in Appendix 5 and at www.cyberangels.org and www.familyguidebook.com. The rest is up to you.

What Parents Ask Me Most Often About Online Safety

Parents have questions, lots of them. Luckily, in most cases we have the answers. I thought before we get into the nitty-gritty I'd answer the questions most frequently asked of me.

All I hear is about the junk, violence, and pornography online. Why should I bother getting Internet access for my kids?
You *have* to bother.

The Internet is the largest library of information available to mankind. More than a billion pages exist at all levels online. Most mid-level jobs require computer and Internet skills, and almost all of them will require these skills by the time our children look for employment. Our children need this skill for their future careers.

The Internet is a big help with homework and school assignments. It's also a terrific way for your children to get to know people from other countries and cultures. It's the cheapest ticket for worldwide travel you can get.

It's also a wonderful place for your children to share their creativity with others. They can write, they can report on things, they can draw and share their artwork and music with millions of people around the world. It's the world's biggest soapbox.

It's no longer an option. The Internet is now *essential* to our children's future.

I know my kids will do nothing but surf the sex sites because they're so easy to find online. Are my worries justified?

Kids tell me that after the first few exposures, most adult content becomes boring. Interestingly enough, when kids surf "inappropriate" sites, they are generally surfing gory sites, not sex sites.

In addition, although there's still too much hard-core sexual content available to everyone, more and more of these sites are requiring proof that the viewer is over eighteen.

Education and building a solid and trusting relationship with your children is the first line of defense against these dangers. So is finding fun and entertaining appropriate sites for kids, so they have alternatives to surfing "inappropriate" sites.

I trust my kids not to "go there," but I'm afraid that everywhere they go there will be pornography. They won't be able to avoid it, even when they follow my rules. Is that true?

There are many ways to keep your children on the straight and narrow when it comes to choosing websites to surf. To prevent the problems I discuss in "Stumbling into the Dark Side," they can use kid-friendly search engines and preapproved site lists, as well as other special kid-friendly resources.

I hear that the Internet is loaded with criminals. Is that true?

The Internet is a community, and like all communities it has its good and bad actors, its safe and dangerous places. Predators exist everywhere, online and off. The proportion of bad actors in cyberspace is no different from that in the real world.

As long as we have criminals in this world, though, we will have ingenious people who abuse the system through the use of new technology and media. They are often the first to learn how to manipulate the new medium. The trick is knowing how to avoid trouble and taking whatever steps are necessary to protect yourself and your family and prevent problems.

I think that the only way to keep your children safe is to keep them offline. Is that true?

The only thing you are guaranteeing if you keep your children offline is that they will fall behind in knowing how to use and enjoy the most powerful educational and communication medium in the history of the world.

There are many things you can do to protect your children in cyberspace. It's just like protecting them anywhere else. You don't let six-year-olds wander into a big city all by themselves. You know what dangers exist "out there" and you teach your children how to avoid those dangers. You set rules and enforce them.

Protecting your children in cyberspace isn't any different. The only problem is that you don't know what the dangers are. Once you do, you can set the rules and enforce them, just as you do in the real world. It's really that simple.

My children are receiving pornographic e-mail. Does that mean they have been visiting adult sites?

Not necessarily. The e-mail they are receiving is the online equivalent of junk mail, called "spam." The spammers grab any e-mail address they can find online from chatrooms (even child-friendly ones), profiles, websites, instant messages, and e-mail directories. It's called "harvesting." While your children may indeed be accessing adult sites, usually they're receiving adult spam purely by accident.

Okay, you convinced me. But I'm not a techie, and I can't even program my VCR. How can I supervise my children online?

It's easier than you think. I have to confess that even I can't program my VCR, yet I'm considered one of the world experts in online safety. (Go figure!) It's largely common sense once you know how things work. It's not technology, it's mainly communication and education.

I hear there are no laws in cyberspace. Is that true?

No. Generally everything that is illegal offline is illegal online. And while we don't have cyberpolice just for the Internet, we have units of major law-enforcement agencies who do police cyberspace, and any law-enforcement agency who has jurisdiction over the online crime can handle it. The problem isn't the laws, it's getting enough trained law-enforcement officials and enough technology and funding to enforce them.

I'm afraid that my children will be kidnapped or molested by someone they meet online. How serious a risk is that?

The operative term here is "online." No one can molest your child *online*, or kidnap your child *online*. They can only do that *offline*. So it's much easier to avoid than people think. Just teach your child never to meet anyone they know online, offline. Most of the cases where this happens, children willingly meet strangers offline. And that's a *parenting* issue, not an Internet one.

And although even one child is too many, this happens very infrequently—fewer than a thousand child molesters who lured or attempted to lure a child online have been arrested (almost 98 percent of whom were found guilty). (There are 19 million children in the United States alone who are online.)

Isn't pornography illegal? And, if so, why isn't anyone doing anything about it online?

There isn't a legal definition of "pornography." It's what regular people call "sexually explicit materials," and lawyers call "obscenity." Obscenity is material that is hard-core and has no redeemable (like artistic or scientific) value. (Obviously there's more to this, and I've explained this in Chapter 5, "And Now for the Really Boring Stuff: The Law.")

But even when the material online is clearly illegal in the United States, it might be legal where produced and where it resides online. Also, even when something illegal is produced in the United States, there are other risks (such as online predators) that get priority (and should) by law enforcement, who don't have enough resources to handle all legal problems online yet.

Don't porn sites have to require proof that their viewers are eighteen or over?

Legislation was passed making it illegal for any commercial site to show sexually explicit images without proof of age, but it was held unconstitutional. At the time of this writing there is no law that requires U.S. adult-site operators to restrict access to people eighteen or over, or require proof of age.

That's one reason why it's up to us as parents to look out for our kids online.

I don't have lots of money. How am I supposed to afford filtering software?

Most of the filtering tools cost under $30, and many are free. I'll tell you more about these tools—what they do, where to get them, and how much they cost—in the section called "One from Column A, Two from Column B" in Chapter 8.

What Does the Internet Have to Offer for Families and Kids?

For far too many pages, I will talk to you about the dark side of the Internet and the need to protect our children online. But, as I've told you over and over, the Internet is a terrific place, with millions of interesting sites for families and children. It opens up a whole new world to us parents, and to our families.

Families who use the Internet tell me over and over how it has enhanced and simplified their lives. I thought I'd take a minute here to share some of the things our children and we can do online. I hope you'll share your good Internet stories with me, too, so I can share them with others at my website, www.familyguidebook.com.

As children improve their communication skills online and meet people from other countries and cultures, sharing information, photos, and stories with the world and other family members, they learn not only to be creative but to share their creativity. Children can also research school projects right from home, and can keep in touch with teachers. Check out Homeroom.com (www.homeroom.com) to see how Princeton Review has designed a program to connect parents and schools.

Family members can provide online support for each other in tragic and trying times, and share their joys in good times. New parents can learn parenting skills, and can always find an answer to their questions and someone willing to help. Families can plan vacations online. The list goes on and on.

Current Events

Want to check the latest news and weather? There's no easier way to do that than by checking them online. The *New York Times* (www.nytimes. com) offers its publication online for free, and a special web section, too, called CyberTimes. You can probably also find your local paper, and there are portals with settings to give you local news and weather. My daughter's and my best friend's favorite: The Weather Channel (www.weather.com).

Sports Information, Scores, and Sporting Events

You can get it all online. *Sports Illustrated for Kids* (www.sikids.com) is one of the top sites for kids, and *Sports Illustrated* (for adults) (www.sportsillustrated.com) is online, too, and will give you scores anytime you want them. Want to buy tickets for a game? Do it online at Ticketmaster's site (www.ticketmaster.com).

Games

Tired of throwing away so much money on computer and video games for your kids? There are so many great game sites where kids can play for free. Bonus (www.bonus.com), one of the most popular sites for kids and preteens, tells us that their most popular feature is their game section. And what about www.games.com?

Johnny Can Write (and Research)!

When I was growing up (if you ask my kids, that was in the days before electricity and indoor plumbing), writing was something we did because we *had* to. We had to write thank-you notes for birthday gifts. We had to write essays for school. Writing was painful and formal. (Maybe that's why it took me so long to write this book!)

No wonder everyone complained that Johnny couldn't write. But that must have been before Johnny got online. The Internet and online services have changed all that. Kids have to write to communicate. It's how they "talk" online.

In addition, our children are learning how to find things on the Internet. They're finding information as diverse as academic research (www.studyweb.com), travel options, college data, and consumer product and source information. The term paper, which used to contain a bibliography gleaned from the local library, now contains sources from all around the world.

The Internet is also a wonderful option when the only other option is to drive the children across town in the pouring rain. Even the most technology resistant among us will recognize the advantages of having a library open twenty-four hours a day from your own home computer—especially during that rainstorm.

In addition to doing research for school projects, kids are researching schools themselves. Teenagers can check out prospective colleges and can even apply right online, and parents can learn about college financial aid and the application process. They can find help at Princeton Review's site, www.review.com, Kaplan Educational Centers' site, www.kaplan.com, and www.universities.com and www.finaid.com.

Recognizing how well our kids can navigate the Web, many families I spoke with now research their vacations online. Most airlines have websites, and so do most hotel chains. Lots of discount travel services are available on the Web, too. Check out Travelocity (www.travelocity.com, Priceline (www.priceline.com), Best Fares (www.bestfares.com), and Internet air specials at the airlines' sites, such as Continental (www.continental.com). Many families even assign their family vacation research to their teenagers. They research a few travel locations, ways to get there, things to see, and where to stay.

Shopping is much easier on the Web, too. Most of the major retailers have glossy and easy-to-navigate websites, and many are offering consumers the ability to purchase online. This is a particularly useful service for working parents and parents with young children, who may not have the chance to get out and shop as often as they would like. These sites all offer secure transmissions, so your credit card information is safe. Check out www.landsend.com, www.gap.com, www.spiegel.com, and www.toysrus.com.

You can arrange for a family night out by checking out local movie listings, theaters, and Broadway shows, and by buying tickets online. The Web has many movie sites that explain the movie rating system and why the movies you're interested in received their rating. (Check out www.screenit.com for lots of family information about movies and www.moviefone.com for local listings and to buy tickets online.)

The Internet is global, remember? That's one of the best things about it. That's also why it's a terrific way to get your kids ready for their future. The days when the world was broken into little fiefdoms are over. All business is global. Even mom-and-pop grocery stores are buying international goods, and your local businesses are selling to, buying from, and sharing expertise with other businesses around the world. What better way to teach your kids global thinking and painlessly prepare them for their careers than by letting them speak to the world right now?

Want to travel to a different country each month? Do it from your computer chair.

Interested in learning about kids worldwide? There are many good sites for finding international pen pals. (These usually have very strict terms of service, designed to protect kids from adults masquerading as children.)

What about e-mail? On AOL alone, there were 63 million e-mail messages processed on an average day in June 1999. Everyone is using e-mail for so many reasons. And it's fast and free.

Special Families . . . Special Kids

Parenting can be isolating. This is especially true as we find ourselves fractured into different roles at work, at home, and in our communities. The olden days where parents could sit around, compare stories, and chat over a cup of coffee, or over the backyard fence, sharing ideas, visions, and worries are long gone. We barely have the time and energy to get a load of laundry done or drive our kids to soccer.

When families have special needs, the isolation is magnified. Adoptive parents need to be able to talk to other adoptive families. Single parents (no longer a minority in our society, but carrying a special burden nonetheless) need to be able to share with other single parents. Grandparents who find themselves as primary caregivers to their grandchildren need someone to talk with to get them up to speed on parenting (and grandparenting) this generation.

Parents with exceptional children (disabled and seriously ill) need to be able to reach others with similar children and needs. Stepfamilies and foster families have special needs, too, and need to share them with others who have been through these things already. Parents are a great resource for each other, but until now, finding other, similarly situated parents has been very hard.

They can all find help and support online, 24/7 (as my kids say). It's the new backyard fence and community center, and families with special needs are finding more support online than anywhere else. And they don't need to leave their home to get it.

It's not only parents who can share with others like them using the Internet, either. Kids can find resources designed just for them, too. Remember, in cyberspace we have no skin color, wear no special costumes, don't need to be able to walk or run, or see, or hear. It allows us to be what we are under all our physical differences—just plain people.

These are just a few of the terrific things you can do online. I've included many sites at the Family Guidebook site (www.familyguidebook.com) to get you started. Don't worry.

In a Nutshell—What Are the Risks?

Other than risks posed by people trying to meet our children offline (which I consider the most serious of all dangers our children can face online and which I'll discuss in depth in the "Cyberstalkers and Cyberpredators" section in Chapter 4), there are many less serious risks our children face online. These include access to information that may be inappropriate for children, sites that sell contraband or advocate illegal activities, and sites that pose risks to their privacy.

Even though pornography and sexual content are receiving most of the attention, there are other kinds of inappropriate information our children can easily access. These include tobacco and alcohol advertisements, bomb-building sites, sites that advocate taking drugs, as well as sites that contain violence and gore, misinformation, and hate literature. Some sites even sell guns, drugs, poisons, or alcohol, or let your kids gamble online. Others collect and sell private information about your kids and your family, and use unfair interactive marketing strategies that target cybertots. These things may be far more dangerous to your children than being exposed to sexually explicit content.

And, since we're here to discuss risks and how to avoid them, we need to warn you about the dangers your children (and their friends) may pose to *others* in cyberspace, including you. They may give out your credit card information or passwords, share private information about you and your family, buy things and charge them to you, infringe copyrights, commit computer crimes, and access, lose, or destroy your files. In some cases, they may not even know they're doing it, but the dangers are just as real. (Just ask my sister about her cherubic daughter when she was only three years old. I'll share this story with you later on.)

Finally, there are risks that viruses and hackers pose to your computer.

Lots of things to think about. But I provide help, solutions, and tips for all of them in this book. Don't worry. (You'll notice I say that a lot. Is it working?)

CHAPTER 2

The Good, the Bad, and Being Cautious

I get hundreds of e-mails a day from parents who are concerned about online safety. Often they are from parents who just discovered how easily their children can stumble into the bad stuff, and how many ways there are out there to get into trouble. Parents can get pretty angry about this. They feel they've been conned somehow. (And maybe they have.)

There are common ways the Internet is abused and misused. While new ones are developed every day (people who dream up Internet abuses can be very innovative), understanding how these things work generally, and the intent behind the abuses, allows us to stay one step ahead of them. What we need to do is figure out how to take advantage of the positive things about the Internet, while learning how to avoid the negative ones.

Learning About the Flip Side

On one hand, being able to communicate with anyone, search for information, and share diverse opinions is what the Internet does best. On the other hand, the same activities can be abused very easily. Anyone can communicate with you and your children, even those you want to avoid. Your searches may result in finding things you would prefer not to find. And the range of diverse opinions you find online may be more than you bargained for.

As parents, we need to evaluate and manage these risks. That's the challenge. (It's easier than it sounds—believe me.)

19

When We Take Off the Training Wheels

In addition to the range of information they might be exposed to, when our children access certain areas online and take part in certain activities, they face greater risks. These may be fun and valuable experiences once your child is ready to handle them, but they are not without their risks, and the risks vary depending on the children's age and how well prepared they are.

As parents, we help our children handle increased risks every day. It's called growing up. We use training wheels when our children first learn to ride a bike, don't we? Then, when we think they're ready, we teach them how to balance a bike without training wheels. But we watch them, run alongside the bike, and pick them up when they inevitably crash into a tree. Eventually, we let them ride the bike alone, and later ride it downtown. By the time they get to the fifty-mile runs, they don't need us anymore.

The Internet is no different.

Understanding the Basics

You'll need to understand more about the different parts of the Internet and the activities found there (many of which kids love) so you can use common sense, just as you do when your child asks to go to the mall, use a subway, or go downtown alone. Many of those commonsense solutions, like bringing along a friend, checking in frequently, and making sure that we know what they are planning to do, are just as successful as they've always been. (Remember that common sense works just as well online as it does offline.)

The areas online we need to be extra careful about include IRC (Internet relay chats) and newsgroups, and certain activities, like chatting, searching for sites, instant messaging, registering at a site, joining online pen pal programs, posting personal profiles, and building a personal website.

What I'll teach you to do is measure the risks against the benefits so you can make an informed choice about where your children should surf and what they should do online.

Once you understand how the risks arise, you can learn how to manage them and make your own choices. It's rarely an all-or-nothing choice. And remember, nothing is engraved in stone. The key to making this work is finding the fit that's right for you and your child. As your child grows, matures, and earns more freedom, the restrictions and rules should change.

Stumbling into the Dark Side

Even when your children are trying to stay out of trouble and want to follow the safe-surfing rules, they might get into trouble by accident. Remember how I warned you that even if you trust your child you can't trust the Internet? This is what I was talking about.

Searching for Trouble

Being able to find what you're looking for online is essential to unlocking the wonders of the Internet. But when you search for something online, you are likely to find more than you wanted to find. To understand how searching can be abused, you have to understand how it's supposed to work. (I'll try to make this as painless as possible, I promise.)

I've told you that the Internet is a world of fascinating information never before accessible to nongeeks. Millions of sites covering every topic imaginable . . . for free! *Wait a minute!* You should know by now that when a lawyer offers you something that terrific for free, there's *always* a catch.

What's the catch? You've got to find the stuff yourself! But with all the information the Internet contains, finding things online could be like trying to find a needle in a virtual haystack. So how do you find anything on the Web?

By now we are all familiar with the domain names registered by major corporations, such as www.disney.com and www.sony.com and www.nbc.com. (A few years ago, none of us had any idea what "dot com" meant, but it's now become a part of our common vocabulary.) If you're looking for a famous site, you can often just type the company name, add a ".com," and get there.

But what if you're looking for information about something and don't know if there's a website providing that information? Or what if you are looking for the website of a company or person and you don't know the domain name (and the ".com" trick doesn't work)?

In this case, you need to use a search engine. (It's like calling 411 or using a phone book.) There are many search engines on the Web. Some of the most popular ones are: AltaVista, Excite, Go (Disney/ABC's search engine), Hot Bot, Infoseek, Lycos, Snap (NBC's search engine), WebCrawler, AlltheWeb, and Yahoo! After you've been online for a while, you'll find that some search engines work better for you than others. You may also find that you'll use one for certain kinds of searches, and others for a different kind of search.

Search engines let you search for a site by name or by topic. They work the same way a telephone book does. You can use the White Pages if you know whom you're looking for ("I'd like Jerry's House of Flowers") or the Yellow Pages if you only know what kind of business you are looking for ("I'd like a florist who delivers"). Search engines allow you to put in the name or words that should be included at the site (a "search index"), such as "Jerry" or "flowers" or "Jerry + flowers," or allow you to look through lists of sites organized by topic (a "search directory"), like "florists" or "flower retailers."

Most search engines gather information about sites using software programs (called "spiders" or "bots") that scour the Web searching for websites and information contained at the sites. The spiders and bots search every word at the website, and in some cases, all pages linked to from those sites. Then they index all those sites, based on the number of keywords used and how often they're used. If they use a search directory too, the sites are then read by reviewers who put them into the right topical category for the kind of information they contain.

Bait 'n Switch

But there are many problems that occur as a result of how search engines index sites. Webmasters use keywords—and in some cases the first twenty-five to fifty words at the site—to help the search engines categorize a site. These special keywords and descriptions are written in a hidden code called "metatags."

Metatags can be very helpful, since without them some sites might be indexed based on introductions like "Welcome to our site. We update it often and are happy to hear from you. Stop back often to see new articles and all our new features." This tells you nothing about the site, who runs it, or what information it contains, although this might be the first twenty-seven words found at the site and would otherwise be used to index the site by the spiders or bots.

A good webmaster, to help index his site more accurately, might use "skateboards, sporting goods, sports, kids sports, games, athletics, outdoor sports" in his metatags to tell the search engines that his site is about kids and skateboarding. Then, whenever you search for any of those words, his site will come up. Without metatags, you wouldn't know that this site has information about skateboarding.

Many websites make money from the sale of advertising at their sites. The sites with the most visitors can charge higher advertising rates. So they do whatever they can to make sure that they maximize the number of people who come to their site. To a website traffic auditor, a kid's visit to a site counts the same as an adult's visit. Traffic is traffic.

So how else can a website increase traffic? It can use popular search terms and popular topics (like Disney characters or "American Girl") in its descriptive metatags. Try searching for the keywords "girls" or "toys" (typical searches when you are looking for girl-friendly sites) and you'll learn more about the pornography industry than you might be interested in knowing.

They can also "hijack" a site by using special methods to have their fake site appear at the top of the search engine's list, before the real site. You may think that you're going to the site you searched for, but instead, you end up at an adult site.

Even if they're not out to mislead you, some adult sites have "spicy girls" and "Bambi, the buxom blond bombshell" information at the site. If you searched for Spice Girls or Bambi, these sites might pop up when you wouldn't have expected them.

That means that every time you search for something using the index of a search engine, you might find sexually explicit sites and other sites that you consider to be inappropriate for your children.

What Can You Do About It?

An easy solution for these problems is to use a filtered search engine. These give only prescreened kid-appropriate search results. The most popular filtered kid-friendly search engines are Yahooligans! (www.yahooligans.com) and Ask Jeeves for Kids (www.ajkids.com).

Many of the other popular adult search engines also have a child-friendly option you can select when executing a search which filters the search results. (I talk about filtered search engines in greater detail in "Yes, Virginia . . . There Is a Good Side to the Internet!" in Chapter 8.)

Another option is to use the site directories at the popular search engines. Lycos and Yahoo! are two good examples of site directories whose reviewers read and categorize websites under topic headings. About.com is another great resource, whose expert "guides" also review sites and list reliable websites.

But just because the sites in directories are reviewed doesn't mean all directory *topics* are kid-friendly. So make sure you select a kid-friendly directory topic, such as homework helpers or teen sites, or some other child-appropriate topic. Otherwise you might find some sites that, although appropriate for their directory category, are inappropriate for children.

Spelling Counts!

Remember, the name of the game is site traffic when adult sites are concerned. So they can't rely just on keywords to direct traffic to their sites. How else can they increase traffic at a site? They can use a domain name that is the same as a very popular site, and misspell it— so when people who are trying to contact the real site make a mistake in typing or spelling, they end up at the adult site instead. (At least I *think* that's why they do this. Perhaps *they* just can't spell. . . .)

Over the last couple of years, these "typo-scams" have included www.yahhoo.com (which, although now fixed, used to lead to www.rawsex.xxx.com) instead of www.yahoo.com, www.webcralwer.com (a pornography site), instead of www.webcrawler.com (a popular search engine), www.infosek.com (a pornography site) instead of www.infoseek.com (another popular search engine), and www.altheweb.com (a pornography site) instead of www.alltheweb.com (a mega search engine site). Since even our most tech-savvy kids sometimes make spelling or typing errors, it's likely that they would unexpectedly end up at one of these sites or others that have been designed to mislead people on the Net.

What Can You Do About It?

A good website to review, which allows you to check if anyone is trying to use your favorite site names (a great place for trademark owners to search frequently, too) is www.domainsurfer.com. It'll let you know when other sites are using names similar to your children's favorite sites.

If you find adult websites using names that your kids might mistakenly type in when looking for their favorite site, you can teach them to be very careful about how they spell the site's web address. (Also, you might want to let the webmaster of your favorite sites know when someone is trying to trade on their name.)

If you're using a filtering product, you can add the inappropriate sites you discover to your blocked-site lists.

Otherwise, you should bookmark your children's favorite sites using your Web browser (or mark them as a "favorite" on AOL). (I explain more about bookmarking later on, so don't worry.) Then when they want to visit the site, they can just click on the bookmark. That way your children don't inadvertently end up in the wrong place because they mistyped or misspelled the domain name. It will speed their surfing, as well.

Masquerading as a Famous Site: That "dot com" Thing

We see it every day on television, read it in magazines and on billboards, and hear it on the radio. Everywhere we turn we are confronted with the same thing—something-or-other "dot com." Webmasters know this, too. So they use our limited understanding of how domain names work against us. Most of us have learned that if we are looking for an obvious brand or famous name site, we can add a "dot com" to it and most of the time we get there. But not *all* the time.

Quick! How do you find the White House website, or NASA's website? (Don't cheat by looking ahead to the next paragraph.) You'll probably say (unless you cheated) "www.whitehouse.com" and "www.nasa.com." Wrong!

Most government sites have a ".gov" ending (called a "zone"). Two of the most famous instances of someone using a famous name to gain traffic from people making mistakes in the ".com," ".gov," or ".org" are www.whitehouse.com (a pornography site that is still up) rather than www.whitehouse.gov (the real site for the White House in Washington, D.C.), and www.nasa.com (a pornography billboard site that was shut down in 1997) rather than www.nasa.gov (the official site for the National Aeronautics and Space Administration).

All domain names have to use a three-letter suffix (or zone), which indicates the type of organization or entity involved. The ".com" (read "dot com") indicates a commercial organization site, rather than an Internet network (.net), international organization (.int), higher educational institution (.edu), not-for-profit organization (.org), military (.mil), or government (.gov) site. ".Com" is clearly the most popular zone, followed in popularity by ".edu" and ".org."

Websites from countries other than the United States may use a two-letter country code, rather than one of the three-letter zones. Sites without a country designation are assumed to be U.S. sites.

When I was on the MCI Smart Surfing panel teaching parents how to use the Internet safely, we all watched in horror as the resident typist/navigator typed in "whitehouse.*com*" when we referenced the real site and the filter wasn't turned on. While all of us on the panel had to watch the screen in horror, knowing what was about to happen, a roomful of families learned firsthand what can go wrong online. It was a *very* effective lesson.

And it's a mistake most of us would make. How can we expect our children to know any better?

What Can You Do About It?

This is one place where a filtering product would help. These products help filter out certain sites, and this kind of site is almost always caught by filtering software. Young children can also be restricted to a prescreened list of child-friendly sites, or a filtered search engine when they aren't fully sure of the website URL (address). Also, teaching them to know when different zones are used, such as ".com," ".gov," and ".org," makes it less likely that our children will use the wrong one.

You may also want to review all pages your younger children want to access *before* you let them visit those sites. You can then build a list of your prescreened sites in your bookmarks folder, which your children can just click on to access. Using an approved safe-site list, like the American Library Association's recommended sites for children, or any of the others I've listed in "Yes, Virginia . . . There Is a Good Side to the Internet!," can be a big help, too.

Bookmarking—Leaving a Trail of Bread Crumbs

So how *do* you build your own good-site list? You've read the section on finding your way around. You've found a site. Even better, it's the site you meant to find. Congratulations! This site is everything you ever hoped it would be . . . and has all the information you need or has links to "related" sites you want to read. But you don't want to read everything now. Now what? (Hmmm . . . it's sort of a "computer-book cliffhanger," isn't it?)

How do you find your way back without leaving a trail of bread crumbs? Bookmarking is the easiest way to return to a site over and over again. Just as you would slip a bookmark into a book to find your way back to the page you marked, you can do this online, too. Each web browser and online service has its own way to mark a site. (Come on, you didn't expect them to make this easy, did you?) They also call it different things. Netscape uses the term "bookmarking," but with Explorer it is called "favorites." Whatever they call it, it works the same way.

Using Netscape Navigator as our example, you just click on the

"Bookmarks" button on the toolbar at the top of your screen. Then place your mouse cursor on "Add Bookmark" and click. That's it. The software saves the name and address of whatever page you are currently on to a list of bookmarks. Anytime you want to visit the site again, just open your bookmark menu, scroll down to the site you want . . . and voilà! No need to type in the address each time, and no need to remember what letters are uppercase and which are lower! Also, no chance that your child will misspell the site address and end up at a pornography site by mistake.

Remember, though, that if you have a site on your bookmark list that you don't want your child to see (and you don't have software to block that site), you might want to use this option sparingly or rename it something far less enticing than "Bouncy Babes in Bikinis." Something like "Accounting aspects of short form mergers" is likely to guarantee that no one will ever try to use that bookmark. (Remember, there are many things adults can legally access, even if you don't want your children to. This trick lets you bookmark those sites and maintain your privacy at the same time.)

When the Dark Side Comes to Them . . .

Even when your children are taught to avoid adult sites and scams, sometimes those sites come looking for *them*. They do this by sending us unsolicited bulk e-mails known as "spam."

Before the Internet, "Spam®" was best known as the trademark for Hormel's luncheon meat, which became famous during World War II. It was also the central theme of a *Monty Python's Flying Circus* skit, where Vikings make fun of the luncheon meat by chanting "spam, spam, spam, spam" in the background, while customers in a café ordered "Spam® with Spam® and a side order of Spam®."

Probably because of the Monty Python skit, spam may be best known now as the nickname given to the junk e-mail clogging our e-mail boxes, delivering such "useful" information as pyramid-scheme offers, mass marketing, and pornographic links. (A link is special coding contained in a document or e-mail that, when clicked on, transports the viewer to another site, or another location within the same site.)

Spam—It's Not Just
Luncheon Meat Anymore

Everyone hates spam (the e-mail kind—I take no position on the luncheon meat). Most of us open our e-mail boxes (and, increasingly,

ICQ messages and instant messages) to find lots of unwanted messages, many of which contain live links to adult sites. All our children have to do to visit those sites and view those images is click on the link in the message. They are then instantly transported to sites filled with sexually explicit images.

Sometimes these links are clearly labeled as sexually explicit, other times they aren't. For example, while the obvious ones are labeled as "XXXBlondes," others try to mislead the recipient of the e-mail into clicking on the link by saying things like "Hi. Last week I promised to get you the address for this site. Here it is." You might not recognize the sender of the e-mail and are racking your brain to remember who promised you the address for a site last week, but you click on the link and find yourself in the midst of graphic sexually explicit materials. It works the same when our children are involved.

Who's Protecting Whom? Protecting the Sensitivities of the Innocent

I receive more complaints about spam with links to adult sites than anything else. I must receive forty or more complaints a day from parents asking what they can do about them. Many parents, not understanding how the spammers get their children's e-mail, ICQ, and AOL's instant messaging addresses, think their children must have visited the adult sites to provoke the spam. I can't count how many teenagers I have saved from punishment by explaining that you don't have to visit a site to be spammed by it. (Teens I've helped can send their thank-you notes—and gifts—to me at parry@aftab.com.)

But children aren't the only ones who need to be protected from pornographic spam. One teenager recently admitted that although she had a terrific and close relationship with her mother, she worried that her mother might overreact when she learned how much pornographic spam was delivered to her daughter's e-mail box every day. (Her daughter wasn't doing anything to cause the spam; this was just ordinary spam directed to all AOL and other ISP members.)

When her mother decided to use their existing AOL account for the first time, she asked her daughter to set up a screen name for her. Her daughter set up her mother's account with the second most restrictive parental controls available on AOL, the one for young teens. (This blocks all e-mail from everyone other than those on the child's approved e-mail sender list, including all spammers.) Her mother still has no idea that her Internet access is filtered and that her daughter is trying to protect her and spare her feelings.

When I stopped laughing, I realized how much the power has shifted in many of our families, at least when the Internet is involved. Our children often have control over the settings on our access by controlling the main account password. They are also the ones who install the filtering software we buy to protect them. (Thank goodness the filtering products are getting very easy to install. Otherwise, I can hear you now . . . "Jennifer, I've bought this terrific product that will keep you away from all of the interesting things online you like and I don't. Please help me install it.")

And now, *they* are the ones who try to protect us from inappropriate content.

One of my Teenangels (I'll introduce you to them in Chapter 9, "And Now a Word from the Real Experts—the Teens and Kids") told me that when she first encountered pornographic spam a couple years ago, she was shocked and embarrassed. (She's fifteen.) Now it doesn't even faze her. She deletes it without thinking. She tells us that she isn't immune from disgusting things online (explaining that you can never become fully immune to pornography in any form), but she's getting good at ignoring it. (Although we might be uncomfortable with our children becoming "immune" to pornography, it is comforting to know that they frequently delete it without even bothering to look at it. Perhaps it's not the forbidden fruit anymore.)

How Does Spam Work?

The spammers gather our e-mail, ICQ, and instant messaging addresses in many ways. Sometimes they use e-mail addresses captured when someone accesses their sites, but far more frequently they use software and people to collect e-mail addresses, screen names, ICQ, and instant messaging addresses from chatrooms, newsgroups, and online profiles. This is called "harvesting." These millions of addresses are then often sold to other spammers as part of a bulk e-mailing list.

But although the spammers might have known that the e-mail address, screen name, ICQ, and instant messaging address existed at the time it was harvested, they don't know if it is still in use. That is—not until you reply to the spam complaining about it or asking to be taken off the list. Then they know it's a live account. That means your e-mail, screen name, instant messaging, and ICQ address will be far more valuable when they sell it to the next spammers. If you reply in any way, expect to receive an increased number of spammed messages, since they sell the lists of replies at a much higher price.

And You Think YOU Hate Spam!

The only ones who hate spam more than we do are Internet service providers. They spend millions of dollars fighting the spammers in court, trying to get them to stop using their networks for spam. But as soon as they shut down one spammer, another pops up.

The ISPs developed applications to filter out e-mail sent from known spammers. The spammers countered with their own technology and began using sender aliases (pretending to be someone else) to bypass the filters. At the same time, with the growing enormity of bulk e-mailing lists came an increasing number of undeliverable spam messages.

When an e-mail is undeliverable, it is returned to the sender. This resulted in the spammers being deluged with returned spam. So the use of a fake sender's address shifted the deluge to whoever was designated as the sender. The fake "sender's" designated provider then received the undeliverable responses and returned spam. That resulted in America Online, ISPs like MSN, AT&T, and MCI/Worldcom, and other commonly used free e-mail services receiving millions of returned spam messages, which overloaded their systems. To get a sense of the enormity of the problem, consider this: AOL has reported that a large percentage of the Internet e-mails (not sent from real AOL members) they process through their servers every day constitute spam. It costs them a lot of money and slows down their service to their members. Spam is *everyone*'s problem.

What Can You Do About It?

Surprisingly, unlike offline junk mail or phone solicitations, there are no federal laws yet that require the spammers to remove you from their mailing lists or that regulate the sending of spam. The FTC will take action against online scams and multilevel marketing schemes advertised in the spam, but otherwise it doesn't have the authority to restrict spamming itself.

Waiting for the Federal Troops to Arrive

As I mentioned, there aren't any federal laws regulating spam yet, although there are many bills pending. Some states, though, have enacted laws that give their residents rights against spammers who use fake return addresses. You can check www.cauce.org to see if your state has adopted anti-spam legislation yet, and to check the status of federal regulations.

While I generally oppose regulations directed at the Internet, this is one area that I think needs some governmental help. If you agree with me, I recommend that you contact your congressional representatives and senators. Tell them about your experiences with spam, especially when live pornographic links, multilevel marketing, and scams are involved. Ask for their help. It'll take federal legislation to make a real difference.

Self-Help—Learning How to Defend Yourself

Until federal laws are adopted to regulate spam (some states have already taken action to outlaw certain spam), you can take certain measures on your own to limit junk e-mail.

Many ISPs and online services have a special place to report spam. Check with your ISP and find out where you should be reporting it.

There's also a new service that gathers information about spam for the ISPs and for the regulators. The Spam Recycling Center (www.chooseyourmail.com/spam) is a website that allows you to forward your spam on to them, to be reported to Congress and other federal authorities. It's a great resource, since it gives you a place to dump all the spam you get, and someone is actually keeping track of the spammers and what they're doing. There's even a place to sign an e-petition for congressional action (although I recommend you contact your legislators directly).

You can also contact your ISP to see if e-mail filters, which will block some spam, are available. If your ISP can't help, certain websites and online service providers inform spam recipients how to block or filter e-mail. Junkbusters (www.junkbusters.com), the Junk E-mail Resource Page (www.junkemail.org), Netizens Against Gratuitous Spamming (www.nags.org), the Coalition Against Unsolicited Commercial E-mail (www.cauce.org), and the Campaign to Stop Junk E-mail (www.mcs.com/jcr/junkemail.html) are the most popular anti-spamming sites.

The Dual Account Trick

Because addresses are often harvested from public areas, such as chatrooms, discussion groups, and profiles, you can avoid spam entirely by using two accounts—a public one and a private one. By using a public address to post and chat, and using e-mail filters and controls, you can block all incoming e-mail, stopping spam in its tracks. Then you use your real e-mail address for communicating with people you know, privately. You won't need a filter; since this e-mail address is not publicly posted, it'll be much harder to harvest. Using two accounts isn't perfect, but it's a big help.

Using Parental Controls
to Help Manage the Problem

There are many filtering products that allow you to block e-mail from everyone other than the people you include on a list. These allow your children to receive e-mail from their best friend and their aunt Mary, but block e-mail from strangers, including spammers. Unfortunately, it also blocks the e-mail from someone in their class or Aunt Sherry, who weren't on the list.

I haven't found any parental control software that blocks spam entirely other than by restricting *all* incoming e-mail (except from approved senders). If you allow *any* e-mail from unrestricted senders, *some* spam will get through.

So you have to weigh the problems with being too restrictive against the annoyance of spam.

A few filtering products, such as Net Nanny, also block incoming text and would block the text message contained in the spammed message if it contained predetermined filtered words and phrases.

Although few filtering products can block incoming text, as Net Nanny does, most of them can block access to the sites linked in the spam. So even if they don't block the e-mail itself, or the description of the site contained in the spammed message, they can prevent your child from accessing the site it links to.

If you want a special spam-filtering product, you should check out Spam Exterminator. You can find it at C|Net and ZDNet's software libraries. (It's a shareware—which means you can use it and *should* pay for it—and costs $27.95.) It has a Known Spammer List that blocks e-mail sent from known spammers (okay, so some things are obvious). Spam Exterminator will delete the spam before it's even downloaded (a great feature when children are involved). But AOL users should note that it doesn't work on AOL, which has its own mail control filters.

You should also teach your children to ignore and delete e-mail received from anyone they don't know. In addition to containing links to sites you prefer your children not access, they could also include an attachment that is infected with a virus, be embedded with a code that gives a hacker access to your system, or contain a message from someone you'd prefer they not know.

They might not care about the sexually explicit sites or the darker-side correspondents, but our children care deeply about saving their files and games from virus corruption and destruction and hacker invasions. Use that fear as an incentive to get them to follow this rule. An appropriate level of fear can be a powerful help when teaching caution. (I discuss more about how to protect your computer from viruses and back-door hacker attacks in Chapter 3, in the section called "Protecting Your Computer in Cyberspace: Hackers and Viruses.")

Stranger Danger: How Does This Work When You're *Supposed* to Talk to Strangers Online?

We would never allow our children to have a telephone conversation with a stranger who called our home, would we? Yet strangers can contact and communicate with our children through chatrooms, ICQs, instant messaging, e-mail, and pen pal programs, and track them through buddy lists—and we might not think twice about it. This section helps you understand the risks posed by the different online communication methods, and what you can do to make sure your child uses them safely.

Being able to reach out and "talk" to others online is one of the best things about the Internet. But it can also be the riskiest. Most of the dangers children face online come from strangers, not from information. Whenever children are allowed to interact one-on-one with someone you and they don't know in real life, they face special risks.

The real danger online comes from meeting people *offline*.

But don't panic. Remember that the technology has not yet advanced to the stage of allowing a hairy-armed predator to reach into the modem and pull your child back through. In most cases, your child has to be a willing participant if there's going to be a face-to-face meeting.

And that's how the real problems occur. Internet-related molestations don't result from predators sneaking into your home at night. Most victims willingly meet predators in real life. They may not have known the predator's real age or intent, but they knew they were meeting someone offline. Many of the victims are love-struck teenagers. So education plays the most important role here. We need to teach our children about these risks so they can avoid them. Most of the time, that will make the biggest difference. (I've discussed what our children and teens need to know throughout the book as well as in Chapter 7, "Teach . . . Your Children Well.")

Chatrooms

I talk to kids frequently about what they do online. They all tell me that they like chatting more than anything else (other than sending instant messages). They also tell me that they like chatting with their friends from school. Apparently chatting is this generation's equivalent of the telephone. We used to get on the phone with our classmates as soon as we got home from school; they get online with them. The more things change, the more they stay the same.

What Is Chat?

Chatrooms are places online where lots of people can talk to others in real time. They are like a giant telephone party line you can dial into. (You might have to ask your grandparents about what a party line is.) There are chatrooms on online services (such as AOL, which has more than fifteen thousand chatrooms), chat services on the Web (like Talk City, www.talkcity.com), sites that host their own chatrooms for their members—such as Headbone (www.headbone.com), KidsCom (www.kidscom.com), and Freezone (www.freezone.com)—and chats on IRC (Internet relay chat, which requires a special software program to access; on IRC, chatrooms are called "channels").

While many people love to talk to people in chats, others just like to watch and listen to what is being said and who's saying it. These people are called "lurkers," and watching and listening rather than chatting is called "lurking." You might know they are there, since many chatrooms have a list of people in the room, but you wouldn't otherwise notice them. (This is important, since many of the cyberpredators lurk in chatrooms, silently gathering information about our kids. And since they aren't doing anything to call attention to themselves in the chatroom, no one pays attention to them, including the monitors.)

Many chatrooms are organized by topics. Most of the time the chatroom title or channel title tells you the topic. While there are tons of tamer topics, many topics have something to do with romance and "cyber" (that's cybertalk for cybersex discussions, where people engage in graphic sexual fantasies and discussions). That probably accounts for much of their popularity. (On IRC some also have titles like "father/daughter sex," "software piracy," and "kiddie porn 4–6-year-olds." That's why I recommend that children be kept off IRC entirely.)

How Do They Work?

No matter where you find your chatrooms, they all work basically the same way. Everyone types whatever they want to say (that's how they

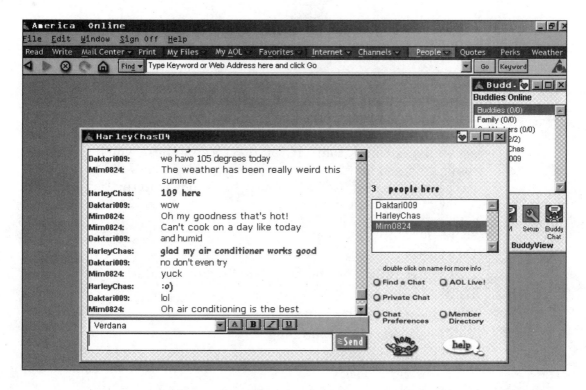

talk to each other online) and other members of the chatroom respond. It can get pretty confusing sometimes, since everything that everyone types shows up on the screen in the order of their having sent it.

Chatrooms come in different sizes, ranging from two people to several hundred (on certain IRC channels). The graphic above shows a typical chatroom on AOL. You can get a sense of how confusing it can become when you're not sure who is talking to whom and who is answering which question.

Can You Control Who's in the Chatroom?

Some chatrooms are public and can be joined by anyone. Other chatrooms are private and open only to invited chatters, by password. Children, and especially teens, set up their own private rooms for friends from school, sports activities, scouting, and camp. It allows them to chat privately.

Many of the pedophile chatrooms are private, too. (There are more pedophile chatrooms than most of us would believe.) They typically invite children to join them by personal invitation. Often the children know they are entering a pedophile chatroom when they agree to go there. (For some reason, the pedophile chatrooms are more often used when the pedophiles are luring boys, rather than girls. They also typically have a homosexual pedophile theme, such as "man/boy love.")

Acronyms

Given the speed of chatting online, certain acronym shortcuts have been invented for frequently used words and phrases. I've included a few below, and a more complete list at the Family Guidebook site (www.familyguidebook.com). If you don't know these, you'll miss most of what's going on and let everyone know you're a "newbie."

Acronyms are also used frequently to cut down on the typing. These are a few of the most common:

LOL—laughing out loud
OTFL—on the floor laughing
ROFLOL—rolling on the floor, laughing out loud
BTW—by the way
OTOH—on the other hand
PMJI—pardon me for jumping in
IMHO—in my humble opinion
BRB—be right back
j/k—just kidding
IGJ—I gotta jet
BB—bye-bye

Now for a pop quiz! (Just kidding. :->) (That's a smiley or an emoticon—you'll learn about those in Chapter 7 in my Netiquette section, "Netiquette: Teaching Your Children How to Behave Properly in Cyberspace." Turn the page sideways and you'll see it's a smiley face, which means I'm joking.)

Is Anyone Watching the Store?

While general Netiquette rules typically apply in chats (you can read up on this in the Netiquette section), the only other rules that apply are the terms of service of the chatroom host, and often these aren't strictly enforced unless someone complains.

Some chatrooms are monitored, but most aren't. When they are monitored, they can be monitored by "bots" or real live humans. Bots are special programs that record what goes on in the chat. Although they can't answer questions they haven't been programmed to answer, they can be used to enforce the chatroom's terms of service or channel rules, by expelling visitors who stray from those rules. Primarily, they are used to monitor the language used in the chatroom or channel.

But when it comes to monitoring activities in a chatroom, nothing replaces real live "chat cops." They are used to what kids say and how kids say it. Only an experienced chat cop can keep up with the kids. Some monitors are parent volunteers; others are paid professionals.

Chatroom Abuses

You're a parent, right? So you could probably write this section yourself. How do kids and teens abuse chats? Let me count the ways. . . .

When they know they are being monitored, they use obscure words, terms, and phrases to try to sneak it past the monitors. As the monitors learn, the kids move on to making up new words, hoping to fool them some more.

They insult each other, and when the language gets too heated, fall back on tried-and-true insults like "You smell!" (These have proven to be very effective from generation to generation.)

They hang out in groups, and some are outcasts, and others are in the "in group," just like at school. They say mean things, talk about things we probably don't want to know and flirt. They sometimes don't care if the person they flirt with is an adult or another kid. It's fun. It's pretend—boys pretend to be girls, and girls pretend to be boys, and everyone pretends to be popular and older than they are. (Except the adults who want to be younger than they are, weigh less, and, where adult males are concerned, have more hair.)

But, since there is no sure way to prevent an adult from entering even the most secure kids' chatroom (since anyone can be anything they want online), your kids need to know that people may be watching them with intense interest. And they don't usually make themselves obvious when monitors are watching. They sit quietly and take notes about our kids. (I've shared more about this in Chapter 4, in the "People Hurting Children—Cyberstalkers and Cyberpredators" section.)

Parents Are Watching . . .
and Other Secret Codes

Kids know that parents might try to supervise their chats and see what's going on in the chatroom. They know that most parents wouldn't understand half of what goes on in a lively chatroom. So they have invented special acronyms to warn the others when parents and others are hovering nearby. These include (in either capitals or lowercase letters):

CTN—can't talk now

NP—nosy parents

P911—my parents are coming in the room! Watch your language!

PA—parent alert

PAL—parents are listening

PAN or PANB—parents are nearby

PAW—parents are watching

POS—parents over shoulder

SA—sibling alert

TA—teacher alert

Remember . . . Being forewarned is being forearmed.

What Can You Do About It?

When you are dealing with preteens and young teens, you should insist that your children chat only in rooms and channels monitored by live monitors, not bots. I also recommend that children and preteens be kept off IRC, which is still considered the Wild West of the Internet, until you're sure they can handle themselves. Even then, make sure they stay in the clean channels.

You should also check to see whether the monitored chatrooms are monitored twenty-four hours a day or just during certain hours. Many parents have complained to me about choosing a chatroom or chat service because of the fact that it monitors chat, only to find that the monitoring is available only during certain hours. Most of the responsible children's chatroom areas post the hours when they are open and when monitors are in attendance. Smart kids' sites have their chat operators close the chatroom whenever monitors aren't in attendance.

You should learn how to log all chats, and teach your children to do the same. You can make a copy of the conversations in the chatroom and channel you're chatting in. When things go wrong, that log can be invaluable in reconstructing the chat. Each log application works slightly differently, so you should refer to your chat service's help files to learn how to set up the log. You don't need special software to do it, since most chat programs have logging capabilities built in.

The secret to keeping your children safe in chat is teaching them not to give out personal information online. But some children still share too much information to be safe. If you've tried everything, and your kids still share too much personal information online, there are software tools that can be programmed to block certain outgoing information, like their names, addresses, and telephone numbers. But you should know that kids also can get around the outgoing blocking programs: instead of typing their name as "Bob Smith," they can type in B*****O*****B and the letter that comes after R*****M****I****and the letter that comes after S****H." They can do the same with addresses, telephone numbers, and other information we don't want them to share. The only way to be really sure you've caught them in the act is by using a program like Cyber Snoop or Disk Tracy, which capture all communications and let you see exactly, word for word, what your kids are saying online. (But many people feel this is overkill. If you resort to products like these, make sure you warn your children that you're using software to monitor their communications—otherwise, it's like reading their diary.)

I discuss these and other parental-control software in Chapter 8, in the "One from Column A, Two from Column B" section. But teenagers and kids alike hate the word-for-word monitoring products; they see them as a severe invasion of their privacy. And I'm not sure I don't agree with them.

E-mail

What Is E-mail?

Join the club. Send an e-mail message to someone on the Internet. It's one of the easiest things you can do online. It's also one of the most popular. Everyone's using it at home, at school, and at work. It's used 150 percent more often than the Web is. Want to send a note to your sister? E-mail it. Want to send a copy of your daughter's report to your husband? E-mail it. Got a photo of the new baby you want to share with everyone in the family? You've got it . . . e-mail it!

And the best part is when they write back. It's instant gratification. You'll soon learn that there are few sounds sweeter than the sound of "You've got mail!" when you sign on to America Online. (My five-year-old niece still chants that line whenever my sister or brother-in-law logs on.)

E-mail is a message you send over the Internet to someone else. It can take just seconds to arrive, unless the Internet is particularly busy, and doesn't take longer to get to the person across the street than the one around the world. It's free (ignore any rumors you hear about impending taxes charged by the postal service on e-mail) with your Internet access. (Some of the new Web-based programs are free, too, without your having to subscribe for Internet access, and are supported by advertising to e-mail account holders.)

E-mail is a great way to stay in touch with geographically distant relatives and friends. It lets people send a message when they want to, and answer messages when they can.

How Does It Work?

Your ISP or online service will supply you with their software, which includes an e-mail program that has to be configured. (There's no additional charge for this software.) Online service providers, such as America Online, automatically configure your e-mail, so you can send it and receive it as soon as you get online. It's a lot harder to configure your mail program when you're using an ISP, since it requires configuring your browser. Browser e-mail programs are a pain in the neck to set up initially, but worth the trouble. Once they're set up, they're easy to use.

Hang in there. I promise that this stuff will be over before you know it.

If you know someone who can configure the browser for you, this is a good time to call and plead—bribes are usually in order. (I understand that Twinkies, Yoo-Hoo, and Cheez Doodles are the bribes of choice among computer geeks "in the know.") Ask them to set up e-mail passwords, so you can control your e-mail account, too. (They may be able to set the clock on your VCR while they're at it.)

One product we tested, Surf Monkey, will even read your child's e-mail messages out loud, using voice recognition software. So children can receive e-mail from approved senders even before they can read. (You can learn more about this in "One from Column A, Two from Column B" in Chapter 8.)

Your E-mail Box

Each e-mail address has two parts—your mailbox user name and the domain name of your e-mail server, separated by an "@." Mine is parry@aftab.com, where "parry" is my user name and "aftab.com" is my e-mail server. But many people using online services, such as AOL, have gotten used to using just their screen name—and those of their friends on the same service—to address mail, leaving out the "@" and domain name part.

These are short-form e-mail addresses that only members of the same e-mail system can use. If you're both members of AOL, you can give them your screen name, and you don't need to add the "@aol.com" part. That's because on AOL, it's assumed that you're e-mailing someone else on AOL, unless you tell them otherwise by giving them the e-mail server name. It's like giving your address to someone you know lives in the same town. You give them your street address but leave out the town part of your address.

It won't work, though, when you try to send an e-mail to someone outside of AOL. Try sending a letter to someone using the U.S. Postal Service with just a name and street address—leaving out the town, state, and zip code. What are the chances of its getting there?

Your e-mail is sent to your ISP's mail server. It's like having all your mail sent to a post office box at your local post office. Instead of having to retrieve your mail yourself from your mailbox, though, you can send your mail program for it. (Now, if I could only train it to pick up my snail mail too—regular old-fashioned postal service mail—I'd never need to leave home again.) You can then leave the e-mail on the server, to access again later from another computer, or remove it from the server after you read it.

Several companies, including Juno, Hotmail, Yahoo!, and Excite, also offer free e-mail accounts. You sign up for them online. Many of them are Web-based e-mail products. That means you don't need special software (you use your Web browser to access your e-mail) and can access it from wherever you access the Web. The free e-mail services sell advertising space to defray the cost of the e-mail service. If you're willing to put up with the advertisements, you can get free e-mail.

You can't access your e-mail from another computer, unless you have the software installed and configured. That's why the new Web-based free e-mail systems can be so valuable. You can access them from anywhere that has Web access, using any browser. That's also why they are so risky for our kids. They can access their e-mail from outside of our homes, at school, friends' houses, libraries, and community access centers. If you monitor your children's e-mail, they can bypass your controls by using Web-based e-mail accounts.

There are many ways your e-mail address can be listed online for people who want to find you. (Read all about how to find people online later in this chapter, in "The World's Biggest Billboard" section.) Make sure your children's e-mail accounts aren't listed anywhere online.

E-mail Abuses

The biggest e-mail abuses take the form of spam, flaming, harassment and cyberstalking, forgeries (when people send e-mail pretending to be someone else) and mail bombs (large quantities of e-mail that flood your system). E-mail is abused in more ways than any other online communication mechanism. (Fast on its heels, though, is abuse of instant messaging.)

Spam is probably the biggest abuse of e-mail. Junk e-mail clogs our e-mail boxes daily, delivering scams, pornography, and pyramid schemes to adults and children alike. (I've dealt with spam in detail in the "When the Dark Side Comes to Them" section.) When we reply to spammed messages, asking to be removed from their e-mailing lists, our e-mail address is sold at a premium price, since they know someone is listening. That means we get even more spam.

If we're not careful, e-mail can also be an open door into our homes and our computers. Flaming, harassment, and cyberstalking can arrive via our e-mail. Viruses can arrive as attachments to our e-mail (or even included in the e-mail message itself) as well. We used to be able to tell people never to open an attachment sent from someone we don't know. But since the Melissa virus, all that has changed. That virus arrived masquerading as an e-mail from a friend. (The Melissa and BubbleBoy viruses worked by copying your e-mail address book and sending e-mails to those people, masquerading as you. It would then take their e-mail address book entries and start all over again.) The BubbleBoy virus can infect your computer just through an e-mail message, without an attachment.

Trojan horses offer a back-door entry into our computers for local (and not-so-local) resident hackers. They allow hackers to steal our files, the financial information we store on our computers, and our passwords, and can even delete everything on our hard drives.

Live links to pornography sites (which advertise sexual images of teens) can be delivered to kids via e-mail, as well. Photos can also be sent to our children by people we don't want our children to correspond with, and photos can be sent back to them by our children. And e-mail is how cyberpredators can reach out and touch our children online and how our children can share personal information with strangers.

E-mail chain letters are becoming a big problem, too. Like their offline counterpart, they promise good luck, riches, or love if forwarded to twenty-five of your nearest and dearest friends online, or dire consequences if you don't forward them. Since offline chain letters require copying the original and putting it in an envelope with stamps, only the most gullible would send them on. But since all it takes to satisfy the "luck gods" is to "cc:" several close friends in your e-mail address book, everyone is forwarding them. The consequences of these mass

e-mailings is clogged servers and slower Internet service. They are the bane of school Internet access systems, too, often causing serious crashes.

Maggie, one of our online safety guides in training (and ten years old), recently came running down the stairs to her parents, her face white, sobbing and hiccuping. She always deletes e-mail sent from people she doesn't recognize. And someone had sent her a chain e-mail that told her she would die if she didn't forward it to three of her friends. She had deleted it without thinking, and since she couldn't get it back and therefore couldn't send it on, she was convinced that she was going to die. It took her parents almost an hour to quiet her hysteria by explaining that the chain e-mail was just a scam.

Even when you weigh the benefits against these risks, though, e-mail still comes out on top as a great way to share information and communicate. But it's one of those things that requires extra supervision and education about online risks.

It also should be limited to children who have the requisite judgment to handle it, which often means children over a certain age. That age usually depends on the children, but generally, unsupervised e-mail access should be limited to children over the age of eleven. Surf Monkey, a free child-safe Web browser, has a great system of delivering e-mail headers to a parental e-mail box. Those that the parent clears can be released to the child. The others are deleted. I discuss this in greater detail in Chapter 8, in "One from Column A, Two from Column B."

Given how valuable e-mail can be, it's sad that it is abused as often as it is. Recognizing the frequency of e-mail abuse, the recently passed Children's Online Privacy Protection Act, which goes into effect in April 2000, requires parental consent before any child under the age of thirteen signs up for e-mail from any site or section of a site directed at children.

What Can We Do About It?

Many of our kids have these free e-mail accounts, and often we don't know that they do. That's a mistake. Even if we don't monitor our children's e-mail, we should always know where they have accounts and their passwords. Also, some of the services publish personal information you provide in member directories or White Pages. Check there to make sure your child isn't listed.

You should know, though, that if your teen has a Hotmail e-mail account, you can't cancel it. The best you can do is make sure your teen doesn't use it for 120 days, when it will automatically lapse. This is one of the biggest complaints I receive from parents, but your children had to tell Hotmail that they were eighteen years old or that they had your consent. I hope the people at Hotmail will rethink the 120-day rule when parents are involved in trying to close a child's account. If your child is under 13, though, the new federal privacy law requires them to cancel if you notify them of your objection and your child's age.

Many filtering products block e-mail entirely. Some can filter the text messages of the e-mail. Many child sites have a closed system for e-mail, using only an in-site e-mail address, and a screening process for all e-mail. Other services (like Surf Monkey) send the e-mail headers to the parent's e-mail account, and if it's from someone the parent approves of, the child can access the e-mail. Still other parental controls can block e-mail from anyone other than preapproved senders. (This often also blocks spam, as well as Aunt Matilda.) There are many products and ways of handling e-mail risks available to parents. We'll discuss them in detail in "One from Column A, Two from Column B."

A few quick tips to remember about using e-mail:

- Change your password often (and keep it in a safe place that your children won't find)
- Don't share the password with anyone (especially your children)
- Don't open any attachments unless they are run through an anti-virus program
- Log off when done
- Don't reply to spam, harassing, or offensive e-mail
- Use common sense and keep personal information personal
- Delete all e-mails, unread, from people you don't know
- Don't be caught by the spammers' favorite trick, "Remember me?"

ICQ and Other Instant Messaging Services

What Are They?

Instant messaging is real-time communication. It's a blend of e-mail and chat (since you send one to someone and get real-time communication), but better. It's also fast eclipsing e-mail as the most popular Internet communication tool.

To give you a sense of their popularity, AOL reports that in June 1999 an average of 63 million e-mail messages traveled through their system daily, compared to 432 million instant messages per day.

ICQ is the original instant messaging product. It's a messaging and chat program that lets you know if your friends or family are online and let's you send them a message instantly. (ICQ stands for "I seek you.") It was acquired by AOL in 1998. AOL users have a similar proprietary product called "instant messages," or "IMs," and AOL Instant Messenger is available for free use by all Internet users (it is expected that the products will be integrated).

AT&T, Microsoft, Mindspring, and Yahoo! are also offering similar products, and kid-friendly companies like Headbone and Disney Blast Pad offer similar services for children. But no matter which you use, instant messaging is very popular and likely to grow in popularity. (In this book, I refer to all of the services generally as "instant messaging.")

How Do They Work?

On ICQ you get a UIN (Universal Internet Number), which is the ICQ equivalent of an e-mail address. That's how others can find and contact you. (You can even chat using ICQ and send attachments like photos or documents to others.) On AOL, you use your screen name as your IM address. And AOL's Instant Messenger and other instant messaging services use their own identifiers, including a screen name or code name.

Using instant messaging is easier than sending an e-mail because the instant messaging programs all run in the "background." That means they can interrupt your other applications by popping the message up on your screen or flashing an icon on your task bar. When you compare it to sending an e-mail, think of it as beeping someone instead of calling them: it finds you anywhere and interrupts you, although just like when you're beeped, you can ignore it. The other method (e-mail) works only if you answer it, like using a phone.

How Are They Abused?

Instant messaging can also notify others when you are online, so they can contact you "live." That's one of the main reasons people use them. It's also one of the greatest dangers where children are concerned. Cyberpredators can add a child's UIN or instant messaging ID to their notify list (AOL calls it the "buddy list"), allowing them to be notified whenever the child is online. Contacting is then as simple as sending them a message. (I explain more about buddy lists later on.)

ICQ also has different modes of "existence," thus giving others even more information. A user can be simply "online" but also "away," in "do not disturb" mode, available for "random chat," and a couple of others.

In addition, if a user is in "online" mode and leaves the computer for a while, the ICQ program sets the mode to "away" automatically. This means that cyberpredators could potentially know not only when the child is online but also when the computer is online but the child has stepped away for a few minutes.

Exactly what does the cyberpredator gain by knowing this? Maybe nothing; then again, maybe something—like the child has left the computer to get a parent. The bottom line is that the child is giving away a little more information and losing a little more privacy.

Luckily, both ICQ and IM allow you to prevent others adding you to their notify list without your permission. ICQ allows you to make yourself "invisible" to one or more users on your contact list, or to everyone. The users for whom you have set this option will then always see you as "offline" regardless of your true status. I recommend that if your children are permitted to use instant messaging and ICQ, you set these features to help retain their privacy.

Most instant messaging programs are free, but you need to download the software and register to use it. You can find ICQ at www.icq.com and find its affiliate, Instant Messenger, at www.aol.com. All you need to install and use the other instant messaging programs can be found at the sponsor's site. For example, Disney's (available just for its Disney Club Blast members) is found at www.disney.com, and Headbone's is at www.headbone.com.

When you register, the providers ask for a lot of personal information, and unless you are careful, that information may be publicly posted. That means you'll be sharing personal information with others without even knowing it.

So, make sure you read about privacy options and click on all the privacy settings, so that information you provide remains private. Also, provide only the information you *have* to provide, not the elective or optional information. (And *always* make sure you check the site's privacy policy to make sure that whatever information you share really is kept private.)

It's a shame that the technology that can be so helpful for productive reasons can be misused as easily for negative ones. AOL's parental controls permit IMs only at the young teen level, and they know best.

Don't allow your children to use instant messaging until they are old enough to use them carefully and responsibly—and you know they are following your rules. And read about how the kid sites are designing programs to give your children instant messaging capability safely. But remember that adults can sign up at most kid sites by pretending to be a child, and can communicate within that service with your child.

So, even in a kid-friendly environment, your children have to use their "stranger-danger radar." Make sure that you have set up your child's account to restrict strangers from being able to contact your children, and to keep their contact information private. Also, check these services' new safety and privacy features frequently. Those features are being added regularly, and you'll want to be able to take advantage of them.

Buddy Lists

What Are They?

Buddy lists are a great way to keep track of friends online. They started on AOL, to allow you to track other members and know when they were online so you could contact them. Now many ISPs and other online services offer them as well. Most instant messaging services and ICQ use them, although these services might call them something else, like "notify lists."

How Do They Work?

Adding someone to your buddy list (or notify list) is as easy as adding an e-mail address or screen name to a list. If you use AOL and your three best friends use AOL, you add their screen names to your list and AOL's buddy list utility will let you know when they sign on, so you can send them an instant message. If you are using AT&T's instant messaging system, you can add non-AOL members to your buddy list, too. (At the time of writing, many ISPs' instant messaging products weren't able to access AOL members, due to a dispute between AOL and these other instant messaging providers.)

It's a terrific feature. Just think how wonderful it would be to have something notify you when someone you want to call gets home. That's what buddy lists do—they let you know when someone's within reach of your instant messages or available to chat online.

Also, if you add your child's name to your buddy list and don't use the same AOL account (only one AOL account member can use the account at a time), you can check and see when they are online while you are at work or not at home. It lets you know when your child might be breaking your "time online" rule. (Again, let them know when you are monitoring them.)

How Are They Abused?

Stalkers, hackers, flamers, harassers, and online predators love buddy lists. The same way you know when your friends are online, they can use buddy lists to tell them when your child is online. They can find profiles of likely victims and just add their screen names and instant messaging addresses to their own buddy lists. When your child gets online, the buddy list alerts the bad guys, who can then step up the harassment, luring, or hacking.

What Can You Do About It?

Make sure that you check any privacy setting that allows you to block others from including your child on their buddy lists. With younger children especially, the only people who should be allowed to have your child on their buddy lists are people you know and trust *offline*.

If someone contacts your child who shouldn't and you suspect that they are tracking your child online, make sure you have blocked incoming messages from that person (or, depending on what technology you're using, included that person on your "ignore list") and check to make sure that all privacy settings are at their most restrictive.

You should also check and see who is on your child's buddy list. Make sure you personally know each of the people who are listed. Go through them one by one on a regular basis, asking your child to tell you who each is.

Also, make sure that they really are the friends the child thinks they are. A common mistake made by children who are using AOL is to include their friends on their buddy list using the personal portion of their e-mail address—such as "Parry"—instead of the complete e-mail address—such as Parry@aftab.com—because people communicating within AOL (which includes half the children under the age of thirteen in the United States who are online!) don't need to use the "@aol.com" part. So they would just type in "Parry" on their AOL buddy list. But since my AOL screen name is ParryA, or ParryAftab, they just added a stranger to their buddy list without realizing it.

Pen Pal Programs

What Is an Online Pen Pal Program?

Online pen pal programs allow kids to find others with special interests and from all around the world as e-mail, instant messaging, and chat correspondents. They are particularly popular when social studies research papers are due. KidsCom (the most popular kids' pen pal program provider) can spot when assignments are given, because hundreds of kids from a particular school will sign up at once, needing correspondents from a particular country. "Help! What's your gross national product and chief natural resource?" is typical of the first message exchange, KidsCom tells us.

How Do They Work?

There are two different ways to find pen pal programs: One is through websites, such as KidsCom (www.kidscom.com), and the other is through school networks, where one school joins a network of schools around the world to create a pen pal program. Most kid-friendly programs use an anonymous screen name and caution the kids not to share information that identifies them personally.

How Are They Abused?

Many of us had pen pals when we were growing up. (I had several, but never wrote back on time, so I didn't hold on to them for very long.) But online pen pals are different somehow. Maybe it's the fact that so much of our children's online correspondence occurs when we're not watching.

Maybe it's the fact that we don't really know where the pen pal lives when we correspond online. The pen pal you think is safely in Hong Kong might really live next door. And even if he lives in Hong Kong, international travel has become commonplace these days. But whatever it is, cyber–pen pals are different. Pen pal programs can be a rich source of potential victims for cyberpredators. You never know with whom you are corresponding.

Yet children who are not allowed to e-mail strangers, or chat in unmonitored chatrooms, or use ICQ or instant messaging, are often allowed to have online pen pals and no one worries about it.

What Can You Do About It?

Until someone develops the technology to allow us to know for sure with whom we are communicating online, children should be restricted to classroom pen pal programs. That's when a classroom or school arranges to exchange pen pals with another classroom or school in another state or country. The only way to know if a child is really a child is by asking the school. Making sure that the school confirms the pen pal participants keeps it safe.

I don't recommend that parents allow children to join any other pen pal program, even at safe sites, unless all pen pal communications are monitored by the program, the child can be trusted to follow the online safety rules, or the parent screens all correspondence. Even then, make sure the pen pal doesn't have your child's regular e-mail address. Set up another e-mail account (free e-mail services, like Hotmail, are good for this) just for the pen pal correspondence. That way, if things go wrong, you can simply close that e-mail address.

Your children can start joining non-school pen pal programs when you think they are old enough to follow your rules and know how to avoid cyberpredators' advances.

When you think they're ready, KidsCom (www.kidscom.com) has a good program, which you need parental consent to join. They have kids from 121 countries who participate at the site, which makes for a very diverse pen pal group. But remember that anyone can pretend to be a child online. They can even register at kids' sites as a child. So meeting them in a child's site is no guarantee of authenticity.

So, even if your children enter a pen pal program you trust, you should still keep an eye on the correspondence. (But always make sure your children know ahead of time when you're going to monitor their correspondence.)

Also, ask your children to talk to you about their pen pals often. Open communication between parent and child is the bane of a cyberpredator's existence.

The World's Biggest Billboard

There's a lot of information we give away online, just by forgetting to click on privacy settings, or by giving more information than we have to. There are three other ways our children can innocently give away information about themselves—by posting personal profiles, by filling out contest and registration forms, and by building a website. There are also many databases that could list your child's address, phone number, and e-mail address.

Knowing how our children can innocently give out information online, and how easily information about them can be found by strangers, is one of the most important things I can teach you.

Online Profiles—
Advertising for Trouble

What Is a Profile?

A profile is a list of personal information that certain services let you post online to allow other subscribers to know more about you, your hobbies, etc. A profile helps you find others with similar interests online. It also helps them find you (or your child).

How Does a Profile Work?

Profiles are often included as a free feature for members of AOL, other Internet service providers, and many free e-mail services. The service may ask you questions that you can answer, and have your answers searchable to others online. Usually they include "A/S/L," cybershorthand for age/gender (sex)/location. (Generally, these are the first questions asked of a newcomer in a chatroom.)

How Are Profiles Abused?

This is what a typical online profile looks like:

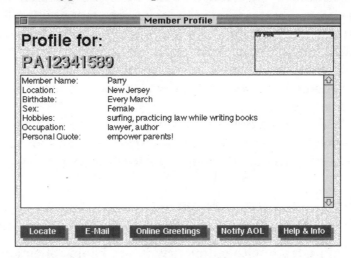

Many unsuspecting children give their real names—and other personal information—on their profiles without thinking twice. These profiles can then be searched online, using a special search feature. While this lets you find others with similar interests, like skateboarding or the Backstreet Boys, it too can be abused. (You aren't really surprised, are you? By now you should be getting a sense of how things work online.)

People who don't have your child's well-being at heart can search for all birth dates by year, so that they can find preteen or young teenagers born in a certain year. Profiles of all thirteen- and fourteen-year-olds could then pop up. They can search further by gender and by state. The technology can help them locate exactly what they're looking for in a geographically desirable location.

Sometimes, although kids may be careful about posting personal information, they post provocative phrases or flame others. (That's cybertalk for being rude, insulting, or trying to provoke arguments with or among others online. I talk about this in depth in the "Dark Side" chapter and in "Ms. Parry's Rules for Correct Internet Behavior" in Chapter 7.)

Teenagers also often play practical jokes on their friends by using their passwords to access their friend's profile and posting something provocative. (And anything provocative gets a quick response in cyberspace.) That's why we teach them not to share their passwords with anyone, even their friends (*especially* their friends!).

What Can You Do About It?

The simplest solution is to make sure your children don't post a profile. The second-best option is to make sure any profile they do post doesn't contain personal information, such as their real names, addresses, schools, sports team names, birth dates, or ages (they can use a grade to confuse the technology search instead), or provocative information. You should review what they want to post to make sure it's generic and scandal-free.

If they already have a profile, review it and make sure they change everything that is provocative or can be used to find them offline. And check back frequently to make sure it stays safe.

Filling Out Forms Online—
Giving Away Personal Information

I deal in depth with online privacy and data collection from our kids in "Protecting Our Kids' Privacy and Our Privacy" in Chapter 4, but you need to be aware that our kids are filling out forms for contests, registrations, and newsletters all the time. Make sure you teach them to check with you first, and to fill out forms only at trusted sites with a privacy policy. If your child is under thirteen, new laws require the site to get your okay first.

Kids' Personal Websites

Many Internet service providers, online services, and other websites (like Yahoo!) provide free websites for anyone who wants one. This gives our children a chance to be creative and express their opinions. Many teachers are encouraging their students to develop Web pages, too.

How Are They Abused?

Kids are always building sites that tell more than they should about themselves. They list their schools, sports teams, even sometimes their telephone numbers, photos, and addresses. They almost always include their e-mail address.

The only good thing is that most of these personal Web pages are difficult to find, since they are normally not registered with search engines, and are too obscure to find in a search. And the harder it is for you to find the website, the less likely it is that anyone else can find it.

If your kids have a website, look it over—not just as a parental cop, but because it might show you how creative your child or teen is, and it might teach you more about your child. See if it includes any personal-contact information. If there's no way of knowing who your child is, or how to contact them online or offline, they can use photos. Otherwise, think about what information it contains. Could you find your child offline by using the information they supply? Think really hard about this. Sometimes we give out clues that, when pieced together, can lead to us. (Don't worry. I'll share information about this later on in Chapter 7, in "Clues We Give Away—Shannon, Now Known as 'Tiffany'.")

Do you know what information is really out there that can be pieced together? Here's how you can find out.

Hello, Information? I'd Like to Know What Information You Have About My Child

There are several directory websites that contain e-mail addresses and, in some cases, home addresses and phone numbers. These are called "white pages." They get their information from public telephone directories, voluntary listings (when people register this information directly with the site), and search spiders. If your kids want to be found, they register their e-mail or home address with these sites.

Some of the free e-mail services also have a members' directory, but the contact information may not be as complete as that with a search directory. The ICQ and instant messaging directories can be surprisingly dangerous, since they include lots of information your child might not even realize is made public.

While your kids may be careful about sharing offline personal information, there are ways information is used to help get more information about a person online. For example, if your child has a listed phone number, their address is probably listed in an online White Pages directory. Sometimes, if they registered at one of the directory sites, their e-mail address is linked to their offline contact info, including their phone number.

There are several websites that provide reverse telephone number searches (www.anywho.com, www.switchboard.com, and www.infospace.com). Just type in the telephone number, and up comes the person's name and address, with handy links to search for e-mail information and a map to their home. If you have an unlisted number, it is less likely that your information will appear.

There are reverse e-mail searches, too, such as www.bigfoot.com, and www.iaf.net. There you can put in someone's e-mail address and it gives you other information about them. (We searched for mine, but nothing came up, so this might not be a serious problem yet, since there are hundreds of websites that contain my e-mail address and offline business contact information.) Still, it's a good idea to check them all out. One site allows you to search several databases at the same time, www.theultimates.com/white/. It might be a good place to start.

What Can You Do About It?

You can check and see if your child is listed anywhere and remove the information if they are.

Here are a few other website search locations you should check:

Finding people: www.1800ussearch.com

Looking up people and businesses: www.databaseamerica.com

National Telephone Book—White Page: www.yahoo.com/
search/people

Also, if your child has ICQ, check their directories and profiles: www.icq.com.

If they use AOL's instant messenger, or another instant messaging service, or any free e-mail service, check their member directories. And if your ISP or online service offers member directories or profiles, search for your child, using their screen name or your or their e-mail addresses. You might want to enlist your children's help—if you think they won't add themselves to these site directories when you're not looking.

Last but not least, you should search for your child's name at the major search engines by putting their whole name in quotes. (For example, "Parry Aftab" will search for me, as opposed to every "Parry" and every "Aftab" mentioned that might appear separately in the search engine.) And if someone is posting about them, or they are using their real names in newsgroups, you can also search Deja News (www.dejanews.com) for their name, also using the same "quotes" search format.

The Wild Wild West: IRC, FTP, Usenet, and Newsgroups

Some parts of the Internet are more free-for-all than others. IRC, FTP, and Usenet are three of those.

Usenet is a worldwide collection of newsgroups. A newsgroup is a discussion group devoted to a particular topic. They aren't located on the Web. They are a separate and much older part of the Internet, without graphics, sound, or animation (other than the lively discussion of newsgroup members).

The newsgroups collect articles, discussions, and other messages on a particular subject, then broadcast them or make them available to users over the Internet. Some newsgroups are moderated, which means the material is screened by a moderator before being posted. Many are not.

As the Web develops, Usenet and newsgroups are becoming less prominent. But with so many die-hard Usenet fans out there, they're unlikely to disappear anytime soon. They can still be a great way to reach people who are interested in the same things that you are, and teenagers may sometimes find newsgroups a good source of arcane information about certain topics for reports. Finding a newsgroup is as simple as searching www.dejanews.com, the main newsgroup index. And posting is as simple as following the Deja News instructions.

But newsgroup participants are well known for their opinionated discussions, and flaming often abounds. (Flaming is when someone insults, annoys, provokes, or attacks someone else online.) Although there are many great newsgroups, especially for special parenting needs (try "misc.kids"), there are many more where chaos and outrageous behavior rule. There are even a few that trade in illegal materials, such as child pornography.

IRC is a non-Web chat area, where thousands of channels, on thousands of topics, give people a place to chat. On IRC they can usually chat without the strict terms of service codes of conduct set by the chat giants, like AOL and Talk City. That means the same unrestricted Wild West atmosphere exists in IRC as in newsgroups, but live. Many pedophile groups use IRC as their chat area of choice. To ensure privacy from prying eyes of parents and undercover FBI agents, chats by invitation only can be set up.

FTP (file transfer protocol) is a method of accessing files located on computers that are connected to the Internet. They are most often used to access game files, but sometimes these computers also house serious hate, pedophilia, and child pornography materials.

Newsgroups, FTP, and IRC are good examples of how an area of the Internet can be both rich with valuable information and lively discussion and full of serious dangers for our children.

What Can You Do About It?

Just remember that given the Wild West atmosphere of many IRC and newsgroup discussions, your children should be carefully supervised when using any of them—or kept off them entirely until they're old enough to look out for themselves. They should also be warned to know the Netiquette and IRC channel or newsgroup rules before venturing forth into any IRC channels or newsgroup. Failure to adhere to the rules can result in serious flaming and harassment of the offender and being "kicked" (thrown off the chat channel for a while) or "banned" (thrown off forever).

You'll be relieved to learn that it's not as hard to keep a child away from newsgroups as it is to keep them away from certain websites. Unless children are looking for graphic information on just about any offensive topic, the newsgroups don't hold much interest for a child. (No sounds, graphics, or animations, remember?) So finding safe and interesting sites on the Web, and warning them to stay away from newsgroups, might be enough.

And since many child-friendly chat areas are easier to use and often more fun than IRC chats, children may not mind staying off IRC altogether.

Talk to them about the FTP sites they access and what they are downloading. Make sure that they are staying away from the dangerous ones and are using antivirus programs.

For those of you who want to filter access to IRC, FTP, and newsgroups, many of the products on the market filter them, as well as the Web. Some can block access to them entirely.

CHAPTER 3

The Dark Side

There's a lot of offensive information on the Internet, no matter how you personally define "offensive." Remember that the Internet is an equal-opportunity offender. But it's important that we keep things in perspective.

Are We Being Cautious Parents . . . or Paranoid Wrecks?

Everything in life has its risks. I remember years ago when I was watching *Sesame Street* with my children, and Grover appeared in a piece where he was afraid of everything. He was even afraid that the ceiling would fall in on him. (Los Angeles earthquakes aside. . . .) He had to be taught how to put his fears (and the dangers) in perspective.

It was a good lesson. It taught us that when we don't understand the risks, how things work, or the likelihood of things going wrong, even ceilings can become the object of terror.

It might help to know what other parents worry about. According to surveys taken by Jupiter Communications (the statisticians I trust—www.jup.com), 72 percent of parents in 1998 were concerned about danger from strangers coming from e-mail and chatrooms. That figure rose slightly to 76 percent in 1999. For dangers from adult entertainment, the 1998 and 1999 figures are 68 percent and 75 percent, respectively—again, not a significant change. Parents seemed to show the most increase in concerns when dealing with marketing and advertising. Privacy issues concerned only 55 percent of the parents in 1998 but 68 percent in 1999, and concerns about advertising aimed at kids jumped from just 18 percent in 1998 to 45 percent in 1999. (Note that different surveys give different percentages, but all show increases in concern about commercial risks.) These opinions are a result of both heightened awareness and an increase in Internet use among parents.

To parents who aren't familiar with the Internet, everything is equally frightening and dangerous. But as we learn more, we can distinguish between real and imagined dangers. This allows us, as Grover did, to weigh the benefits of being shielded from the elements against the risk of the ceiling falling in.

All Risks and Dangers Are Not Equal in Cyberspace

Part of the challenge we face in trying to keep our kids safe online is telling the difference between what's only annoying or offensive and what's dangerous and even illegal. But whether it's illegal or merely annoying, we need to remember that we have the right, as parents, to decide what our children should see and what they shouldn't.

And we have to be realistic about the risks. There's a fine line between being a cautious parent and being a paranoid wreck. We shouldn't see monsters under every cyberbed and in every cybercloset. We need to recognize where the real risks are, and remember that many things are only annoying, not dangerous.

Finally, as our children mature and demonstrate improved judgment, we have to keep moving the bar higher, to give them more freedom and choices online. A big part of parenting is teaching our children to exercise their own judgment. The training wheels have to come off sometime.

Information Doesn't Hurt Children— People Hurt Children

There are two kinds of risks our children face in life. One relates to our children's sensitivities, emotional well-being, and intellectual growth. The other relates to their physical well-being and safety. While no one wants their children's feelings hurt, or their being exposed to disgusting and hateful information, I think if given a choice we would prefer *that* to their being physically molested or hurt. It's *people* who pose the greatest risks to our children online, not information.

But that doesn't mean information can't be a problem. We just need to recognize that not all information is created equal. The information our children can access ranges from information you may consider inappropriate, disgusting, or even dangerous for them emotionally, to how they can buy dangerous substances and guns online.

Some parents believe that their children should have access to *all* information, no matter how outrageous they personally might believe it to be. They believe that it helps their children handle things they face in life and is a matter of intellectual freedom and free speech. Other parents believe that all information should be prescreened for their children since *they*—not the U.S. Constitution—are the final arbiters of their children's intellectual freedom. There's no right answer for *all* children, just a right one for *your own* children.

Whether you decide that your children should have unlimited access to all content online, be limited to only preapproved content, or something in between, remember: It's *your* choice. It's not a political issue, it's a parenting one. One of our few prerogatives as parents is to decide what information is appropriate for our own children.

What Kinds of Risks Are We Talking About?

There are two kinds of risks I'll discuss in this chapter—risks to our children and risks your children pose to others, including you. (Parents with perfect children can ignore the section on risks your children pose to others, as long as their perfect children also have perfect friends.)

Risks to Our Children

There are six types of risks our children face online:

1. They can access information that might be inappropriate for them. This includes pornography, hate, intolerance, bigotry, gore, violence, hoaxes, and misinformation and hype.

2. They can access information, do things, and purchase products that might be dangerous to them. There are sites that offer bomb-building recipes, sites that sell guns, alcohol, poisons, tobacco products and drugs, and sites that offer gambling online.

3. They can be stalked and harassed by people (often other children) who are rude, insulting, and make threats, or may send them viruses or hack their computers.

4. They can give up important and private information by filling out forms and entering contests online, and, as a result, be targeted by irresponsible marketers using unfair marketing techniques.

5. They can be scammed or defrauded when they buy things online, and risk disclosing our important financial information to others, like credit card and pin numbers and passwords.

6. They can be lured by cyberpredators who want to meet them face-to-face.

If you look over the list, you'll see that all but two of the risks are within our children's control. Except when they stumble inadvertently on certain content (as we discussed in the previous chapter), they can avoid information that is either inappropriate or dangerous. They can also refuse to fill out forms and registrations online or make sure the information they provide is okayed by you and is being treated responsibly by the entities that collect it.

Only cyberstalkers, harassers, and cyberpredators are outside of their control. And until someone develops the "Beam me up, Scotty!" technology or ways to shrink our children so they can pass through the modem lines, your child has to agree to meet them, or has to give them information about where they can be found offline, to be really at risk.

I'll give you tips on how to avoid these risks online, but you need to deal with the fact that your children might be *intentionally* accessing inappropriate sites, doing dangerous things, and putting themselves at risk. That's the nature of children. (It's *especially* the nature of teenagers!)

Don't worry, though. We can help you gain more control over what your children do online and teach you how to help them exercise critical thinking and make informed judgments. But in order for you to be able to educate your children about online risks, you need to learn about them first. (I'll try to make this as painless as possible.)

Some of these risks also involve illegal activities. I'll present a brief discussion of the law on this subject later. But right now the focus is on how these risks operate, and some quick advice on what you can do to try to manage these risks inside your home—through technology, safety advice, and talking to your kids. (We'll get to more detailed advice on how to teach your children to handle online risks, and on technological tools and parental controls that might help, in the "Teach . . . Your Children Well" and "Making and Implementing Your Choices" chapters.)

Stuff You Might Prefer Your Children Not See

You will be happy to learn that in my experience most kids are quickly bored with adult sites and other inappropriate information. So, other than their first journey to the dark side to see what it holds in store, most of our kids and teens will wander back disappointed with what they found. (Not that they don't wander back and forth a bit—especially when they are in groups and out to impress others, their hormones are raging, or when violence and gore sites are concerned.)

But the dark side may hold more of a lingering lure to a troubled child or teen. (We've seen that with Littleton and other tragedies.) It's your job to know if your child or teen is troubled. While some of these tips might help you understand more about their surfing habits and control their activities online, helping troubled teens with their pain and anger takes more than using a filtering software. It takes caring and professional advice.

So while I'll help you spot the risks online, you're the one who needs to understand your child. (In "Get to Know Your Kids, and Create a Workable 'Safe-Surfing Contract' for Them," in Chapter 7, I give you a few tips on getting to know your children. I've even included a checklist on some things all of us should know about our children and teenagers.)

Sexually Explicit Content— Adult Pornography

Spicey Girls! XXX-rated! Hot Teens and Bouncing Blonde Bombshells! Very few of us haven't been exposed to this information online. There's no question that there are hundreds of thousands of sexually explicit websites. It's no wonder that Internet sex sites seem to get far more attention than any other content online.

These adult-content sites range from the *Playboy*-type (which some parents may not strongly object to) to lurid hard-core and sexually deviant sites that even the most liberal parents would not want their kids to see. Fortunately, many responsible adult sites do what they can to keep your kids out by requiring a credit card or other adult-verification system to access their content.

But much of this content is legal. Content on the Internet can't and shouldn't be limited to what is appropriate for only six-year-olds. There are many things that adults can legally do and access that may not be appropriate for children. That's our prerogative as adults.

But whatever our tolerance level is and whether it's legal or not, we don't have to allow our children to view what *we* consider inappropriate for them. As parents, it's also our prerogative to decide what is appropriate for our children and what isn't. That's why I wrote this book.

True Confessions

When I did a segment for *Good Morning America* a few years ago, I worked with a group of eight- to ten-year-olds in a suburban school assembly. I asked the kids what they did online that they knew their parents wouldn't like. One nine-year-old timidly raised his hand and shared with us (and potentially the national television audience) that he looked at "naked people."

Gradually, the entire class raised their hands, admitting that they, too, looked at "naked people." I joked that they were probably just studying *biology*, and convinced *GMA* not to use the confession in the piece. But nine-year-olds (and younger) can see naked people and far more with just a click of the mouse.

Children don't have to find a retailer that will sell them an adult magazine. They don't have to scrounge up the money to buy one. They don't have to smuggle one out of a friend's house (or your bathroom). The stuff they can see online is home-delivered, largely free, very easy to find (just use a regular search engine), and in many cases far more graphic than they would be able to buy even under-the-counter.

Although many parents agree that graphic sexual content isn't the most serious danger our children face online, few of us want our children exposed to images of bestiality, rape, or sadomasochism.

What Can You Do About It?

Plenty! All of the options set out in "Yes, Virginia . . . There Is a Good Side to the Internet!" in Chapter 8, are free of graphic sex (although you may learn more about the reproductive life of sea turtles than you might want to know). And all of the products we tested were designed primarily to screen out sexually explicit content. It's what they do best. (You can learn how they work and how well they perform later in that chapter in "One from Column A, Two from Column B.")

But, first and foremost, we need to sit with our children and teach them that while they may have a healthy curiosity about naked people (and more), it's not worth getting obsessed about and after the first thrill may be pretty boring. This is an important time to teach them about your attitudes toward sex, pornography, and degradation and why you consider this stuff a waste of their time.

You have to constantly improve the filter between their ears—their judgment!

Hatred, Intolerance, and Bigotry

Ideas repugnant to many people have found a global audience in cyberspace. We need to make sure that our children become an informed, skeptical, and unwilling audience where hate, intolerance, and bigotry are concerned.

The range of hate, intolerance, and bigotry sites is pretty broad. There are many sites that question whether the Holocaust ever happened. Others mock racial minority groups, ethnic groups, religious groups, and those with different sexual preferences. Some indirectly promote intolerance by promoting racial supremacy. In-groups make fun of those outside their groups—everyone who wants to promote hate can do so online.

Unfortunately, it took the Littleton tragedy to make many people understand how much hate exists online (and offline). And most of it is legal. Hate laws in the United States regulate hate speech only when a certain group or individual is targeted in a way that promotes violence against them in a legally protected environment.

It's ironic that the one medium that should promote equality and tolerance is so often misused to promote the opposite. The Internet strips away everything but how well you communicate your ideas. The Internet is blind to gender, age, physical disability, race, and religion. When you meet people online, you don't know how old they are, whether they are male or female, what color their skin is, what accent they speak with, or how they pray. It's the most egalitarian environment in the world. No geographical borders—seamless global communication. That's the beauty of the Internet.

Biases online can be pretty illuminating, though. For example, people are often surprised to learn I'm a woman, because I have an unusual name and because I'm a lawyer. I'm amazed that their tone online often changes after they find out I'm a woman. Why that should be the case, especially in this day and age, I don't know. But we all do it. We all treat people differently based on their gender, age, or where they're from. It's part of how we're trained.

There are several sites that track hate, bigotry, and intolerance. One of my favorites, The Hate Directory (www.bcpl.lib.md.us/~rfrankli/hatedir.htm), is run by Ray Franklin, a law-enforcement officer from Maryland. As of August 1999, he reports 290 different "hate" websites, 6 FTP sites (where you can access and download files), 18 list servs (e-mail discussion group lists), 34 special hate chatrooms, and 13 bulletin board systems (discussion boards). Unfortunately, hate thrives online, where hatemongers, bigots, and kooks can feel safe and brave while hiding behind their monitors.

What Can You Do About It?

We have to teach our children that many people on the Internet have biases and prejudices that clash with our values. It's a good time to explain what your values are and to explain why you believe what you do. A solid grounding like this is your best weapon against others trying to sway your children's opinions.

When our children are exposed to outrageous bigotry and hatred online or anywhere else, we can help them understand the dangers of prejudice and the importance of diversity and tolerance. The more they have a chance to talk and share ideas with other children around the world, the more they will learn how alike we all are.

Mark Twain put his finger on it when he said: "Travel is fatal to prejudice, bigotry, and narrow-mindedness." On the Internet, our children travel the world every day. We need to make sure that they understand that they are truly part of the global community, and learn to celebrate the differences and diversity the global community represents rather than mock them.

Point out faulty expectations and prejudices with your children by asking them what they think the person they're talking to online is like. Then give them alternative descriptions telling them that the person is fifty, not fifteen, male, not female, and of a different race. Ask them how that changes things—and why. This may be a good way to start to teach them about prejudice and stereotypes.

Also, you should discuss hurtful and hateful things when they happen and:

- teach your children how much discrimination hurts
- remind them that when we call others "names," or say we hate "those" people, we are discriminating against others
- teach them never to condone prejudice or discrimination, whether they encounter it at school, home, or anywhere else
- understand that even if we don't discriminate ourselves, our children can be influenced by the media and others they encounter who may not be as enlightened
- teach your children that they should question the way things have always been done and always try to improve the world

Once the discussion starts, be prepared for some hard questions and even tougher answers.

The Anti-Defamation League and the National PTA have prepared some wonderful information about ways we can all teach our children to deal with hate, intolerance, and bigotry. The Simon Wiesenthal Center is another source of information about avoiding hate, intolerance, and bigotry. (You can access their sites to learn more at www.adl.org, www.pta.org, and www.wiesenthal.org.) In addition to the filtering products we review that block or filter hate, intolerance, and bigotry sites, the ADL has developed a Hate Filter. It retails for $29.99. More information about the Hate Filter can be found at the ADL site.

Violence and Gore

Kids and teens aren't as interested in the sexually explicit sites as parents think they are, but they are much more intrigued by gory sites filled with amputated body parts and people clubbing baby seals and beached whales than any of us would have dreamed. Kids see them as horror movies rather than real life. I suspect the best thing we can do is hope they grow out of it.

One particularly savvy library media specialist I know told me that when the kids are grouped around the monitor with their faces pressed up against the monitor screen, she *knows* that it's a gory site they are viewing.

Our Teenangels (a special team of teenagers I work with who are trained in online safety) tell me that their friends visit gory sites whenever they can. Many teenagers have shared with me the names of sites that purported to show body parts at famous accident scenes. I don't understand the attraction, but it seems to be pretty universal among teenagers in particular. The sites range from just gross to very disgusting. (Some even show human corpses being cut into pieces or posed in grotesque ways.) The violent sites also often try to provoke violence. But since the Littleton tragedy, most of us understand these as "hate sites."

What Can You Do About It?

Trying to educate our children not to "go there" might work. (I have no faith that it will, though.) But here we need education to teach our children that these aren't horror movies, that the whales and seals being clubbed to death are real, and that the accident victims are someone's loved ones. Filtering products also block and filter violence and gore sites. (Our test results on how well the big four blocked our sample violence and gore sites is included in Chapter 8.)

Misinformation and Hype

The Internet is an inexpensive and easy method of publishing information. Anyone can be a publisher, and everyone is an expert. Separating the truth from fantasy in cyberspace is one of the hardest tasks we have. Con artists, scam artists, cultists, and just plain nutcases thrive in this free atmosphere.

How can you tell marketing hype from fact? What information is reliable and what is pure bunk? How do your kids separate Elvis sightings from scholarly discourse? How do we, for that matter? (I guess that's another book.)

Robin Raskin, Internet Mom, sees misinformation as a big problem, too, one that the latest technology can't provide a quick fix for. "Most parental control software," she states, "while it does a decent job of blocking pornographic material, does not do a very good job of blocking kooks, pyramid schemes, racism, or outright lies. These are subtleties that no technology can easily block." I guess that leaves it up to us.

Whether we like it or not, the buck stops here. It's our job as parents to teach our children the difference between hype, misinformation, and quality sources wherever they find them. We also need to teach them that not everyone is what he or she seems to be. Most of us have already started teaching them that. Unfortunately, our children have to learn these things early.

Every time I used to wheel my kids through the supermarket checkout aisle, supermarket tabloids would blast outrageous headlines at them: "Men from Mars Father Children in Indiana," "Four-Hundred-

Year-Old Woman Shares the Secrets of Long Life," and so on. Once they could read, I would have to explain the truth (although I could rarely explain it well enough, since I'm not sure *I* understand how they can get away with saying these things—and I'm a *lawyer*).

Every time a publishing company's sweepstakes envelope would arrive addressed to them and heralding that they had won umpteen million dollars, I would have to explain the small print. But whether we're in the supermarket or handing out the mail, we're there to answer any questions. That's why it's important that we be there when they have surfing questions, too, especially when they are getting online for the first time. But that's the easy part. When our kids are surfing alone, we need to teach them how to do it for themselves. That's much harder.

What Can You Do About It?

Teach them to be smart information consumers. Try to get them to share what they learn and read in cyberspace with you, so you can do a reality check. Surf with them and point out outrageous sources that should be approached with skepticism.

You also have to teach them to exercise their judgment. This is the most important thing we can teach our children, but it takes a special twist online. Other than the professional look of a site, there is very little a child can go on to judge a site's credibility. Terrific groups like the American Library Association (ALA) and others have compiled recommended and safe-site lists, but these amount to no more than maybe forty thousand websites collectively (the size of a typical high school library). There is no *Good Housekeeping* Seal of Approval yet for Internet sites. (But some are coming! The WiredKids site, www.wiredkids.org will be giving a "safe and fun site" seal of approval to qualified sites and Cyberangels gives a safe site seal of approval to sites approved by Cyberangels' Cybermoms.)

So, what about the remainder of the millions of sites on the Internet? How do children judge site credibility when most adults can't? What can they believe? The Teenangels have told me that we should teach younger children never to believe anything they see, hear, or read online. Perhaps that's a bit extreme. But we do need to teach them to be skeptical.

How do we teach children to measure the credibility of a site? How can they tell who's behind the site? Is it a historian or a hate group? Is it sharing facts or fiction? How can we create smart Internet information consumers?

Trusting a Brand Name

Sometimes, until children have developed solid critical thinking skills, it's often best to rely on the judgment of someone you trust. You might try to guide your children to school- and library-approved site lists. The ALA's list of safe and approved sites is one of the best (www.ala.org/parentspage/greatsites). So is the Children's Partnership list and (she says with mock humility) Cyberangels' CyberMoms' Approved Sites list. I've given a list of these approved site lists, and some other places to find reliable sites, in "Yes, Virginia . . . There Is a Good Side to the Internet!" in Chapter 8.

Using a search engine directory rather than the simple index search might help, too. (Remember when I explained how search engine directories worked?) Trained reviewers have reviewed each site and made a decision whether it should have been included in the directory listings.

I often use Yahoo! and Lycos directories for that reason. They do a lot of the screening and sifting I would have had to do at other search engines.

I also rely heavily on Lycos's Top 5% of the Web–awarded sites. (Our law firm site, www.aftab.com, was honored with this award a few years ago.) You can even execute a search just of their award-winning sites. Trusting the professionals is an easy place to begin. The online expert guides on About.com are trusted website evaluators, too. (But make sure you choose a kid-friendly topic, or the reviewed sites may not be kid-friendly.)

Either way, whether you use someone's site list or trust their directories to screen out the kooks, you're relying on a recognized name brand to help you select credible and worthwhile sites.

We can teach our children how to exercise their own information literacy skills by making sure they talk to their librarians and teachers about how to evaluate the credibility of information. I've also set out a few tips in the "Kids Online in Schools" chapter, too. But whether they rely on trusted experts (or you) to help them evaluate information, or develop their own method to measure credibility, we should teach them to always question the source and use their best judgment, online and off. Our children have to become critical thinkers.

Cyber Hoaxes, Rumors, and Urban Legends

We aren't strangers to urban legends. The crazed stalker of couples in lovers' lane. The baby alligator brought back as a souvenir from Florida that, when flushed down the toilet, lived and hunted in the sewers. Some legends live on from one generation to the next. (Do we even have lovers' lanes anymore, and aren't alligators a protected or endangered species?)

Remember Mikey, the kid who wouldn't eat anything? Well, you may also remember the rumor (totally unfounded) about twenty years ago that he died while eating Pop Rocks (the effervescent candy) when he drank a can of soda and his stomach exploded. (I wrote my senior thesis on that and other business rumors.)

Rumors, especially those that sound believable, have abounded for centuries. It isn't any different in cyberspace. In fact, they move faster online than they ever could offline.

Someone went to a movie and sat down on a hypodermic needle that had been left on the seat. She then contracted AIDS. Someone else was drugged by a beautiful woman and woke up in a bathtub filled with ice to find a kidney missing. (Apparently it had been removed and sold to someone who needed a kidney transplant.) Real or hoaxes? You be the judge.

But most good hoaxes and rumors have three main ingredients—they *could* happen, they touch something we know about or think is true (people can get HIV from an exposed infected needle, and people are desperate for transplant organs), and they feed on fear (getting HIV/AIDS, being drugged by strangers, dangers of having sex with strangers, etc.).

The difference between a rumor and a hoax is that while hoaxes are planned fakes, rumors may be believed and innocently passed on. But since once a hoax is passed on by people who believe it, it becomes a rumor, who cares anyway?

Computer Virus Rumors Are
Just the Latest Fad of Cyberhoaxes

E-mail hoax messages warning me about some new virus hazard arrive in my mailbox daily. One night a few years ago, my son, Michael, sent me a list of supposedly infected files that someone had sent to him at college. The list included the upgrade for AOL, among many other unlikely virus-carrier candidates. This is the typical virus hoax that attempts to frighten people who have already installed popular programs, like AOL. (I reminded Michael to reread this section before he forwarded the hoax e-mail to anyone else—and he reminded me to include a chapter like this one in the book to help others.)

One of the biggest Internet rumors in the last few years was the Good Times virus, which was reputed to infect your computer through a regular e-mail. Experienced Internet and computer users dismissed it as a hoax, because they knew a virus couldn't be passed by reading an e-mail message (but they could be passed on by downloading and opening attachments to e-mails). A lot of other people were fooled, though. (You should know, though, that a recently discovered virus can now infect your computer merely by being read in e-mail.)

What Can You Do About It?

Luckily, there are several great websites you can refer to when you get your next e-mail announcing Armageddon, especially e-mails announcing the latest viruses. These sites will help you decide what to pay careful attention to and which to just ignore.

If you want to check, you can go to the experts. Symantec, the maker of Norton AntiVirus (www.symantec.com/avcenter), IBM hype alerts (www.av.ibm.com/BreakingNews/HypeAlert), Carnegie Mellon's Software Engineering Institute's CERT Coordination Center (www.cert.org), and the U.S. Department of Energy's Computer Incident Advisory Capability page (ciac.llnl.gov) are the places you can trust to help you separate fact from fiction.

Before you forward any e-mail proclaiming the latest virus, check it out. It's good Netiquette and a good way to preserve your credibility. And if you know someone who's rumormongering in cyberspace, tell them, too. (Otherwise, ignore anything they send you, or tell them to remove you from their rumor mailing list.)

The Riskier Stuff: When Kids Do Dangerous Things and Buy Illegal or Dangerous Products Online

Mom . . . How Do You Build a Bomb?

There are plenty of harmless books available on the Internet, but *The Big Book of Mischief* isn't one of them. Don't be fooled by its innocent name—the "mischief" it refers to is serious injury and death. It teaches violence, and gives our kids the tools they need to get the job done. To give you an idea of its tone, Part I is subtitled "The Terrorist's Handbook."

Of course it comes with the requisite disclaimer: that serious injury or death could result from any attempt to make the recipes it contains, and that the book is being provided merely for your reading pleasure. (Apparently, everyone has a lawyer these days.)

Then there's *The Anarchists' Cookbook*, which explains how you can buy whatever you need at your local grocery, hardware, and farming supply stores to build a bomb. (It even includes a recipe to make nitroglycerin.)

And who are the terrorists armed with this deadly and easily accessible information? Judging from recent tragic experiences and other, lesser-known cases from around the United States, these "terrorists" include our kids and kids who go to school with our kids.

The *really* frightening part is that thousands of teenagers have told me that they might try to build a bomb just to see if it works. Girls and boys, inner-city, suburban, and rural teens seem to agree on this. So even your *good* kids, may be a bomb threat if they get bored one afternoon.

An illuminating pre-Littleton account of online bomb-building dangers appeared in a *Ladies' Home Journal* article in March 1997 about a mother, Cheryl, whose thirteen-year-old son, Michael, suffered burns over 25 percent of his body when he and a friend were building a smoke bomb from instructions they had found on the Internet. It turned out that while Cheryl didn't have a home computer, her son's friend had Internet access at home, and the boys would go online unsupervised. Learning how to build a bomb turned out to be as simple as typing the word "bomb" into their favorite search engine.

At first, understandably, Cheryl was furious and blamed the Internet. Her anger that this type of information was available to children online, however, softened when she realized that her son could just as easily have found the bomb-building information at their local library. (Although teenagers tell me that they'd never bother to research this in a library. It's the ease of accessibility that makes looking for this information online so appealing . . . and so dangerous.)

But Cheryl didn't overreact. Recognizing the importance that computer literacy plays in a child's life, the family bought a home computer four months after the accident, and subscribed to an online service. But they vowed to protect themselves and their son online.

What did they do to protect themselves and Michael while online? They put the computer in the family room, not in Michael's bedroom. They also set rules for him, such as going online only when a parent is home. They also monitored him closely. They chose not to use any parental controls or filtering software, deciding instead to trust Michael to follow the rules. This is one family's way of dealing with Internet risks, and a good one. Trust and education go a long way with the right child.

What Can You Do About It?

Most of this information is perfectly legal, and protected by the First Amendment. So, what can you do? You can take certain measures to make sure your children understand the dangers of these kinds of things. Let them know that kids can be disfigured, or lose limbs, fingers, and sometimes their lives from bomb-making accidents. Their appreciation of the dangers has to outweigh their teenage curiosity. You can also keep a lookout for signs that your kids may be getting into trouble.

There are several things parents should look out for if they're concerned that their children may be getting into the bomb-building business: pails or buckets, soda or bleach bottles, pipes, ammonia, glycerin, or paraffin. Unfortunately, items like these aren't likely to even raise our suspicions. That's how easy it is for kids to gather what they need to build a bomb.

Parents should also be on the alert for children who collect empty containers or unusual-looking containers, nails or sharp screws, metal pellets, and shotgun shells that may have been broken open and emptied of their powder. Parents should also call the police if they find anything that looks suspicious, rather than attempt to deal with the "bomb" or bomb ingredients themselves.

In addition to education and keeping an eye out for suspicious activities, technology may also be a big help in making sure your kids aren't accessing this kind of information online. You can filter incoming content and websites that use certain words, like "bombs." You can also block sites that have been reviewed and found to contain this kind of information. Restricting younger children to prescreened sites is another way of avoiding this kind of content.

Bomb-building Information, Violence, and Responsibility— Post-Littleton

Especially since the Littleton tragedy, there has been a lot of interest in bomb-building information online. It's significant that the number of questions I receive from parents about filtering products has increased tenfold since Littleton. While sex rarely moves parents to consider filtering, bomb-building, violence, and hate seem to have tipped the scale for many parents.

But the filtering products don't block these sites as completely as they do sites with sexual references. (We review the effectiveness of bomb-building information filtering in "One from Column A, Two from Column B" in Chapter 8.) Be sure to review the product's test results for the types of information you're seeking to block or filter. And remember, all children should be educated about the risks as though you weren't using a parental control product, even if you intend to use one. All children have to be able to handle information "unplugged."

Drugs, Alcohol, Tobacco, Guns, and Poisons

There are two different kinds of sites out there that deal with these topics. One group of sites promotes their use. The online risks of this information really aren't any greater than the offline risks of anyone promoting their use by minors (although there may be more of this information online than is easily accessed by our children offline). The other group of sites sells these things online to anyone who wants to buy them, including children.

Sites That Promote Their Use

Some alcohol, tobacco, and gun sites are set up by manufacturers of these products; other sites, such as those that promote drugs and poisons (generally for assisted suicides), are set up by people who advocate their use.

Many manufacturers have stated that their sites are directed at adults who may legally consume their products, and not at children, but we need to recognize that these sites are often accessed by children. (Many child-protection groups believe that children are even being targeted by some of these companies.) But whether these companies intend to attract children to their sites or not, our children need to be educated about the dangers of drugs, guns, poisons, alcohol, and tobacco.

Hopefully, you have already taught them about some of these dangers. If not, this is a good time to start.

What Can You Do About It?

Education and values enforcement are the best defense against this kind of information—online and off. You may already have educated your children thoroughly on these topics. Ask them. You might be surprised how much they already know.

If you think you need more help than education can provide, most of the filtering products block access to drug, alcohol, and tobacco sites.

Sites That Sell These Things to Kids

There are thousands of sites that sell alcohol online. You can do a quick search on any search engine that isn't a filtered or kid-friendly search engine (alcohol sites tend to be filtered at these search engines) and pull up hundreds of sites that sell wine and other alcohol online. Selling online has become a popular mechanism for small wineries who can't afford large distribution networks to market across the country.

While it's very easy to find sites that sell alcohol and tobacco online, it's a bit harder to find those that sell drugs (usually these sites sell only prescription drugs being sold over-the-cybercounter, like Viagra and weight-loss medications, although some sell drug paraphernalia) or guns online. It's even harder to find controlled substances and illegal drugs and poisons, such as cyanide (although one site that facilitated suicide in Japan was selling some), for sale online. But they're there, and kids armed with money or credit cards can buy them as easily as adults can.

A couple of years ago, a mother opened a package shipped to her son and discovered a semiautomatic weapon he had ordered online. He had charged it to his parents' credit card. (I have no idea what he thought would happen when the bill arrived.) And your children could do the same.

What Can You Do About It?

You need to recognize that the alcohol and drug sites, unlike some of the other riskier content sites, aren't targeting kids. They are targeting adults—for example, wine connoisseurs looking for smaller and unique vineyards, and patients with erectile dysfunction or weight problems looking for prescription medicines.

For the most part, kids aren't buying these products online. Alcohol and tobacco products tend to cost far more online than the over-the-counter alternative (assuming the kids can get some adult to buy it for them or obtain a fake ID).

But in order to make sure your children aren't buying anything from any of these sites, you should check your credit card and bank statements closely, and make sure you are there when packages are opened (or, make sure your kids show you what they have ordered).

Are We Raising Future Riverboat Gamblers in Cyberspace?

There is no doubt that the Internet is an equal-opportunity vice provider. And gambling hasn't escaped cyberspace any more than the other vices have. In fact, gambling is thriving in the Internet arena, even while facing strict governmental controls elsewhere. (The sites are illegal in the United States if they offer gambling to U.S. residents without being properly licensed.)

Most of the gambling sites are hosted offshore, which makes law enforcement more difficult. They require prepayment in the form of credit card advances, debit card advances, or wired funds. A simple search on any of the search engines will result in thousands of gambling sites. And your teenager's money is as good as anyone else's.

Frankly, I was surprised that kids are using the gambling sites as much as they reportedly are. But with more and more children having their own credit card on our accounts for emergency purposes, as well as generous allowances and access to savings accounts that hold their birthday cash, baby-sitting earnings, and paper route money gathered over the years, it's apparently easier than ever for them to gamble it away.

Sometimes they'll even use our credit card and hope we don't notice when the statement arrives. (And, surprisingly enough, we often don't.)

What Can You Do About It?

Keep an eye on your credit card statements and on your children's savings account balances. Blocking their ability to send out credit card information over the Internet might make it harder for them to gamble online. (Some of the filtering products allow you to block certain outgoing information.) In addition, if the computer is centrally located under your watchful eyes, you may be able to keep them out of the gambling dens entirely.

Also, teach them that the only people who make money on gambling are the gambling site operators themselves. (I represented casinos for years, and I know how profitable gaming can be for the gambling establishment.) Let them also know that many of the gambling sites are scams, and many hold on to your winnings under the guise of international currency laws.

Gambling online is a no-win game, especially for children and teens.

Flaming, Harassment, and Cyberstalking

Sometimes, largely because they feel that they are anonymous (hiding behind their computer screens) and because they have a captive audience, people say things online they would never dream of saying to someone's face. They also do things they would never dream of doing in real life. When these messages are directed at our children, we are understandably concerned, and our children may have their feelings hurt—deeply. They range from insults (flaming), to creating fear (harassment), to credible threats of actual harm offline (cyberstalking).

Flaming

Flaming is cybertalk for when people say mean, insulting, rude, or provocative things online to others. Sometimes these are just rude people; other times they are people who want to incite arguments online with others or among others. Some people will post an insulting or provocative remark in one group while pretending to be a member of an opposing group, just to create an online fight.

It's interesting to note that many flamers would never dream of behaving this way offline. They often consider it harmless fun.

What Can You Do About Flaming?

Many parents who have been online for a while have worked out ways of dealing with abusive or vulgar messages (flames) that are sent to their children. One of these parents, Bill Bickel, has several personal websites where he highlights stories about his children. (His websites can be found at www.bickelboys.com.) He posted the message below at his site to help other parents deal with flaming directed at their children. Bill wrote it referring to messages received in connection with his children's sites, but it applies equally to e-mail messages or chat-room flaming. It is reprinted here, with his kind permission. It's good advice, and I suggest following it (whether your child is on the receiving end or on the sending end):

> [Sometimes people send our children] inappropriate, vulgar, or even abusive messages. Aaron's received one of each.
>
> Of course, we all prescreen our kids' e-mail, but it's still upsetting to think that somebody's sending our child this sort of thing. The fact that it's probably just another child doing it isn't much comfort, because it isn't a physical threat we're worried

about. (The abusive mail Aaron received came from Australia. We live in New Jersey.)

My suggestion is: Don't ignore it, and don't wait for a second message. The next message will probably get sent to another child. This sort of thing should be stopped immediately.

Send a copy of the message to POSTMASTER@whatever.com, adding, simply, "Please do something about this." I did this twice, and one account was shut down and the other was suspended (the account holders' little darlings had done this sort of thing before). For good measure, I cc'd my messages to the account holders, leaving the subject blank (so the kids wouldn't be alerted and try intercepting them).

For the message that was merely inappropriate, I just sent a copy of the original to the account holder, again deleting the subject. We received an apology within 24 hours, and a promise that their teenage daughter would not be sitting in front of the computer for some time.

Your older children and teens should be taught to report the flame or ignore it. They shouldn't get involved in a flaming war, no matter how tempting it may be. These things escalate fast, and get out of control quickly. Even if you don't take the action that Bill Bickel did, you should try to screen e-mail so that you can intercept hurtful messages to your younger children.

Then make sure that your child doesn't take the insults to heart. Let them know, and help them remember, that what this person says to them or others online isn't worth paying a second's attention to. It's not easy, but we have to help them develop thicker skin if we are going to allow them to spend time online.

Harassment and Cyberstalking

But many people don't stop at just insulting you or your children. They may make death threats, hack your computer, or send you viruses. They may track your children online, using buddy lists and ICQ technology, and say nasty things about our children to others in chatrooms our children frequent. They may post terrible things in guestbooks on our children's sites, or sites our children visit. They may pose as our children, by using remailer and alias technology (that allow people to appear to be someone else or mask their identity online), and say and do things that get our children into trouble.

It can get really ugly. Sometimes we have to get their ISPs involved, and it might even warrant getting law-enforcement agencies involved, especially if there are threats relating to offline dangers. Always take these things seriously.

What Can You Do About It?

I've written an extensive analysis of cyberstalkers, and what to do if your child is stalked or harassed, in the "'Leave My Kid Alone!'— Cyberstalking and Harassment" section in Chapter 4. But teaching your child to follow the rules of online etiquette ("netiquette"), and to stay out of more volatile chatrooms and discussion boards, may prevent most of these problems. Not including a guestbook or personal information in their personal websites can be a big help, too.

They should also be taught never to respond to harassment or threats they receive online. Ignoring them is often the best way of getting them to go away.

You can also use software or parental controls to block incoming e-mail from unknown senders, or to filter out e-mail from a particular sender.

Cyberpredators

Later on, I present a whole section on cyberstalkers and cyberpredators. We have to learn how they function, and teach our children how to avoid their lures. This is the cyber–Cliffs Notes version. But you'll need to read the real thing in order to pass the one test that all parents have to pass—keeping our children safe.

One of the biggest problems with cyberpredators is that they operate in your home. But improving your alarm system and adding better locks won't keep them out. They enter your living room (or your child's bedroom if you ignore my tip to keep their computer in a public place) through your computer. Your children feel safe in their pajamas and slippers, with you seated a few feet away watching television or reading. Therefore, people who converse with them while they are in this "comfort zone" are safe, too—as safe as any invited guest in your home.

Cyberpredators count on this sense of security in lulling your children into letting down their guard. There is a sense of intimacy online that cyberpredators take advantage of to convince your children that they are not strangers at all.

What Can You Do About It?

It's your job to teach your children that these people are strangers, no matter how friendly they sound. If you're close at hand when problems arise, and make it a point to get to know their online friends, the cyberpredator's task will be much harder.

Protecting your children online is like buying an antitheft device for your car. Although it can't completely prevent thieves from stealing your car if they really want to, you may have made it hard enough that they go somewhere else. (And if all parents do the same thing, the cyberpredators will be out of luck everywhere.)

Our children too often believe what others tell them. And when they want to check it out, they go to online profiles posted by the cyberpredator. It's like the old adage "you lie and I'll swear to it," but they can lie and swear to it all by themselves. We need to teach our children not to trust so easily. It's a sad, but necessary, lesson.

Our children have already been taught stranger-danger techniques, but nice people aren't strangers—only hairy, smelly, and dirty ones are. Ask your child to describe a stranger, and you'll see I'm right. (Unfortunately, most cyberpredators don't fit that description at all. Most are educated and successful men.)

Report any attempts to lure your child into a face-to-face meeting to law-enforcement officials immediately. For more information, check out the "Where Do You Report Trouble and Cybercrimes?" section in Chapter 5. You can also report it to your ISP's security department. I've included the security department e-mail addresses for each of the ISPs at www.familyguidebook.com.

The Big Three . . .

The topic of cyberpredators and cyberstalkers is so important that I've given it its own chapter (where I've also included substantial details about how cyberstalkings occur and how cyberpredators function, as well as how to avoid them). In addition to that topic, there are two other risks to discuss, ones I consider very important and which require more than common sense to fully appreciate. These are risks to privacy—including marketing that requires your children to divulge personal information about themselves or your family—and commercial risks from unfair online marketing and cyberscams. These three risks are discussed in the next chapter. Before I get to them, though, let's discuss the risks your computer faces and the risks your own kids can pose to you or others online.

Protecting Your Computer in Cyberspace:
Hackers and Viruses

What's a Virus?

A virus is a special computer code, contained within a computer program, that is designed to infect a file and, when executed, do something bad to your computer and spread. Your computer may crash, it may not be able to turn on (boot up), files may become corrupted, the entire hard drive may be wiped out. . . . There are a lot of ways a virus can wreak havoc.

The odds of catching a virus on the Internet are small. But they can do lots of damage if you do catch one. (You can't get one just from visiting a site. You'd have to download something before your system could become infected.) Most viruses have been especially designed to damage computer systems, and are very successful at it. They also replicate themselves, infecting file after file once they've embedded themselves into a program.

A far greater danger lies in sharing infected floppy disks (something kids inadvertently do all the time) and by running infected programs. When my law firm's website was first being built we were drafting a lot of articles, from home and from our office. We kept the articles on one disk and took it back and forth, sharing it from computer to computer. One morning, none of those computers would boot up. The virus was on the disk, and it had infected each and every computer it touched. Luckily, we had just purchased Norton AntiVirus, which we quickly installed. That program, coupled with our prayers, saved our system.

There are also applications called "trojan horses." A trojan horse (also known as a back-door oriface) is used by a hacker to infiltrate your system. It doesn't replicate itself (spread) like a virus, however. It opens a "back-door" to your computer that can be accessed when you're offline, giving the hacker control over your computer. Hackers can steal your accounts and obtain password and credit card information that way.

What Can You Do About It?

To avoid viruses and trojan horses, practice safe computing! Luckily, there are a few good virus-protection programs available (which also protect against trojan horses and back-door orifaces) that scan your hard drive for viruses and get rid of them. The two most popular ones for PCs are Norton AntiVirus and McAfee Anti-Virus. All of these rid your system of any existing viruses and scan it regularly for new ones that you may have contracted unwittingly.

All products update the software frequently to stay on top of the latest viruses. You can update them from the Web, with free downloads. (Your antivirus product is only as good as your frequency of updates—remember that!)

Both McAfee and Norton let you try out their products by giving you a free download for a trial period. They know that once you try them, you'll like them.

To make sure that I'm covered for the latest viruses, I have recently begun using both products. It's belts and suspenders—you can never be too careful these days.

Smart and safe computing means being careful. Preventive medicine is the best medicine. You'll be fine if you remember to:

- Use a good antivirus program and update it regularly.
- Set it to run automatically on each boot-up.
- Remember to update it frequently online.
- Run each Internet-downloaded document/program through an antivirus program before installation.
- Check each floppy disk for a virus before loading anything onto your computer.
- Never open a file sent to you by someone unless you know them, and then only after running it through your antivirus program. (The Melissa virus worked by posing as an e-mail from someone you know. It used people's e-mail address books to spread to friends of the owner of the infected computer.)
- Scan your system regularly for viruses.

To make sure your computer stays well and virus-free, practice—and make sure your children always practice—safe computing.

Risks Your Kids Pose to Others—Including You

Since we're here to discuss risks and how to avoid them, we need to warn you about the dangers your children (and their friends) may pose to others in cyberspace, including you. They may give out credit card information, share private information about you and your family, infringe copyrights, commit computer crimes, and lose or destroy your files. In some cases, they may not even know they're doing it, but the dangers are just as real.

"Because I Can"—When Kids Act Out Violent Fantasies Online

All kids act out fantasies online, pretending to be someone or something they're not. But sometimes they act out violent fantasies online, too.

Twenty seventh-graders sat quietly in the library, not quite sure who I was or why they were seated there. I looked around at the group. These were typical suburban, well-mannered kids. They lived in a town with good schools, safe streets, and PTA bake sales. I didn't expect any surprises. (Now, for you parents and teachers out there, you know what happened next.)

I asked them how often they used the Internet and what they did online. Each responded that they used it daily. Most admitted to chatting online, surfing music and sports sites, and sending instant messages and e-mail to friends. Some had set up their own websites. I received typical responses to my typical questions.

Then I asked them what they did online that their parents wouldn't want them to do. (I am always amazed how many kids confess outrageous things to me, just to be helpful.) That's when it got interesting. A few kids admitted to setting up a website that made fun of an overweight girl in the school. They told others in school about the site, and the girl was very upset, understandably. They put up a fake profile on AOL, pretending to be her. (These kids had *way* too much time on their hands.)

A few others admitted to using a parent's credit card to access adult sites. (It had somehow never occurred to them that a bill would eventually arrive for the pornography service.) Some had been thrown off AOL for using vulgar language or provoking fights online.

But the one story I will always remember was from a soft-spoken, shy and intelligent boy, with sandy-colored hair. He was a top student, the kind of kid you knew never got into trouble. He raised his hand and confessed to sending out death threats via e-mail. This got my attention quickly.

We talked a bit about his life. He said that he doesn't get into trouble in "rl" (real life, for us nongeeks). His homework is turned in on time, and he comes straight home after school and listens to his parents. But he sends out death threats online. When I probed more, he said that he would never do anything wrong, because he's afraid of getting caught and getting into trouble. He also likes being a "good kid." He thought that it might be fun to act out his fantasies online. He also was convinced that he couldn't get caught.

When I asked him why he did it, he said simply, "Because I can."

He *is* a good kid. He's the kind of kid that you'd want your children to be friends with, the one we refer to when we say "Why can't you be more like . . . ?" He never forgets to say please or thank you. He'd never dream of threatening anyone offline. But online he's not a well-mannered honors student. Online he's the tough and violent kid he always fantasized about being. He plays at being someone else. It's the cyberspace version of Dr. Jekyll and Mr. Hyde. And he does it from the safety of his bedroom, after his homework is finished.

The only problem is that when a death threat arrives via e-mail, the recipient doesn't know that this innocuous honors student sent it—to the recipient, it's a serious threat. It's also a serious threat when law enforcement traces him to his house and knocks on the door.

"Dear Jennifer, I am going to kill you."

At Cyberangels, we help cyberstalking victims find their stalkers and prosecute them. They usually come to us when they are already hysterical with fear. One case, where the stalker threatened to kill a terrified mother and her teenage daughter, became a personal quest for Kelley Beatty, my deputy executive director and head of our cyberstalking team.

The mother sent us a frantic e-mail. She had been stalked online. The stalker threatened to kill her and her daughter. The stalker also knew personal details about her—offline details, such as her address and full real name. He also knew her telephone number. She had already been to her local police, but they didn't seem to take her fears seriously. She was afraid for her safety and that of her teenage daughter. She had missed several days of work, and was under medical treatment for the stress.

It didn't take Kelley long to figure out how the stalker had this information about the mother. She had included it in her ICQ profile. Getting her telephone number was as easy as accessing the White Pages online and looking her up, using the name and address she had voluntarily supplied to the world—and her stalker. She had also mentioned her daughter in chats, and the stalker apparently had picked up this information. (The mother was immediately advised of this, and removed the personal information. Kelley taught her how to surf anonymously.)

When an online stalking reveals that the stalker has offline information, the case is taken very seriously by us, and should be taken very seriously by law enforcement. Kelley stepped up the investigation. Luckily, the stalker had left a trail of personal information as well. This allowed Kelley and her cyberstalking team to identify him easily. Kelley contacted the stalker and confronted him with the fact that Cyberangels knew who he was, and that what he had done was a crime. He lived in Canada, and the victim lived in the United States. But it's against the law in both countries. (I warn parents not to do this yourselves. Don't contact the cyberstalker. It almost always escalates the stalking. Instead, contact law-enforcement, groups like Cyberangels or their ISP for help.)

He immediately was contrite. He admitted that he was a teenager and was just fooling around. He thought it was fun to try to scare people, and didn't consider it a serious problem since he had no intention of acting on his threats. He promised never to do it again. Kelley shared this information with the victim, who called the home of the stalker. (Again, I advise against doing this.) His grandmother answered and immediately understood the seriousness of her grandson's actions. The victim and Kelley were both satisfied that the matter would be dealt with appropriately, and didn't think that legal intervention was necessary.

When Kids Hack and Commit Computer Crimes

Some children, armed with powerful computers, have proven themselves very good at manipulating others' computer systems and cyberspace. They are breaking into other computer systems, sending e-mail, and pretending that someone else sent them (remailers). Because they do this from their home, they think they are anonymous. Many don't understand how serious these activities may be.

There are two major types of hackers: those who do it for fun and glory, and those who do it for financial gain or to hurt others. Many kids fall into the first of these two types. They take pride in being the ones to break into the CIA computers or take over the *New York Times* site. They hang out in private rooms you can't find unless you are highly skilled as a hacker. It has become an Internet "badge of courage" to be known as a hacker.

But the biggest part of the problem is that hackers are considered the heroes of their Internet generation even by some adults who should know better. According to *Fortune*, a manager at Panasonic said that hacking is how computer experts learn. "You break into programs, commit piracy, all kinds of wild and crazy things." ("Who's Reading Your E-mail?" *Fortune*, February 3, 1997.) The fact that adults who are computer experts can classify these acts as "wild and crazy things" is the essential problem.

Kids don't understand that hacking is a crime, and a serious one. (Frankly, neither do many adults. When I was giving a television interview about the capture of the Melissa virus perpetrator, several "men in the street" who were interviewed commented that he would make a fortune for some major computer company as soon as he is released from jail.)

Sending viruses to others is considered a hacking crime as well. Anyone who has ever had a file or computer infected with a virus can attest that having a virus can be heartbreaking in the amount of information lost, but too many kids don't take it seriously (until *they* have been victimized).

Some kids will send each other viruses the way our generation made crank calls and sent anchovy pizzas as a spoof to our friends (and often to our enemies and the cranky old woman down the street, but that's another matter).

At the first White House Summit on Children and the Internet, several kids were assembled on the stage to talk about how they use the Internet. One young boy said that he used it for sending e-mail bombs (e-mail bombs occur when so many e-mails are sent to your e-mail box at once that your e-mail system crashes), among other things. (Since few people understood what an e-mail bomb was, the audience laughed instead of reacting appropriately.)

Although it rarely happens, some kids will destroy a site or commit a financial hacking crime. They may not be thinking about the risks involved in serious hacking, but hacking is nevertheless a very serious matter. The FBI estimates that financial losses from computer crimes run over $10 billion per year. What's even scarier is that a vast percentage of these crimes, according to FBI estimates, go undetected.

Several years ago, new laws were passed making it easier to prosecute hackers. More and more frequently, law-enforcement groups are using these laws to charge kids with Internet-related crimes.

Men in Black

A woman I know shared a story with me recently about several "men in black" who appeared at her door asking for her son. It appears that he was one of the first hackers who had developed a program that broke credit card codes. No charges were ever brought, and he always denied misusing his program, but this mother has never fully recovered from the visit to her house by the U.S. Secret Service. We laugh about this today, and her son is a well-paid computer specialist, but it was frightening at the time.

Even so, kids tend to think that they will never get caught. While that might have been true a few years ago, it's not true any longer.

What Can You Do About It?

It's our job to teach our children not to hack or commit other computer crimes. In order to make kids understand how serious hacking is, they need to identify with the victim, since to them hacking is a victimless and faceless crime.

If you try to "bring it home," showing your kids how horrible it would be if a hacker got into your computer at work and destroyed all the work you'd done, or got into your home computer and destroyed their files or their favorite websites, they may be able to appreciate the seriousness of the crime.

Last year, when I was speaking to a group of students and their parents, a fifth-grader lamented the loss of all of his games, and his research for a report, when his computer had been infected with a trojan horse. All the kids took this story to heart. No one joked about hacking or viruses. It was the most effective session I had ever given, thanks to this one boy. It brought the story home.

You should talk to your kids about hacking. Let them know how serious it is. Schools may want to have local and federal law-enforcement officers come and talk to the kids about hacking crimes. Schools should try to spot the budding hackers and give them productive challenges for their hacking urges.

Parents should realize that keeping an eye on their children's computing makes it a little harder for them to commit computer crimes. Look over their shoulders from time to time, and don't put the computer in their bedroom.

Keeping the computer in a central family location is one of the best tips I can share with you. If your kids, huddled together in front of a computer, suddenly get quiet when you walk into the room—beware! (Remember what I told you: This isn't any different from parenting them offline.)

On the Other Hand . . .

But not all "hackers" are bad. Ethical Hackers Against Pedophilia ("EHAP," www.ehap.com) are people with hacking-level computer skills who devote their time to finding and reporting predators and child pornography online. (They use the term "hacker" in its original sense, which means people with high-level computer skills.) Many kids with hacking skills are being recruited to become white-hat hackers . . . which means they turn their skills toward helping, not hurting. They may find holes in computer security systems, and even help their schools find and investigate computer break-ins. The good thing about white-hat hacking is that they don't have to wait until they get out of prison for a job. (Just kidding.)

Sticks and Stones— Defaming Others Online

Sticks and stones will break their bones, but words will never hurt them—right? Wrong! While the First Amendment gives us the right of free speech, it does not give us the right to say false and horrible things about others. In the United States, someone whose reputation is damaged by a false statement made by another can sue that person for defamation. (Libel is when the defamatory statement is written, and slander is when it is spoken.) Under rare circumstances, such statements may rise to the level of harassment, generally considered a crime.

Unfortunately, since the advent of the Web, many kids are taking their grievances to the public, online. They are building defamatory websites and posting defamatory comments online. While initially the victims of the defamation ignored the postings and websites, they are starting to take action more and more frequently. Sometimes even the schools are trying to get involved, often to their detriment. (See the "Kids Online in Schools" chapter.)

Our kids need to know that the online services and ISPs will provide their identity pursuant to legal process. And they can be found and sued for what they say online.

Hey! That's My Intellectual Property!

Many people forget that the laws that apply on the ground apply equally in cyberspace. U.S. and international intellectual property laws and treaties protect copyrighted material, and copyrighted material doesn't have to have been filed with the Copyright Office to be protected by the copyright laws. It doesn't have to be labeled as "copyrighted" and doesn't need the © mark. Under intellectual-property laws, if you write it and publish it, it's protected against infringement.

Given the ease with which anyone can block, cut, and paste anything from any website, or download and save it as a document or graphic on his or her computer, people sometimes forget that anything more than "fair use" is an infringement. Our children need to learn to attribute material (using correct bibliographies), and not use more than a simple quote or two.

Recent changes in the U.S. copyright laws, to bring them in line with the world community, make copyright infringement a crime, even if the infringement was not for the purposes of making a profit. Many kids swap software, trading a copy of something for a copy someone else has of something else. The new law changes make this a crime. Although it's unlikely that the FBI will start arresting our children in droves, it's a risk that didn't exist before.

The movie and music industries have been very active recently, trying to stem the tide of kids pirating movies and music online. But aggressive enforcement can have embarrassing results in cyberspace. One in-house counsel for the *Star Trek* movies lamented finding out that she had sent a cease-and-desist letter to an eight-year-old. Our kids have become very good at using the available technology to pirate media.

And it doesn't stop with media. Kids pirate software all the time, often without thinking that it might violate the law, or be considered stealing.

If we teach our kids how terrible they would feel if someone ripped off their designs, they might do it less. (But in view of the number of college students I hear are buying term papers online, this might be a hopeless proposition. We need to take some quick and radical action to teach ethical behavior.)

Teach your children to respect others' property, even if it looks like it's available for everyone to use freely. The Internet works because people are willing to publish proprietary information for public enjoyment and learning. It's important that the rights of those people are protected, or the flow of information might slow—to everyone's detriment.

Risks to You from Your Kids and Their Friends

So far, we have focused on protecting your *children* from others in cyberspace. But dangers exist to you and others as well. And these dangers may be caused by our children and their friends, whether inadvertently or intentionally.

Pranks That Can Cost
You Your Internet Account

All of the Internet service providers and online service providers, such as AOL, have their own rules. Often referred to as the "terms of service," or "TOS," these are contractual arrangements with you, as a user of the service. If you (or anyone using your account) break these "house rules," you risk losing your account.

One of the favorite pranks of teenagers is accessing someone else's account and making up funny or provocative profiles. Many teens share their passwords openly with their friends. One teenager laughingly told me that she had used her friend's password to access her friend's account, and had changed her profile to say that she wore a 38DD bra size and was looking for a boyfriend. Her friend hadn't noticed until she started getting lewd e-mail from strangers who had accessed her profile. The friend had to change her screen name to avoid the harassment. I can only hope they both learned from this.

Warn your children not to share their passwords with anyone. Also warn them not to perform pranks like this using anyone else's password. Had this prank been reported, the girl would have lost her (and her parents') account, and her friend might have been very seriously harassed or stalked online.

If this doesn't sound like something one of your children would do, remember that other people's kids can create problems for you, too. Remember that even if you trust your own kids not to break the rules, you need to be able to trust their friends, too. Their friends may be using your account when they visit—friends who may not know your rules, or if they do, may not follow them. I wish I had thought of this before learning the hard way myself.

When I hosted several boards in an AOL legal forum, I was expected to be online regularly, monitoring activity while policing my boards. One night, when I tried to log on, I learned that my account had been closed. I was told that someone had violated AOL's terms of service. Not able to reach anyone in AOL administration in the evening, I had to open a new account just to get online. The new account didn't have my board tools, so I couldn't police the discussion boards. I was angry, and my forum suffered. It took days to get things sorted out, and all my e-mail was returned to their senders during that time.

Apparently, friends of my daughter had been over and had used my AOL account to get online. These kids had gotten into a flaming match in a teen chatroom (remember, "flaming" is when you insult or act in a discourteous manner in an online discussion), and when their bad behavior was reported to AOL, my account was closed for violating the terms of service.

When Kids Use Our Credit Cards to Buy Things Online Without Our Okay

A close friend of mine, one of the first cyberspace lawyers in the United States and very tech-smart, called me complaining about his children. Apparently they had found his credit card information stored in a computer file for his easy access. They called their friends and together ordered a big-screen TV and surround-sound system from a vendor on AOL.

Luckily, AOL staff, noticing that the delivery and the billing addresses were different (the kids were smart enough to have it delivered down the street to their friend's house), called to confirm. My friend was able to cancel the order before too much damage was done.

Knowing a lot about computers doesn't always prepare you for what your kids, or their friends, will dream up next. Remember that.

And keep an eye on your credit card statements, and don't store this information on your computer or where it can be easily found (and misused) by your children.

Protecting Your Job: Don't Use Your Business Account for Family Computing

It is estimated that half of the people on the Internet access it in connection with their work. Problems for employers from misuse of their Internet access by employees, or others using an employee's account, include defamation, copyright infringement, trade-secret protection and confidentiality, harassment (including hostile work environment issues), and criminal accountability (such as for hate crimes and hacking).

As easy as it might be to use your business Internet account at home to get online with your children, don't. Just to save $19.95 per month (the cost of an Internet service provider account), you might jeopardize your job or risk your business. Get another account.

With more and more employers being held liable for actions of their employees online (cybertorts), many employers are setting up Internet use policies to regulate their employees' Internet access. Most of those policies prohibit the use of the account by nonemployees, and substantially restrict the online activities of employees.

In addition, Big Brother may be watching you. All but a small minority of states permit an employer to monitor electronic communications of their employees, if the employer supplied the equipment and access or the employee consented to the monitoring. (E-mail policies contained in your employee handbook may be deemed consent.) That means that they are permitted to intercept and monitor your e-mail and where you (or your kids, for that matter) go online.

If employers discover a misuse of their Internet accounts, they may be able to discipline or fire you. So be careful.

CHAPTER 4

And Now for the Really Serious Stuff

In the next three sections, we'll discuss in detail the three greatest risks to our children online: misuse of their (and your) personal information, financial risks, and risks to their personal safety.

Protecting Our Kids' Privacy and Our Privacy

How many of you were Howard Johnson birthday club members? (Don't be embarrassed—I won't share this information with anyone. I promise.) I was. On my birthday, if we went to Howard Johnson I got a free meal and ice cream. (To this day I can't eat Howard Johnson fried clams without humming "Happy Birthday.")

Whenever my daughter walks into a store, the first thing she does is sign the guest book and add herself to the mailing list for sales and special promotions. In the United States we regularly give up bits and pieces of our privacy to receive certain perks, like fried clams and ice cream and special insider sales and catalogues.

Looking Over Their Shoulders

But we don't expect that anyone will try to gather personal information directly from our children. The examples I used above about Howard Johnson and my daughter filling out the mailing-list forms when she shops are very relevant. (Aren't you happy that *one* of my diatribes is relevant?) How many kids *choose* to visit Howard Johnson? It's where parents or even grandparents might want to eat, not usually the first choice of a teenager when dining with friends. That means your parents were usually there at the table when you filled out the birthday-club card.

Also, we usually go shopping with our children when they're younger. We make sure that they're ready, before we let them go shopping by themselves. By the time the kids are old enough to go shopping alone, they should be aware of the aggravation of postal junk mail and phone direct marketing. That means they can usually weigh the benefits of getting sale notices against the risk of others getting their address or calling them to sell things.

Thankfully, my daughter's careful. But this didn't happen by accident. She's careful because I taught her to be. She never gives her real telephone number. She'll either leave it blank, or if she has to give a telephone number to qualify, she'll make one up or use my law firm telephone number.

How did I teach her to be careful? When I saw her filling out her first form, I went over and asked her why she was doing it, checked out the information she was asked for and was supplying, and explained the risks involved.

When she was still a teenager, I made sure she checked with me first, and we decided together which store could be trusted and which one couldn't. (This is a family tradition, apparently, because my mother checked over my birthday-club form, and might even have had to sign it in the prehistoric days of my youth.)

The Internet and Online Data Collection Are Different

While you might be perfectly comfortable with your children and teenagers giving out personal information offline in your presence or at places you trust, how comfortable are you when your kids fill out *online* forms asking for personal information? If you're not there with them, how are you supposed to know when to guide them about reliability and trustworthiness? Or when to tell them to pass up the contest because the risk of loss of privacy outweighs the value of the free T-shirt?

How do we know that this site is really what it says it is, and not a scam artist trying to gather credit card numbers from unsuspecting online shoppers? In real life we can visit the storefront. Someone is paying rent for space and for telephone lines, and perhaps employees. But online, bogus operations look as big as IBM does. It's merely a matter of graphics and website design, and $50 per month for webhosting.

In addition, online data collection is different from offline data collection. The online information can be collected from many sources and aggregated to allow a substantial dossier to be compiled on your child very quickly. Technology allows information to be collected without your even knowing it—information about where you surf, where you live, and how long you spend at any site or site area. Within minutes this information can be used to help tailor advertising to your child—even during the *same* surfing session.

How Big a Problem Is This?

When I wrote my first book, *A Parents' Guide to the Internet*, one reviewer commented that I had devoted more pages to commercial risks to children than I had to pornography. While I couldn't believe that anyone would actually count the pages, the amount of time I devoted to each reflects my belief of the relative risks posed by each.

And apparently most parents agree. Parents who were surveyed see collecting personal information from their children as the most important issue where their child's online well-being is concerned. It's more serious, as far as they are concerned, than any online safety issue. (I've already given some survey results showing how important parents think privacy is. These statistics, although a bit older, focus on what aspects of data collection bother parents most.)

- Sixty-four percent of parents surveyed said it is not acceptable to ask children to provide their e-mail addresses to gather statistics on how many children visit a site and what they do at the site.

- Fifty-six percent say it is not acceptable to ask children to provide their e-mail addresses along with their interests and activities in order to gather information for product improvement.

- Seventy-two percent say it is not acceptable to ask children to provide their real names and addresses when they purchase products or register to use a site, even if this information is to be used only within that company.

- Ninety-seven percent say it is not acceptable to ask children to provide their real names and addresses when they purchase products or register to use a site, then share those names with other companies.

(Source: "Commerce, Communication and Privacy Online," Louis Harris/Alan F. Westin Survey, Privacy & American Business, 1997.)

What Are They Collecting and How Are They Using It?

The information collected online from our children and from us, and how it's used, falls into three general groups:

- *Tracking Your Preferences.* This occurs when the site operator tracks your activities at the site and your preferences for internal marketing purposes (knowing when to send you a newsletter about music groups, as opposed to one about computer software, based upon your surfing preferences) and designing customized content and services for you (making sure you get notices about upcoming concerts and new mystery novels first, because you go to those places first when you visit the site).

- *Tracking Group Preferences and Demographics.* This occurs when the site operator collects everyone's preferences (girls at the site prefer red lettering and music, boys at the site prefer yellow lettering and games) and demographic information about the group as a whole (how many girls, boys, 13-year-olds, kids from New York, etc.) and shares them with third parties (like advertisers) without identifying any particular individual's information. It helps them attract the right advertisers by giving the advertisers a snapshot of their audience as a whole, and helps the advertisers develop relevant promotions.

- *Sharing Your Personal Information with Others, in Personally Identifiable Form.* This occurs when the site operator or advertisers at the site collect personal information from someone and share it with third parties. (For example: Robby Smith lives in New York, is eleven years old, has a Pentium MMX 300 computer, uses AOL, and spends two hours a day in the game section of the site.)

Databases allow advertisers to use the personal information collected to target certain kids very efficiently, and get their attention by using personal information to customize the ad. We're all familiar with the personally customized junk mail ("Hello, Parry, we know how much you enjoy Howard Johnson's fried clams on your birthday!"). This is like that, but is much more customizable because it's interactive.

Big-Company-That-Sells-To-Kids (I'll call it "Big Company" for short) buys information from a few unethical websites that have collected it from their registered kid members (don't worry, none of the kid sites I mention in this book do that), and discovers that Johnny has two siblings and a golden retriever, and lives in Montclair, New Jersey. He plays shortstop for his local Little League and likes the Backstreet Boys. He's eleven years old. Now, when Johnny logs into one of those sites, or others where he is identified by the Big Company as "Johnny," customized ads can be sent to the pages he is viewing. Big Company's ads can come with the Backstreet Boys music in the background, and show an eleven-year-old boy in the suburbs with a golden retriever wearing Big Company's sneakers. Perhaps Big Company will use a shot of Little Leaguers eating the brand of macaroni and cheese they want to sell to Johnny. Or an e-mail arrives in his e-mail box: "Hi, Johnny. Tired of having to share everything with your two brothers? This new computer game gives you privacy. No one can play it but you. Put in your password, and everyone else is locked out. It's the official computer game of the Backstreet Boys. And you can buy it at The Big Computer Shop in Montclair."

You have to decide if it's fair for advertisers to use this kind of personal information to reach your kids. You also have to decide if you trust these advertisers with this kind of personal information. Do you really want them to know this much about your eleven-year-old? The FTC doesn't. (At least not unless you know about it and say it's okay. But we'll discuss the law in a minute.)

There's no right answer here. Some parents don't want their children sharing personal information under any circumstances, while others may not have any problems with websites and advertisers collecting any of this information, or even with their sharing it, if it provides enhanced product information and customer service.

But it needs to be *your* choice. You need to be told what's being collected and why, and be able to trust the website operators when they promise that they will respect your decision, especially when younger children are involved. Advertisers and websites need to recognize that an informed parent can be their best ally.

How Do They Collect Information?

Essentially, there are two ways you give up anonymity online—voluntarily, by supplying information when you register at a site or fill out a form sharing that information, or automatically, through "cookies" or other similar technology.

Giving It Away Voluntarily: "Yes, Ma'am . . ."

We raise polite children. (I didn't say polite *teens*, just polite *children*.) When children are still young (the FTC has determined that this includes all children twelve and under), they don't fully appreciate the importance of keeping their personal information private. If someone asks them for their name and telephone number on a form online, it's likely that they won't think twice about giving it to them. Add a chance to win a contest for an 'N Sync CD, or a trip to meet MTV's *Real World* cast, and children and teens will sell their *souls*, much less give away personal information.

What They Give Away for T-shirts

Many sites require that children register in order to participate in certain activities. Free T-shirts and baseball caps might be given away online if your child fills out the registration forms at certain sites. CDs and autographed pictures provide the encouragement for giving away information at other sites. The kids see it as getting something for free. It never occurs to them that they are paying for these "prizes" by sharing their personal information, and teaching the advertisers how to market to them by using the personal information they provide. It never occurs to them (or us) that extensive databases are created about us to track our preferences through our lives—just so marketers can sell us "things."

Until recently, the registrations asked for our kids' full names, and often their e-mail address and their regular address, phone numbers, birthday, gender, and sometimes information about their family (how many siblings, pets, etc.). Some even asked for their social security number and where their parents invested their college funds. And these sites normally didn't even tell the kids to check with their parents before giving this information away. But, thankfully, this is changing.

Using Technology to Collect Information

What's a Cookie?

Cookies are text files (just information, not programs) that a website server passes to your computer through your Web browser. It's installed in a "cookie file" on your hard drive and stores certain information. The stored information can then be transferred back to the server upon request. By using a cookie, a website operator can tell where you've been and a lot of information about you and your computer.

Cookies aren't all bad, though (especially the chocolate-covered-mint Girl Scout kind). Many perform helpful functions, like making it easier to access a site that requires you to register. It stores the information you gave the website when you first registered, and recalls it when you type in your password and screen name for your next visit. If you didn't have a cookie, you'd have to completely reregister every time you visited the site.

In addition, if you're shopping online and want to purchase more than one item, you need a cookie. It's one of the ways you can collect all your purchases to transmit to the server at one time (in a cyber-shopping cart). Otherwise you'd have to select and purchase the items one by one.

Webmasters use cookies to track where you go on their site, and how you use the site. They know that you like the music pages, and the fashion and computing pages, and are online after school until about 5 P.M. every weekday. They also know you're a sixteen-year-old girl because you told them that when you registered at the site. This helps them to design better sites with your needs in mind, and provide enhanced service when you use the site.

Many services use cookies to allow them to customize content to you, as well. If you regularly buy murder mysteries online at one of the big booksellers' sites, they keep track of that information and they can then make sure that you know about the new murder mysteries when they are released. It's like having your own personal shopper who knows what you like, what sizes you wear, and things you're looking for.

Big Brother

Almost all advertisers install cookies on their ads and track where you go after having clicked through to their ad site. (A click-through is when you click on an ad to visit the advertiser's site.) With special information-sharing agreements, some advertisers share information they collect with other advertisers and websites. When this information is shared, several companies know a lot about your surfing habits—probably a lot more than you'd like them to know.

They know when you visit the golf page of a sporting-goods site, and then click on an ad for a sports utility vehicle, followed by checking the movie listings for your local theater's showing of Disney's latest movie where you buy three tickets for the matinee show. Next you check out your local newspaper online (where you had previously registered) and read the car ads.

So, what have they learned about you from your surfing? They know you golf or might like to, and are in the market for an upscale car. They know you have one child, maybe two, probably a young child. They know you have an American Express card, which is how you paid for the tickets, and what town you live in, or near. They add this information to the information the newspaper collected when you registered at the site, which includes your name, and sometimes your address, profession, gender, and income.

The information they have about your address tells them that you live in an upscale neighborhood where the average home sells for $350,000. The neighborhood is predominantly Caucasian, generally populated with young professionals with children. You might now start receiving spam with advertisements for cars or from other companies who are seeking a young, upscale professional earning more than $X per year. You might also start getting junk snail mail (the non–e-mail postal mail—remember, the kind delivered to your house by a postal worker, the kind with stamps?)

If they have arrangements with offline marketers to aggregate the information they have on you with offline information available on you, they might find out that you are thirty-four years old, weigh 160 pounds, have blue eyes and brown hair, and wear glasses. (Many driver's license databases are available to marketers.)

These are real examples of how much information is collected about us and shared among advertisers and others. As uncomfortable as this may make us, knowing how much information about us is "out there," think about how unhappy we would be to have this same kind of information collected about our children.

The balancing act we face is between allowing websites to customize their information delivery to match your and your children's needs and allowing certain unscrupulous companies to invade your and your children's privacy just to collect data about you for their own purposes. The secret to resolving this when cookies are involved is to let you make the choice as to when your children should accept a cookie.

What Are Cookies Telling Others About You, and What Can You Do About It?

There are websites that help you test what information is available to others from your computer through cookie technology. Junkbusters (www.junkbusters.com) has a wonderful site about cookies and privacy. (I also use them as a spam information resource.) When you visit the page, it lets you know what information is available from your Web browser about you and your computer. It also tells you what others can determine based on that information. You may be unpleasantly surprised.

You can look into your hard drive Web browser's directory and probably find several cookies sitting there now. Most of them use the word "cookie" in their name. There are ways to remove cookies and ways you can surf anonymously. Before you remove any, though, you should make sure you don't need the cookie to access any particular site with which you're registered. For example, the *New York Times* site uses a cookie. If you remove it, you won't be able to access their site and will have to reregister.

Ideally, advertisers and website operators will ask before attempting to install a cookie on our computers. But, while we're waiting for them to teach pigs to fly, we have other, more realistic methods of giving you the opportunity to decide when to accept a cookie.

Web browsers, versions 4.0 and higher, allow you to reject all cookies. They also, along with the older versions of 3.0 and higher, allow you to reject cookies one by one as they are offered. You can learn how to do this by checking with the www.netscape.com and www.microsoft.com sites.

Do They Need Everything They Collect, or Are They Just Being Pigs?

We may appreciate the benefit of having services customized for us based on our personal preferences, but are website operators and advertisers collecting more than they have to?

To track your surfing activities and customize content or services for you, the website operator doesn't need to know your real name or where you live. They don't need your name and offline address to send you an e-mailed newsletter that matches your hobbies and interests. And advertisers don't really need your name, address, or telephone number to know what you like. They need to know that ten-year-old boys who live in New Jersey like hightop sneakers in blue, and ten-year-old boys who live in Kansas like lowtop sneakers in black. They don't need to know that a ten-year-old named Robby Smith who lives at 21 Jump Street likes hightops in blue.

While we may want advertisers to be able to improve their products and offer services that fit our needs, we don't have to put our personal information at risk for that to happen. We can help them understand what we like without giving them our phone numbers and full names. It means they have to think a little harder to figure out what information they really need and how to collect that information honestly.

And children should always be reminded by a website operator to check with their parents before sharing personal information. Surf where your kids do. Check and see if these sites tell your children to check with you when they provide personal information online. If they don't, tell the website operators how you feel. (Send an e-mail to webmaster@[the address of the site].)

The FTC to the Rescue!

The Federal Trade Commission is in charge when it comes to issues of children's online privacy where commercial sites are concerned. They are one of the most Internet-savvy regulatory authorities in the United States and have been working on these issues since the Web was launched. The FTC has done several surveys of children's websites over the last few years. They have concluded, more than once, that many of the sites that cater to children don't tell parents (or children) what information they collect from children or how it will be used. In addition, while many of these sites use this information only internally, others are selling this information or otherwise sharing it with advertisers and direct marketers who would use it to target children directly.

Over the last few years, the FTC has been begging and pleading with the Internet industry to self-regulate, but to little avail. No matter how often they said that they *really* meant it this time, some members of the Internet industry didn't take them seriously.

That's why the Children's Online Privacy Protection Act was enacted in October 1998. (It takes effect in April 2000.) This law applies only to commercial websites and makes sure that you know what's being collected about your children (if they are under thirteen years of age) so you can decide how it can be used and with whom it can be shared. (The FTC has been essentially enforcing these guidelines since July 1997 under its existing consumer protection authority.)

This act applies only to children under age thirteen, and requires that website operators contact parents and get their verifiable consent (which is more than just a reply e-mail) to their children's participation in chats or other one-to-one communication systems, or to pen pal programs. The FTC believes that since these are higher-risk activities, parents should know when their children are participating in them. I agree.

Websites also have to get the parent's consent *prior* to collecting information about children that personally identifies them. This information includes the child's e-mail address—under most circumstances—as well as their full name, address, etc. (I've given a complete analysis of the law and what constitutes personally identifiable information at the familyguidebook.com site.) Parents also have the right to review the information a site has on file about their children and have it removed.

We also plan to set up a spot at the Cyberangels site (www.cyberangels.org) to "blow the whistle" on the kid sites that don't adhere to the law. We'll review it and try to encourage compliance. If all else fails, we will share this information with the FTC.

Whom Do You Trust?

Some sites are trustworthy, but others may not be. Parents need to decide whether a site is trustworthy or not. And just because you trust a site with your child's personal information doesn't mean you trust the advertiser they share the information with. So check for a privacy policy at the site. If they don't have one, or it isn't clear, don't let your children surf there until they post one or clarify their privacy policies.

If they post a privacy policy, have they told you what they collect and how it's collected? Are they collecting more than they need? If they are sharing information with third parties, do they share it only in aggregate form? (That means they don't provide any individual information, only information about the group as a whole—for example, how old the group is, how many are boys or girls, how many prefer red backpacks or blue ones.) Or do they share it in a form whereby your child can be identified as an individual: Johnny Smith is eleven years old and likes blue backpacks?

Whom do they share it with? Advertisers or unnamed third parties? Who are their advertisers, are they reliable, and do you trust them not to misuse your child's information? Do the advertisers post a privacy policy telling you what they do with the information they receive about your child? If not, ask them. Let them know that your child's privacy is important to you.

If they haven't provided contact information at the site (although the Children's Online Privacy Protection Act requires them to), send an e-mail to the webmaster, who will pass it along. Webmasters can usually be contacted at webmaster@[whatever site you're trying to contact]. For example, the Family Guidebook webmaster can be contacted at webmaster@familyguidebook.com.

Protecting Ourselves from Cyberscams and Unfair Marketing Online

Targeting Cybertots: Advertising to Children Online

Now you know that as more and more kids are getting online, more and more advertisers are marketing to kids online and seeking private information about them and about you in order to better define that marketing. Online advertising, unfortunately, when compared to television advertising, is still the Wild West when it comes to marketing to kids—the Wild West during the early Gold Rush days.

How Enticing Is the Kids Market?

Although advertising on the Web hasn't panned out as advertisers originally hoped, it's the next frontier. And the statistics are very appealing to marketers:

- Children control over $150 billion in purchasing power annually.
- Children's television advertisers spend $700 million annually.
- Sales of children's computer products exceed $5 billion each year ($1.6 billion in hardware and $3.5 billion in software).

Jingles . . . Jingles All the Way

To understand the impact advertising can have on children, we need only think about how many commercial jingles our kids know, and remember how young they were when they could first identify the Toys "R" Us sign and McDonald's golden arches. (My kids were under a year old.)

And our kids aren't much different from us when we were young. Remember Soupy Sales? In his most famous (infamous?) TV show segment, he asked his viewers to go into Mommy's and Daddy's wallets, take out all those little green pieces of paper, and send them to him. A lot of kids did. It created a scandal for Soupy and proved how susceptible children are to media influence.

You should be teaching your children to be smart consumers—

"buyer beware" should be the motto. Teaching them to be smart consumers online is the same as it is offline, with one exception. Online, the ads are customized to your kids. They're designed to reach one kid only—yours—and can use his name, your pet's name, and the town you live in to help customize the sales pitch. They are also interactive and can be mesmerizing.

It's our job as parents to help our children separate advertising fact from fiction and limit the amount of hype delivered to our children online. It's also important to help make these distinctions even when the ad "talks to them." Our kids need to become ad-savvy.

Helping Your Kids Understand Where the Ads Start and the Content Ends

One of the biggest issues relating to children's advertising is helping kids understand when the show ends and the ads begin. Ever wonder why we hear "Now a word from our sponsor . . ." during children's programming? Television advertising directed at children has been specially regulated by the Federal Communications Commission since 1974. During children's shows, commercials can be aired only after a five-second gap, called a "bumper," from the program itself. It marks the end of the show and the beginning of the ad. That's the reason for the announcement.

In addition, the amount of time, in aggregate, devoted to commercials during a children's program is limited. Finally, to keep their favorite cartoon character from turning the entire program into a commercial, other restrictions exist that are aimed at separating the show's content from the advertising. Products cannot be promoted as part of the television show's content, and characters from the show cannot be used in commercials aired during their show.

But these restrictions have not yet been adopted in cyberspace. At this time, other than the requirement that all advertising and sponsored pages at kids' sites be identified as "ads" or promotional materials, and FTC and state regulation of deceptive advertising, there are no laws specifically applicable to online children's advertising. That's why it's largely up to us.

What's Being Done to Address Parents' Advertising Concerns?

KidsCom (a very popular website for kids under fourteen and one of the earliest websites designed just for children) is way ahead of the pack when it comes to helping children identify advertisements online.

It has introduced the Ad Bug, a cartoon character who identifies advertisements and promotional material at the KidsCom.com site and on other sites participating in the program, like Avery Dennison Corporation's Avery KidsSite, www.avery.com/kids. (Due to KidsCom's generosity, WiredKids.org, the website for all kids' online issues in the United States—which I run—will be able to offer the Ad Bug to other sites as well.) It's particularly helpful with early readers, who might not be able to read the word "advertisement" yet.

How Is the Advertising Industry Policing Itself?

The Children's Advertising Review Unit (CARU) of the Council of Better Business Bureaus was created twenty-five years ago by the National Advertising Review Council (NARC) as part of an effort by the advertising industry and the Council of Better Business Bureaus to be responsive to the concerns of parents and to provide an advertising industry standard for children's advertising. They have guidelines relating to online advertising to children, in addition to privacy and data-collection guidelines.

CARU's first rule is that "children should always be told when they are being targeted for a sale." The guidelines (found at www.caru.org) also call for advertisers to make a reasonable effort to see to it that any purchase by a child is done with the parents' knowledge. Otherwise, parents should be able to cancel the purchase and receive a full credit.

CARU also warns advertisers that under existing state laws, parents may not be held responsible for sales contracts entered into by their children. (Thank goodness, since when I was twelve I signed up for every monthly book club that existed.)

The advertisers are voluntarily complying. Many truly care about children. And all of them realize that unless the companies promoting to children online start addressing parents' concerns regarding privacy and advertising to children, they may have to face tough government regulations aimed at advertisers' marketing to children online—and the even tougher scrutiny of a disgruntled parent.

In the end, advertisers have nothing to gain by alienating parents. The smart ones know that. Let the website operators (and me) know if you think they're doing a good job in balancing promotion and content, and make sure you let them know if you think they're marketing irresponsibly to your children. If cleaning up their act means that they'll sell more products, it'll get cleaned up faster than any of us could have imagined.

Chant after me: "Parent Power! Parent Power! Parent Power!"

Spending Money—What Kids and Teens Do Best

The amount of money teens are spending online has been rising almost exponentially, and current estimates suggest that this trend will continue. In 1999, teens alone will spend 120 million dollars online. According to Jupiter Communications, that figure is expected to rise to $274 million in 2000 and to a whopping $1.16 billion by 2002.

There are three different ways kids and teens can buy things online. (There's even a way or two they can sell and trade things online.) Many of the tried-and-true retailers and manufacturers sell their products online. There are also sites especially designed for kids' commerce, which allow kids and teens to have their own accounts and use them to buy from many approved vendors. (Expect to be hearing a lot more about this kids' e-commerce alternative over the next year or so.) And finally, they can buy (and sell and trade) things at auction sites, like eBay and Onsale.com.

There's No Free Lunch: How You Can Pay for Things Online

Before we get into what you need to know before your children and teens are allowed to shop online, I thought I'd give you a quick overview of how we can pay for things online, and what you need to be careful about in this respect.

There are essentially four ways you can pay for things online: checks (faxed or regular); credit cards; debit cards; and stored-value cards/electronic money (like a prepaid calling card) that may actually be in card form or in electronic form stored on your computer. Most of the security issues online are the same as those offline (don't share your credit card information with third parties, make sure your debit card password isn't stored where others can easily access it, check your credit and debit card statements for any unauthorized charges, etc.), but there are a few that are unique to cyberspace.

First of all, never use a check when you buy something online. There aren't enough protections for purchasers who use a check when buying something online. If someone demands a check or a faxed payment, do business elsewhere. (There are ways of using an escrow agent to process payments if the seller doesn't accept credit cards, but we'll discuss that a bit later.) The preferred way of paying online, if you want maximum protection, is by credit card.

Credit cards have certain consumer dispute procedures that apply, by law, when they are used. These allow you, under most circumstances, to get a full credit if something goes wrong. Because of this increased consumer protection, if you don't have a credit card, see if you can borrow one from a friend. Debit cards don't give you the same level of consumer protection, although if someone accesses your debit card account illegally, you may be protected as long as you act quickly.

Stored-value cards allow you certain privacy protection, but they may be as vulnerable as cash. Unless they are part of a special online payment system (like iCanBuy.com's, which I'll describe shortly), if you lose them, you lose everything. Think of them as a prepaid calling card. If you lose them, generally anyone who finds them can use them—just like cash.

How Secure Is It?

Most hackers and criminals don't care about your credit card information. They care about *entire databases* of credit card numbers, so intercepting a single e-mail may be more bother than it's worth because of the methods used to transmit information online. (Information larger than a virtual breadbox is broken into smaller pieces, called "packets," when you transmit it. These packets are then sent through different Internet routes and reassembled at the final destination—the online vendor.)

But your kids might care about your credit card info. So if you store it online, password-protect it. (Earlier, I shared a story about a cyberspace lawyer friend whose kids found his credit card information on his computer and used it to buy a home theater system.)

Everyone who really understands the risks realizes that credit card transactions are at least as safe online as they are offline. (How concerned are you when your waiter or gas station attendant takes your credit card and walks away to process it out of your sight?) But there are certain precautions you should take to make sure that your transaction is as secure as possible.

Always use a "secure" server or transmission. You can tell if a connection is secure by the little key or the padlock on the lower corner of your Netscape browser or Microsoft's Internet Explorer. You can also look at the website address. Does it say "http:" as most sites do, or does it say "https:" which denotes a secure server?

What does the site tell you about security and the transmission of financial information, like a credit card number? What does their privacy policy say about how they treat and secure this data? (Never shop at a site that doesn't have a privacy policy you feel comfortable with.)

And make sure that you review your credit card and bank statements regularly, and keep all records and copies of all orders you've placed online. (I recommend printing them out and filing them along with your offline receipts and orders.) If you discover an irregularity, contact your credit card company or bank immediately. Do it by phone and send a *certified mail* letter to the address contained on your statement for disputes (not where you send your payment). Your legal rights may depend on how quickly you report the irregularity or fraud. So don't sit on this—do it right away. And remember that the certified mail letter has to be sent in time—the phone call may not count.

How Do You Know Whom You're Dealing With Online?

Check out the seller before you buy from them. If you're dealing with a known vendor, like Toys "R" Us, the GAP, or Spiegel, you can probably trust them to use the same level of care with their online customers as with their offline customers.

There are also certain vendors who may not be as familiar to us yet because they do all their business online. These are the new brand names and business models online (which I'll discuss later), like iCanBuy.com, Priceline.com, and Onsale.com. These are generally just as trustworthy as your trusted offline brand names and vendors. There are others that are "vouched for" by names you trust, like AOL's approved vendors or vendors linked from your portal (where you start your surfing from).

But what about the millions of other sites online? Just as you would normally check out a mail-order company with the Better Business Bureau, you can do the same with an online vendor (www.bbb.org). You can also check them out with Internet Scam Busters (www.members. tripod.com/netcommand) and other similar online consumer information and help services. That way you can obtain information about previous consumer complaints, and judge the vendor accordingly.

Don't deal with individuals unless you understand the risks. The consumer protection laws don't usually apply to individual sellers, only to businesses. That means you're on your own when it comes to enforcing your rights. The FTC can't help. In addition, most individuals don't have a merchant account (which would allow them to accept credit cards). So you are forced to pay using checks, cash, money orders, or similar means. This means that when payment is disputed, the level of consumer protection you get by using a credit card doesn't exist.

Auction sites have helped develop an escrow system, whereby the escrow agent (for a fee equal to about 5 percent of the purchase price) collects your payment and the merchandise and, when they are sure that everything is on the up-and-up, forwards the merchandise to you and the payment to the seller. This can be very valuable when you're dealing with an individual. You may want to have the merchandise delivered to a post office box, as well. This keeps your real address private. But if you've paid with a check that has your address printed at the top, you've already given them your real address, so don't bother.

And make sure that you report any problems you've experienced, as well. The more we share with others, the faster we'll be able to improve cyberspace commerce and put the con artists out of business.

Shopping Online

When you're shopping at a website, always check the site's privacy policy and see how they plan to treat the information they collect from you.

Some sites, such as Toys "R" Us, eToys, and the GAP, offer merchandise kids want to buy. You can purchase from them directly online, the same way you would have purchased anything from an offline catalogue. They're a trustworthy way to shop for kid items. But how comfortable are you trusting your child with your credit card information when toys or hot new clothing are involved?

Kids eCommerce—
Where Kids Can Buy Safely

Many parents didn't want their children using their credit cards to buy things online. They also wanted to know that their children were shopping at reliable sites. A new e-commerce model has been developed specifically to address these concerns. There are a few sites that are leading the pack—iCanBuy.com, DoughNET.com, SurfMonkey.com, and Rocketcash.com.

I work with iCanBuy.com, one of the biggest of the kids' e-commerce sites.

iCanBuy.com allows parents to deposit a credit line (by charging it in advance) for the kids. With a unique parental permissions system I helped design, kids can save, shop, create a wish list ("electronic gift registry"), and donate to charity from a secure online account.

iCanBuy.com was the first to invent and launch a kids' commerce site. They have also "walked the walk" by requiring their vendors to agree not to market to their members, and not to use the contact information for anything other than processing an order and providing customer service in connection with a service. Because this cuts down on direct marketing spam, it is an important feature to many parents.

iCanBuy.com's parental permissions also ensure that kids and teens use money only in a manner that is approved. For example, iCanBuy can restrict the places you use your money and how much can be used at one time. It's a great alternative to a gift certificate. When grandparents want to know what Little Susie really wants, the gift registry "wish list" tells them, and they can just charge it and have it sent directly, using the preprogrammed shipping information. (Many e-commerce sites have "wish lists.") Parents can even arrange for weekly allowances to be automatically deposited into their child's account.

But there are many kids' commerce sites and I expect many more to be launched. No matter which one you use, when you rate these kids' e-commerce sites check three things:

1. Are they putting children's privacy first? Do they tell you everything they collect and how it is being used? Do they get your consent for kids under age thirteen?

2. Do they make sure vendors don't sell adult products to the child (like a *Playboy* video)?

3. Do they require that vendors sign an agreement not to use your or your child's contact information for promotions, e-mail solicitations, or newsletters? Do they make their vendors adhere to their strict privacy rules?

If the answer to all three isn't "yes," shop elsewhere. That's the good thing about having lots of choices. And let them know if you decide to shop elsewhere, so they can be responsive to your concerns. If you find that their vendors are spamming your children with e-mail offers, let the site know that their vendors are violating their privacy rules.

What You Need to Know About Online Auctions

If you love bargains, garage sales, auctions, or flea markets, you'll love online auctions. You can buy everything, from new computers to beanie babies, often at bargain prices and in your pajamas. You enter a bid, and if you're the highest bidder, you win!

Although there are many great auction sites (I now book hotel rooms only through Priceline, www.priceline.com), which I'll list at familyguidebook.com, there are two that lead the market in their niche—eBay and Onsale.com.

eBay (www.ebay.com) became popular pretty quickly. But since Rosie O'Donnell started promoting it as the place to buy things benefiting her charities, it has risen to become one of the top sites on the Internet (with more than 50 million viewers and 250,000 new items listed for sale daily).

eBay is a great service, since anyone who wants to can sell anything they have to anyone who needs it. It's like buying a table at a virtual flea market. They sell lots of collectibles, lots of new stuff, and some junk (unless it's the *treasure* you've always wanted). If you browse it, you'll buy something. Trust me.

Onsale.com was the very first online auction site. It started out as an auction site for small businesses. (There are now 575,000 visitors to the site daily.) While it still is the site of choice for small businesses, tech businesses, and home offices (selling computers, faxes, scanners, and printers), it has now expanded to offer travel and other auction services, and is very popular among ordinary consumers as well. Because of its special niche, Onsale.com has become one of the online sales leaders in technology and computer equipment. It even offers a special program that sells computers at "cost."

Online Auctions: Going . . . Going . . . Uh-Oh!

Online auctions are great places to find bargains. But unless you're careful, you can get less than you bargained for. The most frequent complaints received from purchasers are that the goods were never delivered, or that the item was misrepresented, was damaged in shipping, or was defective.

Here's a checklist of things you should do if you want to buy at an auction site:

- *Make sure it's a reliable auction site.* Auction fraud complaints were more numerous than any other online fraud complaints received by Internet Fraud Watch in 1998, accounting for five out of every seven complaints they received. Check the site out with the consumer protection information sites, and if you don't like what you learn, shop elsewhere. Also ask around at discussion boards, and do some basic research at websites you trust to help you find tried-and-true auction sites. (A few I like are included at familyguidebook.com.)

- *Become familiar with the auction site*—how it works and its rules, including return policies (are there restocking fees?), shipping and handling costs, insurance options, warranty (look for one year parts and labor on electronics, a defective-product replacement, and a thirty-day no-questions-asked full-refund policy), as well as customer service and complaint mechanisms. Make sure you have all contact information, including offline contact information for the auction site and the seller. (E-mail addresses can be changed very easily.)

- *Avoid individual sellers and get to know the seller you're buying from.* If you *have* to have something that this individual is selling, check him or her out carefully. Get offline contact information and an e-mail address that isn't from a free Web-based service, like Hotmail. Check to see if the online people finders link to the same information. Run their e-mail address and telephone number through the reverse searches I shared with you in Chapter 2, in "The World's Biggest Billboard."

  If the site has a seller reviews page, check it out and see what other buyers have to say about this seller. But you should know that many sellers plant good reviews to mislead buyers into believing that they are reliable. And competitors often plant negative comments, too, trying to steer you away from their competitors. So take all comments in stride.

  Recently, eBay and others have agreed to start keeping track of the feedback and complaints received from buyers and terminate sellers who have a history of failing to deliver. But don't rely on the auction site to protect you from any unreliable sellers. You have to look out for yourself.

  Also, if you're a member of a certain special-interest collectors' group, you might want to ask the group if any have been burned by a particular seller, or if any members find another to be more reliable. And report what you have experienced, good and bad, so others can benefit from your experience.

- *Make sure you understand the payment terms before you start bidding.* If you submit a bid, you are accepting the terms as offered, whether you knew them or not. Ignorance of the terms, assuming they are posted, is no excuse.

- *Don't believe everything you hear.* If they promise you a collectible, get a reliable appraisal, and buy only from a trustworthy source. Many sellers try to pass off counterfeit goods as genuine goods. If the sale seems too good to be true, it's probably a scam. Don't suspend your common sense and street smarts just because you're online. If you wouldn't fall for something offline, don't fall for it online. Don't let anyone pressure you into buying "right now."

- *Don't buy illegal goods online*—you can be easily traced. And even if you aren't investigated by the police, do you really want these kinds of people having your home address and credit card information? People sell term papers, fake IDs, and just about everything else you could imagine online. (Recently, we even found someone selling what purported to be child pornography videos on one of the online auctions. It was removed the moment the auction learned about it from us, but it gives you an idea about some of the people out there.)

- *Use a safe payment method, and try to use an escrow agent and insurance, if available.* (Auction Universe, a very popular auction site (www.auctionuniverse.com), doesn't charge for escrow intermediaries.) Some auctions offer a special service to their shoppers to protect them against small losses. eBay protects its shoppers from the first $200 of loss, with a $25 loss deductible. Since, according to Internet Fraud Watch, the average loss reported to them in 1998 was $211, this may have covered most of the average losses.

- *Plan ahead.* Check competitive nonauction prices. Decide how much you can spend and stick to it. Many of the new auction sites allow you to preset a maximum spending limit for any particular item. This is a good idea, since many people get "auctionitis," bidding higher than they should because they get caught up in the excitement. This is especially important when our children might be using auction sites. We need to cap their spending and make sure they don't get carried away.

Some online auctions have even instituted a bidding proxy program, which bids for you up to your maximum even when you can't get online and watch the bids yourself.

People Hurting Children: Cyberstalkers and Cyberpredators—The Real Bad Guys in Cyberspace

"Leave My Kid Alone!"— Cyberstalking and Harassment

Cyberstalking isn't when an adult tries to meet a child offline to molest them. (That's a luring, or a cyberpredator.) Cyberstalking is when someone harasses and stalks someone online, or uses the Internet as a means to provoke a harassment or confrontation offline.

There are three different kinds of cyberstalking situations:

1. Online cyberstalking and harassment that stays online.
2. Online harassment and stalking that ventures offline or has an offline component, too.
3. Offline harassment and stalking that has an online component.

Although all are terrifying, only the offline harassment and stalking is physically dangerous. (Any offline component qualifies as offline harassment and stalking.) However, the laws in your jurisdiction may cover only offline stalking and harassment.

Cyberstalking usually occurs when a woman is stalked by a man, although a child can be targeted as well. A very famous case of cyberstalking involving a child occurred when neighbors got into a dispute and the stalker posted a message in a newsgroup announcing that his neighbor's young daughter was interested in sex. He also gave the neighbor's telephone number and address. Many of us are familiar with the "name on the bathroom stall wall," but this bathroom stall is 86 million people wide, and that's just in the United States. The family was forced to move, after learning that even if the case were prosecuted, the crime amounted only to a misdemeanor.

Because of this case, federal legislation was enacted to protect children from adults doing these kinds of things when sexual activities are encouraged or implicated by the harassment. Adults who are stalked in a similar manner have only the harassment and cyber-stalking laws, if they exist in their state, to fall back on.

Recently a woman in California was stalked by someone who used the Internet. This was the first case prosecuted under California's new cyberstalking law. The victim herself had never used the Internet. The stalker went online and announced in a sexual-topic newsgroup that this woman was interested in group sex with men. He also gave her address. Men showed up at her door. Luckily, they understood and left when she asked them to. But this is frightening. The Internet can be a very powerful tool when it comes to harassing someone.

Who's a Typical Victim?

Typically, a cyberstalking victim is new online, and inexperienced with the rules of Netiquette (online etiquette). And typically, the stalker feels empowered by the perceived anonymity online. They feel they can hide behind their monitor. But, unless you have found a truly sick and depraved stalker, or one with an ax to grind, most lose interest quickly if they don't get the reaction they seek.

What About Online Stalking
That Moves Offline?

Although most cyberstalking cases start online and stay online, some move offline. That's when it can get very dangerous. The cyberstalkers often find the victim offline using all the people-finding tricks I shared with you earlier. They'll find your home address and your child's school or telephone number, and generally make a threat either by telephoning you or sending a note offline, or by sharing your personal contact number with others online to encourage them to harass you.

And it can be very frightening. I've shared the "Dear Jennifer, I am going to kill you" story, where the woman involved couldn't even leave her house to go to work. Very recently a mother called me in a panic—her fourteen-year-old son had been receiving threats online, which became offline phone calls and threats. Her son was frightened, and she was going to keep her children under close supervision until the cyber-stalker was found. She was also going to step up her home's security by adding a burglar alarm.

The cyberstalker seemed to know more about her son than anyone who had only known him online would know. We went through the typical information risks. I asked her if her son had a profile. He did. But he said that it included only his first name and age, nothing about where he lived or went to school. He also said that he didn't share any of this information online, and normally just chatted online with his friends from school.

The latest threats had been called in from local pay phones, which took it from being a cyberstalking case to being a real-life one. The police were already involved and contacted AOL to get the cyberstalker's real identity. (AOL will provide this information only pursuant to a subpoena or a valid police investigation, and will give the member a chance to take legal action to block the disclosure before doing so.) Once the cyberstalking moves offline, most police officers are more confident and more willing to investigate.

It's Scary Being Stalked . . .

It's a mistake to let the cyberstalking go until it becomes an offline stalking. But getting anyone to take you seriously can be hard. You'll hear things like "Just turn off your computer," "Sticks and stones may break your bones, but words will never hurt you," and "It's just words" from people who haven't been the target of such an act, who don't appreciate the fear and terror of being a victim of someone who is targeting you, someone who is trying to evoke fear.

As anyone who has ever been harassed online can tell you, cyberstalking is just as frightening as offline stalking. It can be more intimate, too, since the cyberstalker infiltrates your home through your computer.

In most cases, the person cyberstalking your child is another child or teenager. It might also be someone your child provoked, looking to retaliate. But since most cyberstalking occurs in connection with sexual harassment or a rejected flirtation, cyberstalkers usually lose interest when they find out they are dealing with someone who is underage. Pedophiles, who target underage victims, operate not by harassing or frightening their victims, but by seducing or tricking them.

As more and more teens get involved with casual cybersex, they risk becoming more frequent targets of cyberstalking. And the percentage of teenage girls who engage in casual cybersex is increasing every day. (I'll share more about what teens tell us about cybersex in Chapter 9, "And Now a Word from the Real Experts—the Teens and Kids.")

Most cyberstalkers prey on "newbies," people who are inexperienced online. Any place where newbies hang out is a likely place to find a cyberstalker. They try to choose people they can terrorize, people who will react when their buttons are pushed. That's what many cyberstalkers live for, watching their victims react in fear. It empowers them.

Sometimes cyberstalkers have a vendetta. It might start as a flaming match that escalates into online harassment and cyberstalking. It can just as easily be directed at someone because of their religious or political beliefs or their racial or ethnic group. The victim may have done something innocently to set off the vendetta. Learning and following Netiquette may reduce the likelihood of this happening.

Most teens we surveyed have told us that they do things online they would never do in real life, and are often far less considerate of other's feelings online than offline. They admitted to using vulgar language when they ordinarily would never use it, and to being rude when they are normally polite. Because of the lowered inhibitions most people experience online, many teenagers express themselves in a much more inflammatory manner than they would ever dream of using offline. While this might be a liberating experience for teenagers who are spreading their cyberwings, it can also provoke online harassment and cyberstalking.

We also need to realize that some cyberstalkers have nothing against the particular victim. Anyone will do. These types of cyberstalkers choose random targets usually to impress others with their power and online skills. This type of cyberstalking might result in hacking as well.

Ignoring the cyberstalker usually works best. It's not as much fun to provoke someone who ignores you.

Kelley, my cyberstalking expert friend, and the deputy executive director of Cyberangels, advises:

> If your teen starts getting a lot of "unknown name/unknown number" phone calls, seems too anxious to answer the phone, or the opposite—doesn't want anyone to answer it—or if she seems upset or moody after being online, she could be a stalking victim and may not even realize it.
>
> What often starts out as a boyfriend/girlfriend relationship can shift to a power struggle and the victim feels trapped and helpless. The victim struggles to get the relationship back "the way it was," or just thinks that the boyfriend is jealous.
>
> As a parent, you have the right and duty to protect your children. If you suspect your teen is being harassed or stalked online, talk to them about it. Often they blame themselves for it and won't come to you first until the situation is out of hand. Assure them that it can be stopped.
>
> If necessary, pay to have your e-mail address changed to prevent contact from the offending party. If the harassment has moved to the telephone, you can change your phone number as

well. If at any time any threats are made to your teen, contact the local authorities.

Don't take the chance that it is just "kid stuff." Teens are very trusting of other teens, but as parents we know that sometimes trust is misplaced—by all of us. Let them know that it's not their fault, and that occasionally bad things happen to very good people.

What Can You Do About It?

Don't be a victim, and don't allow your child to be one. If you get the sense that the person may try to stalk either of you offline, call your local police immediately. Keep a record of all the details, and make sure neither you nor your child responds, even with more threats. That fuels the fire, and many harassers and cyberstalkers are looking only for the thrill of frightening you and your child. Don't give them the satisfaction.

So how do you arm yourself and your child? Know the cyberstalking safety rules:

- Don't respond to flaming (provocation online).
- Choose a genderless, nonprovocative screen name.
- Don't flirt online, unless you're prepared for the consequences.
- Save offending messages and report them to your service provider.
- Get out of an online situation that has become hostile—log off or surf elsewhere.
- Use caller ID.
- Get help! Call the police if there's any indication that the stalker knows where you live and has threatened to hurt you.

The Anatomy of a Cyberpredator: Protecting Your Children from Molesters in Cyberspace

There have been many cases recently where pedophiles and other adults have lured children into offline meetings and molested them. Luckily, there are even more cases when such attempts to lure a child have brought about the attention of law-enforcement groups. I debated whether I should discuss any of these cases, because I did not want to sensationalize them. But if explaining the methods used by offenders might make parents more aware, and their children safer, it's worth it.

Cyberpredators, just like their offline counterparts, usually aren't the scary, hairy monsters in trench coats we imagine standing on a dark street corner. Many are the kind of person you would be inviting to your home as a guest, and often have. They are pediatricians, teachers, lawyers, clergy, vice cops, welfare workers, journalists, Boy Scout leaders, baseball coaches, scientists, etc. They are almost always men. (Sometimes women are accomplices, but rarely are women the molesters.) They are often articulate and well-educated. They come in all shapes, sizes, and colors, and they can be very rich or out of work. But they have one thing in common: they want your child.

Most of us are sickened at the thought of an adult having sexual relations with a child, but to be able to protect our children, we must get into the mind of the predator.

First of all, predators often don't see themselves as predators. They see themselves as loving partners with the children they molest. To them this isn't rape, it's a seduction.

And, as with any seduction, it's a slow and painstaking process. (Predators have been known to wait more than two years, collecting data on a particular child, before striking.) That's what makes them hard to detect. They don't appear to your child to be dangerous.

An FBI agent who shared a panel with me recently said it best: "Before the Internet, these people had to get physically close to your children. They had to lurk near schoolyards, or playgrounds. Kids would see them. Adults would see them. It was a dangerous situation to be in for them, because everyone would notice an adult male lurking around children. They often had to take jobs and volunteer positions that allowed them to work with children in a position of trust in order to reach their victims. Now, however, the personal risks the pedophiles had to expose themselves to in order to be around children are gone. Now they can be 'one of the kids' and hang out with your kids online without exposing themselves. As long as they don't say or do something in the public room that makes them stand out, they can stay there forever, taking notes."

Many of them do. They have been known to create large databases on children. They track the children's likes and dislikes. They track information such as whose parents are divorced, who doesn't like their father's new girlfriend or their mother's boyfriend, or who likes computer games or a particular rock group.

Kids often share personal information about their lives in chatrooms or on profiles. This is one reason why they shouldn't.

It Doesn't Take Torture for Them to Spill Their Guts

Here's a mock chatroom discussion that my law-enforcement friends and I agree is pretty realistic. Imagine a predatorial pedophile sitting and taking notes on this child, and using this information to lure them later. Would your child fall for this? Most, unfortunately, would.

Child: I hate my mom! I know it's her fault that my parents are getting divorced.

Predator: I know. My parents are getting divorced, too.

Child: We never have any money anymore, either. Every time I need something, she says the same thing: "We can't afford it." When my parents were together, I could buy things. Now I can't.

Predator: Me too. I hate that!

Child: I waited for six months for the new computer game to come out. My mom promised to buy it for me when it came out. She promised! Now it's out. Can I buy it? Nope. "We don't have enough money!" I hate my mom!

Predator: Oh! I'm so sorry! I got it! I have this really kewl uncle who buys me things all the time. He's really rich.

Child: You're sooooo lucky. I wish I had a rich and kewl uncle.

Predator: Hey! I got an idea! I'll ask my uncle if he'll buy you one too. . . . I told you he's really kewl. I bet he'd say yes.

Child: Really!? Thanks!!

Predator: BRB [cybertalk for "be right back"] . . . I'll go and call him.

• • •

Predator: Guess what? He said okay. He's gonna buy you the game!

Child: Wow, really? Thanks. I can't believe it!!!

Predator: Where do you live?

Child: I live in NJ. What about you?

Predator: I live in New York. So does my uncle. New Jersey isn't far.

Child: Great!

Predator: Is there a mall near you? We can meet there.

Child: Okay. I live near the GSP Mall.

Predator: I've heard of that. No prob. What about Saturday?

Child: Kewl.

Predator: We can go to McDonald's too if you want. We'll meet you there at noon.

Child: Okay. Where?

Predator: In front of the computer game store. Oh! My uncle's name is George. He's really kewl.

Child: Great . . . thanks, I really appreciate it. You're so lucky to have a rich and kewl uncle.

Saturday arrives, and the child goes to the mall and meets an adult outside the computer game store. He identifies himself as "Uncle George" and explains that his nephew is already at the McDonald's waiting for them. The child is uncomfortable, but the uncle walks into the store and buys the $100 game. He comes out and hands it to the child, who is immediately neutralized and delighted.

Stranger-danger warnings are not applicable. This isn't a stranger—he's "Uncle George," and if any proof was needed, the computer game is it. He gets into Uncle George's car without hesitation to meet his friend at McDonald's. The rest is reported on the 6 o'clock news.

It's disgusting. It makes us sick to our stomachs, but it happens. Not very often, but often enough that you need to be forewarned. (Several hundred cyberpredators are caught and arrested each year.) Even once is too much, though, if it's your child. Knowing how they operate and the tricks of the trade will help you teach your child how to avoid being victimized.

The Script—How They Operate Online

Each case differs, but the pedophiles tend to use the same general tactics. Aside from the "bait and switch" scam discussed above, they often attempt to seduce a child. They want the child to "want" them.

They begin by striking up a conversation with the child, trying to create a relationship of trust and friendship. They often masquerade as another child or teenager, typically of the opposite sex, unless the child has indicated homosexual interests. (The child may or may not know the "seducer's" real age by the time they meet face-to-face.) Phone calls usually start at this point. Sometimes gifts are sent to the child as well, which may include a Polaroid camera and film.

Once they have broken down barriers of caution, they begin introducing sexual topics gradually, often with the use of child pornography to give the child the impression that other children are regularly involved in sexual activities.

Then they begin to approach the child's own sexuality and curiosity, by asking questions and giving them "assignments," like wearing special underwear, sending sexually suggestive photos of themselves to the pedophile, or performing certain sexual acts.

These assignments eventually broaden to the exchange of sexually explicit photographs (using the Polaroid) or videos of the child. Finally, the pedophile attempts to arrange a face-to-face meeting. (He may also have divulged his true age or an age closer to his actual age at this point.)

Why It Works

All the lectures we have given our children from the time they are very young about not talking to strangers aren't applicable online, where *everyone* is a stranger. A large part of the fun online is talking to people you've never met.

In addition, our children's stranger-danger defenses are not triggered when other kids are involved. The warnings apply only to adult strangers, not to other children. If any of us walked up to a child in a playground and tried to strike up a conversation, they would ignore us and probably run away. But if an unknown eleven-year-old came up to another eleven-year-old in the same playground, they'd be playing in ten seconds flat! That's how the pedophiles get in under our kids' stranger-danger radar—they pretend to be other kids.

And children often believe what they read and hear. They "know" things about the predator because they believe what he told them. They also believe what they read about him in his "staged" profile, which supports what he told them. So it's not just true, it's confirmed.

There are many stages at which the pedophile can be thwarted by an observant parent. In addition, children with healthy friendships and a strong, open, and trusting relationship with their parents are less likely to fall victim to pedophiles online. Pedophiles typically prey on a child's loneliness. They feed the child's complaints about her home life—creating an "us-versus-them" atmosphere. "Your mom is so mean to you! I don't know why she won't let you _____." (Fill in the blank with whatever we regulate: makeup, malls, concerts, etc.)

This atmosphere does two things: It creates a distance between the child and her parents, at the same time bringing the child into a special secret alliance with the pedophile. (You should know that boys are almost as often the victims of molestation as girls are.)

Anatomy of a Real Case

I have followed many cases over the last few years. In my role as Cyberangels executive director, I've also been responsible for reporting a few of these to law enforcement and for helping many families through the pain of prosecution. Sometimes we just help the families survive what the molestation has done to them. (The child isn't the only victim—entire families are torn apart in the aftermath of a molestation. Parents feel guilty for not having protected their child, siblings don't know how to treat their fellow sibling—the pain can continue for a lifetime, and even more.)

When cyberpredators are involved, I work very closely with the FBI, particularly their Innocent Images Unit. Innocent Images is the FBI's response to the problem of pedophilia and child pornography on the Internet. Started in 1993, during the Web's infancy, it is now an integral part of the FBI field offices, all coordinated through the FBI's Baltimore office (the home of the first case where someone used the Internet to lure children). To find pedophiles, the Innocent Images Unit investigates tips and also goes undercover online, posing as children. Since it's a federal crime for someone to cross state lines to have sex with a minor, they target people in chatrooms who are willing to travel to meet the "child" they are chatting with. They also pose as adults with an interest in child pornography, and find and arrest those distributing it.

One case I reviewed several years ago involved a New Jersey teenager and an Ohio adult predator. It was one of the earliest reported cases of cyberpredatorial conduct. Luckily, the liaison was discovered before the girl met the man face-to-face. But it had gone on for a year and a half before being discovered by the girl's mother. As you read the details, think about what could have been done to discover the situation earlier and how you can use these precautions to protect your children.

Paul Brown, Jr., an Ohio resident, was forty-six years old. He was also unemployed, weighed over four hundred pounds, and lived in a basement. He had accounts with AOL, Prodigy, and CompuServe. Mary (a hypothetical name for the young girl involved) was twelve when her mother, a schoolteacher, bought her a computer, reportedly because Mary was having problems making friends. When she got online, Mary posted a message on Prodigy, in the spring of 1995, looking for a pen pal. In her message she described herself as a teenage girl. Paul Brown, Jr,. responded to the message, using his real name (something they often do, surprisingly) but identifying himself as a fifteen-year-old boy.

Brown and Mary maintained an e-mail and telephone relationship for several months. As the relationship became more involved, they began writing letters, and Mary sent Brown a photograph. He told her that he was living at home with his mother and was hoping to find a girlfriend. In early August, Brown asked Mary for a "favor."

"If I sent you a roll of film, could you get one of your friends to take pictures of you in different outfits and maybe hairstyles? Makeup if you use any, and different poses. Some sexy, if possible. Please. Baby for me. Thanx. You're the best. Love Ya."

Mary complied. For the next eight months, they continued to converse and correspond, and Mary sent additional photos. Brown encouraged her with juvenile antics, such as using stickers in his letters to her saying things like "Getting better all the time!" In May 1996, Brown sent Mary a special love note. "Saying I love you . . . seems to be an understatement. At the age of 14 you have captured my heart and made it sing . . . I love everything aboutyou. . . ."

Shortly thereafter, Brown confessed to being in his twenties. He also suggested that Mary videotape herself in sexually provocative poses. She did. After Brown had reviewed her videotape, he returned it to her with instructions to redo the tape and include views of her genitalia and breasts. He later admitted to being divorced and in his thirties.

He reportedly also sent her small gifts from time to time. A few months later, in response to Brown's promise to pass copies of the tape to four members of a rock band Mary admired, she sent additional videotapes to Brown. (Brown told Mary that he knew the band members very well.) Each tape sent to Brown was designated for a different member of the band and contained sexually explicit conduct.

Brown apparently had also sent her his size 48 underwear. When her mother discovered the underwear, the authorities were notified. Tracing Brown through phone records, special agents of the FBI in

Cleveland seized the videotapes and photos of Mary and of more than ten other teenage girls from across the country.

Mary was fourteen when this was all discovered. Brown pled guilty to enticing a minor to produce sexually explicit photos and videos and was sentenced to a little less than five years in prison (the maximum penalty for a first offense). In a written statement to Brown following all of this, Mary said, "I trusted you. I thought you were my friend."

There are several things that stand out in this case. One, interstate phone calls were made by Mary. Parents should always be reviewing long-distance bills for suspicious calls. Two, Mary was lonely. These kinds of children are often the most vulnerable; a parent should be involved in their online friendships, and monitor their online lives. And, three, as hard as it is to know what our kids are doing when we're not around, especially if you are a single parent, a year and a half is a long time for a relationship to be going on undiscovered. You should spend time learning who your children's friends are, online and off.

But Monday-morning quarterbacking is always easier than playing the game in real time. We may look at the situation and say that could never happen to one of our kids. However, there but for the grace of God go all of us. . . .

Knowing your child is lonely and has problems making friends is the first sign that the child may fall prey to a pedophile or cyberpredator. Predators can spot lonely children. They can also spot kids who are new online and may not yet know all the rules. Most teens, when surveyed, admit to having been propositioned online. But what may be obvious to a cyberstreetsmart kid may not be so obvious to a child not yet familiar with cyberspace.

Pedophiles befriend these kids and patiently build trust and a relationship—looking toward the day when they can meet face-to-face.

Encourage your children to make online friends, but keeping the computer in a central location and learning about their online friends is an important way to avoid these secret relationships. Education is important in avoiding this danger, too. (Had Mary been forewarned about how pedophiles operate online, she may have been more attentive to how old Brown sounded on the phone, and been more aware of his classic tactics.) So is control over incoming and outgoing information when younger children are involved, using technology blockers, monitors, and filters. These kinds of situations can be avoided if you plan ahead, educate and communicate with your children, and keep your eyes open.

Getting in Under Your Radar: Even When
You're Watching, Bad Things Can Happen

I included the Paul Brown case in my first book, *A Parents' Guide to the Internet*. (He was sentenced in 1997, when I wrote the book.) I included it because it was a good example of how cyberpredators typically operate, and suggested that if the mother had been a bit more attentive, it might have been discovered earlier. I was right about how cyberpredators operate. I was wrong about how being attentive might have avoided the sexual exploitation. It takes more. It takes both an attentive parent and a teenager who has been taught how these pedophiles operate online.

In November 1998, I met a mother who did everything right. She was attentive and inquisitive about her daughter's online relationships. She asked the right questions. She had a good relationship with her daughter, and yet Charles Hatch, a child molester from Utah, got in under everyone's radar and sexually exploited her thirteen-year-old daughter.

Jennifer (not her real name) was eleven and a half when she first met "Charlie" online. She thought he was a few years older, and was intrigued about befriending a slightly older teenage boy. Jennifer was an honors student and had already been taking advanced college courses while still in middle school. She lived in a loving and warm household with her mother and father. She also had siblings and half siblings from her father's previous marriage. They were all close.

Jennifer's mother, Sharry (also not her real name), talked to Jennifer about her online friend, Charlie. She insisted on talking to Charlie himself, by phone, once he and Jennifer had started calling each other. He passed the phone call test, and Sharry was convinced that he really was the teenage boy he professed to be. Either he had manipulated his voice to sound younger or he had a younger person make the call.

Charlie even called and spoke to Jennifer's brothers, talking about when he would be their brother-in-law someday, after he and Jennifer were married. He pleaded with Jennifer to come and visit him in Utah. Sharry invited him to visit them instead. But Charlie always had a reason he couldn't come.

As things progressed, Sharry insisted on talking to Charlie's mother. He first avoided it by saying she was sick, later that her sickness had become cancer, and that eventually she died from the cancer. The family fell for this, hook, line, and sinker. Most caring families would.

Although the "relationship" progressed for almost two years, it remained relatively tame. Charlie was romantic rather than predatorial, and he sent her expensive gifts, including a Polaroid camera. (Remember the Polaroid camera Paul Brown sent?)

Jennifer was inexperienced with boys and dating, and Charlie seemed to know not to push her too fast. But about a year and a half after they met online, Charlie sent her sexually explicit photos of himself from the neck down. She became very uncomfortable and pulled back.

But several tragedies occurred around the same time, which made Jennifer easier prey. Her father was hospitalized with a serious illness, and her sixteen-year-old half brother died of a brain hemorrhage. Charlie, like all good predators, knew when to strike. He told Jennifer that she owed him sexually explicit photos of herself, since he had sent those of himself. When she refused, he told her that she would be left alone, since her family was dying or would die—and he threatened to leave her. Reluctantly, after fighting against it as hard as she could, she acquiesced and sent him sexually explicit photos of herself.

When Sharry was cleaning Jennifer's room, she discovered a letter in which Charlie had set forth the sexual poses he wanted Jennifer to photograph. Sharry sent him a letter, confronting him. She said that he didn't sound like a teenager in the letter. She told him that if he ever contacted her daughter again, she would inform the police. He never replied, and Jennifer was not permitted to use the Internet for months.

One day, just when Jennifer and Sharry thought that the whole episode was past them, the phone rang. It was a detective from Utah, who informed Sharry that Jennifer's photos had been discovered in Hatch's day planner by a coworker. He wasn't sixteen—he was thirty-six. He was a former teacher who had been dismissed by the school after having been accused by a student of sexual abuse. (The school hadn't taken any other action.) He was currently employed by the welfare office in Utah, and was married with children and step-children.

Six months later, Charles Hatch was convicted of sexual exploitation in a Utah federal court. He began his six-and-a-half year sentence in early June 1999. As a condition of his plea, he will not be permitted to use the Internet.

This mother has become a dear friend of mine, after seeking Cyberangels' help in getting through the prosecution of this case. She is a wonderful and warm mother, and her daughter is an inspiration to us all. What this tells us is that some cyberpredators (known as "travelers" to law enforcement) seek out the good kids, the smart ones, the ones who are not street-smart and are from sheltered suburban or rural families. Many of our children match that profile perfectly.

A Mother's Plea at the Sentencing
of Her Daughter's Predator

The following statement was read to the court by a lawyer for the government at Charles Hatch's sentencing. Sharry was too distraught to read it aloud in the crowded courtroom. It could easily be my daughter's or son's tale, or yours. We need to listen to what Sharry has to say, and teach our children that some people are not what they pretend to be in cyberspace. Hug your children close tonight, and rejoice in the fact that this man will be spending time in prison.

In her own words, this statement is a mother's plea for her daughter and for all our children:

I never knew life would be altered forever until the moment I read the misplaced letter to my daughter written by Charles Hatch. In that moment, I realized that he was an impostor and not the 16-year-old boy who had lost his mother to cancer as he had portrayed himself to be. In that moment, all the missing pieces of an Internet relationship between him and my daughter and my family fell together. I finally saw that for over a year my daughter had been stalked and slowly manipulated by him.

Finally she was exploited just when my husband was gravely ill, and we lost one of our children to death. He waited and intruded for over a year, and struck when my family was in crisis.

I've been committed to my children from the day I knew of their conception, and have worked harder than anyone I know to eradicate the seeds of hatred planted in their hearts. These seeds are blown by the winds of our society, and can easily land anywhere. We see their fruits from their having taken root years ago, today manifested as violence, war, poverty, apathy, fear, and hatred for one another.

The actions taken by Charles Hatch have undermined my efforts and humiliated my family and me.

I must passively resist the instinctive urge to strike out if I am to remain committed to the guidelines of moral conduct that I have painstakingly taught my children in this world of ours. But as a human, I continue to suffer and be haunted by what may come in the future for all of our children because some of us cannot seem to resist the irresponsible urge to prey on and violate another, exploiting the weaker ones, younger ones, innocent ones.

These are the seeds that bear fruits and perpetuate the same or worse action, generation to generation. Try as I might to forget this whole thing, I can't. It WON'T go away. It continues to haunt me in my sleep and occasionally creeps into my thoughts when I'm awake. Recurring in my dreams, he comes to pick my daughter up at the curb of my home, and drops her off hours later . . . and she is changed . . . and I'm frozen and unable to intervene.

It continues to haunt my daughter. Even this past week my daughter shared a nightmare with me about being taken from her home by "Charlie"—but he wouldn't bring her back. I prefer the nightmare to the reality, so she will not appear here today. She is attempting to continue with as normal a life as possible, and tonight I will be home again for the dance recital that she has worked hard on this school year.

As for my only daughter's dreams, I can't say.

The effects of this incident are still coming out. This child advanced from honors to pre-baccalaureate status in middle school, but I am watching her grades slip slowly, compromising her determination for an academic scholarship to college. The little girl who could once play openly with her friends now notices that she no longer has relationships with her peer group.

Before this incident she was fully self-expressive. Now her grades have dropped because she can't speak out or make eye contact during presentations. Now she doesn't trust anyone. She has become more dependent, leaning on me. No matter how I tell her she did nothing wrong but made a mistake, she filters it through her experience.

Her brother, younger than she, remains outwardly angry at the betrayal he personally experienced. Her father, angry at the violation of innocence, was prepared to hunt this man down and destroy him. I will remain both disturbed and more than disappointed at something I see cannot be healed in Charles Hatch and others like him. I continue to arrive over and over again at this conclusion: We MUST take responsibility for those who cannot be responsible for themselves. We must protect our children, and we must incarcerate people who prey on other people out of compulsion and incurable illness. We have no other choice but to do so.

Charles Hatch will suffer one way or the other. His trouble is a mental one that we can't fix. I am sorry for him and many others affected by his choices. This may be my only opportunity to be heard, and given the statistics there are innumerable mothers and daughters in the world, and families, whose lives are devastated by adults who stalk and prey on children and never have the chance to have their voices heard.

According to the Cyberangels' website, there are 21,317 pedophile sites listed on the World Wide Web. According to U.S. Customs and the FBI, one adult predator travels daily to meet a victim face-to-face. According to our local law-enforcement agencies, there are even more.

My request is that Charles Hatch be separated from children for as long as possible and held responsible and accountable for his actions. In this case incarceration is the only way to protect. My daughter and I both express our sympathy to his family and children. I don't know what is fair anymore.

There are still many outcomes that I don't know yet. I only know what the responsible thing to do now is. Please, please protect the children.

I can't think of a better way to end this section than with Sharry's plea: Please, let us protect the children.

CHAPTER 5

And Now for the Really Boring Stuff: The Law

Since so many of you have asked for information about what laws exist in cyberspace—and how to tell the difference between what's illegal and what's just annoying—I had to include this section. If knowing the law isn't important to you, skip it. Don't worry—it's not essential to understanding anything else in the book. Some things make more sense, though, when you understand what can be regulated and what can't.

Notwithstanding the fact that I've tried hard not to sound like a lawyer in writing this book (the "notwithstanding" is a dead giveaway that I'm putting my lawyer hat back on), this is one area where being a cyberspace lawyer comes in handy. I'll try not to bore you, but it's hard to make law stimulating. If you tend to fall asleep easily, I recommend you skip this part. On the other hand, if you have insomnia, it's just what the doctor ordered.

Global Access Means Finding a Global Solution

Remember that the Internet isn't owned by anyone or controlled by anyone, and it doesn't exist in real space. So, before we begin discussing the laws, we need to understand how limited they are when it comes to regulating the *entire* Internet.

The Internet is global. Whatever you put up in New Jersey is immediately available everywhere else in the world. (No New Jersey jokes, please . . . I live there.) That means in order to control what is accessible on the Internet, we have to regulate it globally. That involves setting global standards and being able to enforce the laws on a world-wide basis.

But the biggest problem with worldwide efforts is the difference in worldwide standards and laws. U.S. laws and constitutional standards don't cut it everywhere else in the world. What's acceptable and legal in the United States may be criminal elsewhere. In addition, many things that are illegal here are legal in other countries of the world.

Probably the greatest difference involves child pornography and child sexual exploitation laws.

For example, until recently Japan outlawed only pornography that showed genital hair. Since younger children haven't yet developed genital hair, child pornography fell through the legal cracks. Many child pornographers took advantage of this loophole and housed their sites on Japanese Web hosting servers to escape the laws of their native countries. Japan recently enacted laws that closed this loophole. The newly-enacted laws should help considerably in the fight against online child pornography—and give Japanese law enforcement the legal tools they need to prosecute those who abused their hospitality.

This problem isn't limited to the Far East, either. What we consider "child pornography" is legal in many European countries. This is creating a serious problem when it comes to shutting down child pornography sites. In the United States we can't do anything about those sites unless they break U.S. laws and we have jurisdiction over the people or companies that operate those sites.

Even in the countries that do recognize child pornography, the legal age restrictions vary considerably. In the United States, children must be under eighteen to qualify as "children" under these laws, while in some other countries the age is as low as thirteen. So we can't do anything about sites housed in those countries unless the children do not meet the requisite age test for that country.

You can begin to appreciate how complicated this is. When a site is put up on a server in a country that doesn't criminalize conduct or content, whose laws apply? The laws of the country where the server is located? Those of the viewer's home country? These are some of the unique questions posed by Internet content in a worldwide setting. And they are questions that will have to be answered over the next few years as we struggle to find common ground.

What's the UN Doing to Help?

Until now, there was no worldwide effort to enforce crimes against children in cyberspace. But the United Nations (through its agencies) is now getting involved in the child online safety issue.

UNESCO (the United Nations Education Scientific and Cultural Organization) handles Internet matters for the United Nations. In January 1999, UNESCO held an experts' conference on pedophilia and child pornography online. As a result of this conference (at which I presented information about policing the Internet), UNESCO created its "Innocence in Danger—Children Online" program. In the United States, we've incorporated it into our "Wired Kids" project.

The Innocence in Danger project calls for leading experts from all around the world to join forces to make sure that all children will have safe access to the Internet. A child advocate and mother, Homayra Sellier, has been named by UNESCO to create the project and run it worldwide. She has inspired many others around the world to donate their time to this wonderful cause. (I know, she inspired me.)

Pursuant to her plan, each country will form a national action committee to pinpoint the key issues for their children. They will then undertake projects to implement action plans in their own country. Then the national action committees will work together to implement worldwide solutions. The U.S. National Action Committee operates through a nonprofit entity called "Wired Kids." Wired Kids is broader than the original UNESCO mission and will focus on equitable access (making sure that all children share the wealth of the Internet), online safety and Internet training, and helping teachers and schools use the Internet effectively. You can learn more about these efforts and how to get involved at www.familyguidebook.com and www.wiredkids.org, as well as www.innocenceindanger.org and www.unesco.org/webworld/innocence).

It's Not Totally Lawless—It Just Feels That Way

Just because it's global and hard to regulate doesn't mean that there are no laws in cyberspace. Too many people think it's a giant lawless place where people can do anything they want without being held accountable for their actions. But they are wrong. Most laws apply equally online and offline. With few exceptions, if something is criminal offline, it's also criminal online. And the same people who enforce these laws offline do it in cyberspace, too.

Our Founding Fathers, and the Law

Any discussion about pornography on the Internet has to start with the Bill of Rights and a recognition that much of the sexually explicit content we encounter online is protected by the First Amendment. That means we can't prevent others from viewing it online or offline even if we don't like it, or consider it disgusting and inappropriate for our children. That also means that if we want to prevent our children from being exposed to this information, it is largely up to us, as parents, to control our children's access to this information. That's because anything the government does to try to censor this material will be unconstitutional and a waste of their time and ours.

What Do You Know About Free Speech, Really?

We often refer to the First Amendment and constitutional free-speech protection. But many people don't know what that really means. (I was famous for telling my mother that I had the right to say anything I wanted. After all, I had *free-speech* rights!) The U.S. Supreme Court has made it very clear that cyberspace deserves the greatest free-speech protection available.

The First Amendment to the U.S. Constitution gives everyone in the United States the right to free speech, unrestricted by government interference (with a few very carefully crafted exceptions). It doesn't give you the unlimited right to say anything you want, at any time or place. It also doesn't prevent a *nongovernmental* entity or individuals, like your parents (so much for my arguments—luckily, my mother just ignored me anyway), from controlling what you say or what information you can access. (Free speech works both ways, giving you the right to say things and to hear what others have to say.)

Sexually explicit information, generally, may be protected, but certain *kinds* of sexually explicit information (defined as "obscenity") are not protected by the First Amendment. This is called "unprotected speech." If something is obscene, the government can regulate it and criminalize its use, production, and distribution. If it's only "indecent," they can't, because indecency, unlike obscenity, is protected by the First

Amendment. (For those of you still with me, I wish I could tell you it gets better.)

Although to many of you they may seem the same, there's a big difference between "obscenity" and "indecency" legally. (Lawyers never speak the same language as normal people—you should know that by now. If we did, you wouldn't need us, and we'd all have to write books about online safety to make a living.) Very simply, indecency is what makes a movie PG rather than G. Obscenity is what makes a movie XXX or worse, depending on where you live.

Congress keeps confusing obscenity with indecency, too. (I guess they haven't learned the movie rating tip.) That's one of the reasons their attempts at regulating content online have consistently failed. In each case, the courts have held these laws to be unconstitutional. (So much for my lecture about how lawyers don't speak the same language normal people do—since most members of Congress are lawyers, too.)

These rulings are good news for free-speech advocates, but they often make things more confusing for parents and educators. If the law can't protect their children from certain information, what options are available to them? What content is illegal? Aren't there any laws to help parents?

This is the *United States*, remember? We have laws that cover just about everything! Otherwise, how would we employ all us lawyers? (It's Congress's job to make sure that the rest of us lawyers are fully and gainfully employed. Otherwise we, too, might run for office!) (For those avid *Court TV* and *Judge Judy* viewers out there, and any others with insomnia, I have included even more about the law and how free speech works at the familyguidebook.com site.)

Child Pornography—It's Not Only Disgusting, It's Very Illegal!

Child pornography was almost eradicated in the United States about ten years ago, and what remained were mainly pictures produced years before that were constantly recirculated. But since the advent of the Internet and the popularity of the World Wide Web, child pornography has rebounded, becoming a booming business and its production and distribution an emerging cottage industry, even in the United States. And the children who are being used to produce it are *our* kids.

Child pornography isn't pornography that is made available to children. It's pornography that uses (or appears to use) children in sexual acts or in a lewd manner. (The age of consent differs from state to state and from the state to the federal levels of government. For example, it's seventeen in New York, and eighteen federally.) It is illegal throughout the United States and in many countries around the world.

Child pornography was deemed to be a separate unprotected speech category under the First Amendment. Instead of having to determine whether the child pornography is "obscene," the courts now can simply focus on:

- whether the depiction focuses on the child's genitals or pubic area
- whether the setting is sexually suggestive
- whether, taking into consideration the age of the child, she or he is depicted in an unnatural pose and inappropriate attire
- whether the child is only partially clothed or nude
- whether the depiction suggests sexual "coyness" or is designed to elicit a sexual response

Now that you know the tests, I expect to be receiving many more tips from concerned parents who find, or think they find, child pornography online.

But I should warn you in advance that the spam you receive that claims to contain "teens" having sex usually actually contains eighteen-year-olds having sex, not underage children. Child pornography is too illegal to be advertised in spam. It would be like a drug dealer placing an ad in the Yellow Pages. (I get about twenty questions a day from parents asking that question, or trying to report regular adult sites as child pornography based on their advertising. But advertising that you are offering child pornography, even if you aren't, is illegal, too.)

You should also know that it's not illegal to produce or distribute photos of nude children, unless they are posed in such a way as to suggest a sexual tone. The laws define this differently at the state and federal levels, but depictions of a nude child, without more, aren't illegal in the United States.

Laws That Protect Your Child from Sexual Predators in Cyberspace

In the United States it's illegal, online and offline, to:

- entice or coerce a minor to engage in sexually explicit conduct
- import or transport obscenity

- knowingly receive child pornography
- advertise child pornography
- depict minors engaged in sexually explicit conduct (even virtually)
- depict someone engaged in sexually explicit conduct who appears to be a child
- advertise or promote sexually explicit conduct by giving the impression that minors are engaged in sexually explicit conduct

The federal laws also protect children against luring or attempts to lure them into an offline meeting for the purposes of performing illegal sexual acts, or coercing them to provide sexually explicit photos of themselves.

This is one of the biggest problems with sexual predators online. While online sexual predators may ultimately want to meet your child face-to-face, in the meantime they often coerce a child into taking and sending to them sexually explicit photos of themselves, and even more often send children sexually explicit photos of themselves. (When cyberpredators coerce or seduce a child into taking sexually provocative pictures of themselves, they violate the law.)

Sexual abuse has always been a very serious crime, but in the past the penalties for child sexual abuse were not as high as they should have been. Thankfully, Congress has recently enacted laws that increased penalties for conduct involving sexual abuse of children and child pornography.

Cyberstalking Kids

Several years ago an Illinois adult, who was feuding with his neighbors, posted messages online indicating that his neighbor's young daughter was available for sexual activities. He also posted her name, address, and telephone number. The phone calls started arriving immediately, even in the middle of the night, from strangers looking for a young and willing sexual partner. Everyone was surprised to learn that this heinous act was merely a misdemeanor under Illinois law—and that no federal law applied.

Instigated by that horrible incident, Congress enacted a law that prohibits anyone from intentionally transmitting the name, address, telephone number, social security number, or e-mail address of any child under sixteen to entice, encourage, or solicit illegal sexual activity (which is any sexual activity with a minor). Had this horrible neighbor committed the same act now, he could be prosecuted under the new law.

Otherwise, cyberstalking is usually only a misdemeanor (a charge with a maximum sentence of a year or less in jail). And it's only covered by state law, not by federal law. Yet fewer than half of the states have statutes that expressly cover cyberstalking.

Many states stipulate that a "credible threat" must exist before an act is punishable under the law. So, unless the cyberstalker threatens you offline, or indicates that he knows where you live and has been watching you (for example, "I noticed you didn't turn your bedroom lights out until midnight last night"), most local law-enforcement agencies won't even investigate the case. (In their defense, it isn't always easy to tell the difference between someone just spouting off and a real online stalker.)

What About Sites That Advocate or Promote Sexual Abuse of Children?

Unfortunately, in the United States sites that promote and advocate sex between adults and children, even those that contain non-provocative photos of nude children, are generally not illegal.

SOC-UM (Safeguarding Our Children—United Mothers, www.soc-um.org) and Cyberangels have compiled a copyrighted list of sites that advocate pedophilia or support pedophile groups. In August 1999 this list, known as KIDList (Kids in Danger List), contained more than 30,000 websites. For more information about this list, you can go to www.cyberangels.org/kidlist.html. It is available without charge to law-enforcement agencies, and for a licensing fee to filtering companies. Net Nanny licenses the list.

Laws Against the Sale of Drugs, Alcohol, Guns, and Tobacco

Guns, Alcohol, and Tobacco

The legal outlets that sell these products are heavily regulated already, either by purchaser's age restrictions, licensing of dealers, or both.

For the most part, alcohol and handgun sales can only be made through licensed dealers. In addition, neither alcohol nor guns can be shipped from state to state other than to authorized and licensed dealers. For example, gun dealers cannot ship guns sold to a purchaser in another state unless the purchaser is another licensed gun dealer. (That's because the dealers need to do applicable background checks.) It's also a crime to transport alcohol between states unless you have the right license or permits for both interstate transport and the importing of alcohol into the state. So the fact that these products are being sold online is, in most cases, legally no different from their being sold offline via mail order or phone orders.

Apart from interstate shipments, though, the biggest issues arise when proof of age is required in the sale of any of these products (such as the sale of tobacco products to minors).

But how can anyone prove their age online? If we use credit cards as the proof of age, any of our kids armed with our credit cards can look like an adult online.

Handguns generally can't be sold to anyone under the age of twenty-one. Dealers can check proof of age and use common sense when trying to determine whether a buyer is twenty-one or over, but the same tried-and-true methods don't work online. That's why dealers need to be extra careful when dealing with online buyers.

I suspect that most online gun sales to minors are the result of lack of care rather than intentional targeting of kids. But there are a few loopholes that allow online gun shows to bypass current laws that regulate sales to minors. Problems arise when online gun shows allow online sellers to be paired directly with online buyers, who may not be qualified to purchase a gun because of age. Without a responsible intermediary (such as the online gun show entity) involved, unscrupulous sellers might not be as careful about the age of the buyer.

This is a new issue, and no laws have yet been adopted to prevent online gun shows and services from sharing personal information on sellers at the site. Senator Charles E. Schumer of New York has proposed legislation that would restrict the sharing of this information publicly at the site. It makes sense to me.

If you want to know more about this issue, you should contact Senator Schumer's office directly. They can send you information about his findings and the status of the legislation.

Alcohol works the same way. Attempts to regulate alcohol sales aren't really directed at children buying alcohol online. It's really an issue of the alcohol wholesalers worried about losing business to the online merchants, and the states worried about the loss of tax and licensing revenues.

In New York, for example, it's illegal to ship alcohol directly to a

New York consumer from another state. It can be shipped only to a specially licensed wholesaler in New York. Therefore, any sales on the Internet to a New York consumer, of *any* age, are illegal if they involve shipment from any other state. This law applies whether the alcohol is purchased online, by phone, or by any other non–face-to-face means.

What About the Sale of Restricted Poisons and Illegal Drugs Online?

These things are illegal whether sold online or offline. Special rules apply, though, when things that are legal where sold are illegal where bought. Typically, the matter falls under the jurisdiction of the U.S. Customs Service when the goods are imported from another country, whether they are brought in by the purchaser or sent pursuant to an Internet order.

My Legal Disclaimer

I warned you that legal discussions can be very boring, but so many of you have asked me to include this information that I have broken my rule about trying not to sound like a lawyer. If you're still awake, here are a few more legal items. These laws, remember, are currently in effect, and are only a small sampling of laws regulating child pornography, child exploitation, and cyberspace regulations. In addition, these laws may change, or may *already* have changed since we published this book. Finally, you should not rely on this discussion as legal advice. For that you need to consult with your own lawyer.

Cybercops: Who Enforces the Law in Cyberspace?

Remember that if something happens in cyberspace that would constitute a crime in real space, it's still a crime. Some U.S. law-enforcement agencies have been designated as the first line of defense where U.S. laws apply in cyberspace, but there is no law-enforcement group specifically charged with enforcing the law on the Internet.

A few years ago when I wrote my first book, *A Parents' Guide to the Internet*, there were very few cyber–law-enforcement efforts. The FBI had formed its Innocent Images Unit, the FTC was regulating Internet advertising directed to and data collection from children, and U.S. Customs had formed its Cybersmuggling Unit.

Two years later, these are still the three leading federal cybercrime and Internet regulatory agencies. However, over the last few years, several state and local law-enforcement agencies have created cyber-crime units that have risen to national prominence as well. (The New York Attorney General's effort has been a model for state cybercrime enforcement around the country, and Detective Bob O'Leary and the New Jersey State Police, the Bergen County Prosecutor's Office in New Jersey, and the Seattle vice squad's Leanne Shirey are some of the leading cybercops and cybercrime investigators in the country.) But knowing how to enforce laws and investigate cybercrimes was the ex-ception, not the rule, among most law-enforcement agencies.

Part of the problem in enforcing laws online is the lack of cyber-training and resources for law enforcement. It's hard enough for law-enforcement groups to locate criminals in their own jurisdictions without having to track website operators and cyberpredators located anywhere in the world.

Luckily, as the Internet has expanded, so have law enforcement's efforts to police cyberspace. The Department of Justice has created special regional task forces to address the problem and train local law-enforcement agencies around the country. The typical local police officer who had a family AOL account, and was therefore the agency's expert on the Internet, is quickly giving way to new high-tech teams. But budgetary restraints, lack of high-tech tools, and the need for training have made it a struggle for law enforcement to keep up.

The U.S. federal government has now made protecting our children in cyberspace a priority. Both the FBI and the U.S. Customs Cyber-smuggling Unit have received much-needed funding (not enough, but it's a start), and high-tech training centers are being built to train law enforcement in cyber-investigations.

The FBI Innocent Images Unit is the premier law-enforcement agency charged with finding predators in cyberspace. (They call the predators "travelers" since they travel from state to state to meet their victims.) While Innocent Images also handles an occasional child por-nography matter, their main focus is on the people who lure and sexually exploit children online. Innocent Images was formed in 1993 as a result of the first reported cybermolestation—that of a young boy from Maryland. It is still run from Baltimore, Maryland, under the watchful eye of one of my favorite women, U.S. Attorney Lynne Battaglia. (The rest of the FBI generally is run from Washington, D.C.)

Jorge Martinez, a devoted and caring man, has been an important force in steering this elite FBI team into the twenty-first century. Their local teams are also a great way to coordinate local, state, and federal operations in cyberpredator investigations, and make their special expertise available to communities. (I have a special affection and respect for the regional team that operates from New Jersey.)

The Cybersmuggling Unit, a special task force of the U.S. Customs Service, has been set up to handle Internet child pornography cases. It has just recently been organized as a separate unit of Customs. While it also handles the predator cases that emerge from child pornography investigations, its primary jurisdiction is limited to child pornography. The Customs connection is very important to the worldwide effort, since U.S. Customs has more agents outside of the U.S. than does most other federal law-enforcement efforts. This team works tirelessly to help protect children and to eradicate child pornography.

The FTC (the Federal Trade Commission) is the agency that handles consumer fraud, advertising, and data-collection issues. It handles these cases both online and offline and is one of the most expert Internet regulatory agencies. I think what makes them special is the special people who work there. I don't know any other federal regulatory agency that works shoulder-to-shoulder with the industry to try to improve the environment for children. They really care about children and about the Internet. In addition to their people, their website (www.ftc.gov) is a wealth of legal and practical information for website operators and consumers alike.

However, even these elite agencies can't possibly handle the problem without help. The bad guys spend twenty-four hours a day, seven days a week trying to abuse the system and find new ways to lure kids, defraud senior citizens, or steal what isn't theirs. A typical law-enforcement officer works eight hours a day, five days a week.

Who's ahead in the cop-and-robber game? Just do the math.

That's why they need our help—parents, teachers, and child advocacy groups alike can help level the playing field. Each of us can bear some of the responsibility for cleaning up illegal sites and stopping illegal practices by reporting them when we find them.

How Do They Find and Track People Online?

People mistakenly think that they are anonymous online. But wherever you go online, you leave a trail of electronic bread crumbs that track where you've been. Each time you surf online, you are identified by an IP number (Internet protocol). When you have your own server, or use certain ISPs, you have a static IP address. That means it's always your

IP as long as you use the same computer and the same ISP access. Tracking you is then as simple as tracking your IP address.

When you use AOL and other service providers to access the Internet, you have a dynamic IP address, which means it's yours for a temporary period, rather like subletting from the server's IP address pool. But the only way it can be tied to you is by knowing when the IP was recorded and tracking who was using the IP at that time. For that they need the cooperation of the ISP or online service, which has to check their records to tie the IP to you, as their customer.

The problem arises when law enforcement needs those IP records and they are no longer being stored by the ISPs or online service providers, who normally maintain them for only a week or less. Unless the predator or child pornographer is found quickly, important evidence is lost that links the suspect to the cybercrime.

Law enforcement is always lobbying for extended data-retention periods, and ISPs and online services have a problem with the cost of maintaining huge databases for extended periods of time. We can only hope they can work out something that balances law enforcement's needs against the costs. Some statutes permit law enforcement to send a letter to the ISPs requesting that they maintain their records on a particular user for ninety days, and that request can be extended for an additional ninety days, if necessary.

Many people also think that getting rid of evidence on your computer is as simple as clicking on the delete button. But all that does is take it off your desktop so you can't see it. But your computer knows it's there and can retrieve it with the right programs. The only way to know it's really gone is by reformatting your hard drive. That means you write over the old information, like recording over an old audio- or videotape. (Law enforcement can often still retrieve it after reformatting.)

Last but not least, your Web browser keeps a record of where you've surfed. These are called cache or history files. If you check them, you can see where your children have been surfing.

Where Do You Report Trouble and Cybercrimes?

Knowing where to report a cybercrime or where to turn when you need help online is key to cleaning up the Internet. Here are some important tiplines you should know about. As new ones are added, I'll post them on www.familyguidebook.com.

1-800-BE-ALERT (1-800-232-5378) is U.S. Customs' twenty-four-hour hotline, and it will route your complaint to the right law-enforcement agency. (Many states are also setting up similar tiplines. You should contact your state attorney general to find out whom you should contact locally.)

One of the best tiplines in the world is the National Center for Missing & Exploited Children's CyberTipline, a national tipline established by the U.S. Congress. The CyberTipline is accessible by telephone at 1-800-THE-LOST (1-800-843-5678) as well as online at www.cybertipline.com. They get thousands of child-exploitation tips a year, and turn over more than 2,000 tips of child pornography, alone, to U.S. Customs quarterly.

Their website is www.missingkids.com. They were formed under special federal legislation, and the tips sent to them are officially shared with the FBI Innocent Images Unit U.S. Customs' Cybersmuggling unit, the U.S. Postal Inspection Service and, in many cases, local law enforcement.

Other tiplines worldwide have modeled themselves after the National Center's cybertipline. And while they have some of the most devoted and talented professionals of any child-safety group, National Center wouldn't be National Center without Ernie Allen, a visionary when it comes to children's safety.

Several not-for-profit organizations are also devoted to child online safety and helping parents protect their children in cyberspace. The ones I've described have tiplines and work closely with law-enforcement agencies. Many of these are particularly noteworthy, and have great websites devoted to this subject as well.

I'm biased, of course, but Cyberangels has been helping people who need help online for more than four years (www.cyberangels.org). It was formed in 1995 by Curtis Sliwa as a Guardian Angels program. (I've been running Cyberangels since June 1998.) It's the largest of the online safety groups and receives hundreds of cybercrime tips each day, ranging from child pornography sites to cyberstalking cases, cyberfraud, and child-luring and sexual exploitation cases. You can report a cybercrime directly from the site, or by e-mail to tipline@cyberangels.org.

SOC-UM (Safeguarding Our Children—United Mothers, www.soc-um.org), one of the first child advocacy groups devoted to protecting children from cyberpredators, is run by one of my favorite people in the world, Debbie Mahoney. Debbie is the mother of a young man who was sexually molested as a preteen by a trusted neighbor who was an early expert in computers and online networking.

Although her son wasn't lured online, she realized how easily the Internet could be used to find and lure child molestation prey. Since then she has devoted her life to making sure children can surf the Internet safely. Her work predated the World Wide Web, beginning with Internet discussion groups formed by pedophiles online. She also chairs the Online Child Advocacy Task Force Advisory Committee for the Wired Kids project. SOC-UM's tipline can be accessed from their site. Their tipline accepts tips on child pornography, missing children, and online sexual exploitation and luring cases.

EHAP (the Ethical Hackers Against Pedophilia, www.ehap.org) is a select group of computer experts who band together to fight online child pornography and cyberpredators. In June 1999 they numbered only seventeen. But their success and the help they have provided to law-enforcement agencies worldwide belies their size. Notwithstanding their name, they do not break the law by hacking. Instead they use their skills to work with law enforcement to track down the child pornographers and predators in cyberspace.

Cyberscams and fraud can be reported to the FTC at their website, www.ftc.gov, by filling out the electronic complaint form.

Securities cyberfraud can be reported to the Securities and Exchange Commission at their help@sec.gov e-mail address.

Harassment, cyberstalking (that hasn't risen to the level of a credible offline threat), and hacking should be reported to the ISP that is used by the perpetrator. Also, if you report child pornography to the companies that house the site, they have to report it to law enforcement—assuming they are in the United States. I've included the e-mail addresses to report trouble to each of the major ISPs and online services in the ISP and online service directory at familyguidebook.com.

How You Can Make a Difference

We parents are really a very powerful group. If we act together, we can make a huge difference. And law enforcement needs our help.

Report What You Find

Even if you don't want to get law enforcement involved, you should let the ISP know when one of its members is attempting to contact your child with inappropriate intentions. The FBI tells me that when they seize a computer used by a cyber–sexual predator, invariably they find e-mail messages that had been sent to them from parents threatening them for having attempted to lure their child. Had these parents done more than just complain to the predator, someone else's child might not have been molested. We need to start building our own cyber–neighborhood watches.

Also, if you find an objectionable site, let the rating and blocking software companies know about it. To get this movement started, at www.familyguidebook.com and www.cyberangels.org, we have set up a form where anyone can notify the major parental-control software companies about a site they want to be reviewed or added to their "bad-site lists." We will also have a form you can submit if you think a site has been improperly listed in the "bad-site list" and should be removed. You fill out the form once, and we submit it to all the companies for you. It's a start.

If you visit a site you enjoy, ask them to make sure it's rated using a PICS-compliant standard (a Webwide rating system standard that allows sites to be rated by rating agencies, as movies are rated, based on content). We have a form you can use for that, too, which notifies the webmaster that you want their site rated so you can access it using the PICS standard ratings. It also copies the biggest rating agencies with your request so they can follow up.

And, if you find a site you love, tell the sites that produce good-site lists so they can be reviewed and added to these lists. If you fill out the form for great sites you want to recommend for the great-site list, it'll notify leading website review programs, including Cyberangels' Cybermoms.

If you learn about a student's website that threatens violence to others, let the school and local law enforcement know. I talk about this more in the "Kids Online in Schools" chapter.

It's not a perfect system, but it might get things moving. And within the next few years, with the help of interested parents everywhere, I suspect that we will make a difference. (Even if you oppose filtering, rating the Internet and reviewing and collecting great sites for children are the best defenses we have against attempts to regulate free speech online.)

Volunteer Your Time

You can also volunteer to join one of the online safety groups. Cyberangels (www.cyberangels.org) and SOC-UM (www.soc-um.org) both have online volunteer application processes and allow their volunteers to work virtually while online. (That means you can do it at night in your pajamas, once the kids are in bed.)

Drop by their sites to read more about what their volunteers do, and how much of a time commitment is required. Both groups train. (EHAP doesn't recruit or allow volunteers to join. They are a very select and closed group. They work only with those they trust. I am honored that they are willing to work with Cyberangels and with me.)

If you're not interested in working with a larger group, you can help by educating children in your schools about online safety, or by working with children in tech centers and community groups. Your school and library could use your help, too. Help your school become a Wired Kids Cyberschool by joining the Cyberschool program at the Wired Kids site (www.wiredkids.org).

You can create your own website or community newsletter with online safety information or links to other sites. You can even rate websites for the rating groups, or help raise money for child advocacy groups. The ways you can make a difference are limited only by your imagination and your caring.

I'm also interested in what you're doing. At Wired Kids (www.wiredkids.org), we'll be listing parents' efforts and linking to sites we think are helpful. Drop by familyguidebook.com and let me know what you're doing so we can share it with others.

Help Me! What to Do if the Unspeakable Happens

I hope you'll never need to use the information in this section. But sometimes horrible things can happen, and knowing what to do—and what not to do—and having a community response plan in place can make the difference between a child's being returned safely or not.

What to Do if Your Child Is Missing and You Suspect a Cyberpredator Is Involved

- *Don't panic.* I know that's next to impossible, but you need to be thinking clearly to be able to help law enforcement. Don't touch the computer or let anyone else touch it. This is not a time for your neighbor who is a computer expert to be fiddling around with your computer trying to find evidence. That should be left to the professionals.

- *Call your local law-enforcement agency first.* They know your community best and are located right where you need them. Don't let them touch your computer, however, unless they have a cybercrime team.
- *Pull together the information they will need.* Gather recent photos of your child and make sure that someone is talking to your child's friends to see if they have any information about the abduction. Make sure you have the e-mail account passwords available, and information about which ISP and e-mail service you use. If your child has an e-mail account with the school, gather that information as well. Does your child have an ICQ account? If so, make sure you have the ICQ number and their ICQ password. Do you use filtering or monitoring products? Find the manual, and make sure you have your passwords accessible.
- *Call the National Center for Missing & Exploited Children or the FBI.* The National Center can be found at 1-800-THE-LOST, and you can get the number for your local field office of the FBI from the phone book. You can also find it, in advance, online at www.fbi.gov/contact/fo/fo.htm.

Fast methods are available to law enforcement to obtain information from the ISPs. They also have very good working relationships with the Internet service providers, since many of their security officers worked for the FBI and other federal law-enforcement agencies before joining the private sector. Sophisticated cybercrime teams can find almost anything online these days.

The Community Response

Debbie Mahoney, founder of SOC-UM (www.soc-um.org), is deeply involved in missing-children issues. She developed a guide for creating an Effective Readiness Plan (ERP) after having worked with the community of Lodi, California, in helping find a child who had been kidnapped in 1994. Although the child was not abducted by a cyberpredator, this guide works equally well should that happen. Debbie credits the community's enthusiastic response with the safe return of the child. Make sure that if something horrible happens in your community everyone will respond as enthusiastically. And make sure your community is prepared.

Every community and school system should have an ERP. Typically, a task force is appointed by the city management working in coordination with local law enforcement. When Internet issues are involved, it's important that a cyber–law-enforcement agency be involved as well, even if that means contacting and coordinating with the state or federal law-enforcement agencies. Debbie advises that the task force that designs the ERP consider the following:

- stationing a police liaison in the volunteer center
- securing space for the volunteer center
- having city and county maps available at the volunteer center
- making arrangements with the local phone companies to provide phones in the volunteer location immediately
- making arrangements to copy and distribute flyers as soon as information is obtained

I've added a few additional suggestions for when a cyberluring or abduction is involved, or the Internet is involved somehow:

- Local law enforcement should make sure that the emergency contact numbers for the major ISPs and online services are gathered in advance. They don't want to find out that they can't reach someone in the security department over a holiday or weekend, or that they have to work their way through voice-mail mazes.
- Law enforcement should compile a list of the major filtering software companies and their security department contact information. If the parents used a filtering product, the product's security and tech people might be able to help access information that is otherwise unavailable.
- Last but not least, the tech-support or systems manager and library media specialist from the school system should be contacted to brief law enforcement about their systems and what information is available to them. Does the school use a filtering product? If so, what reports are available on surfing practices? E-mail and ICQs? What about websites authored by the students—what information is available about them?

Preparing in advance makes all the difference in the world. Time is the most important element in finding a missing child and capturing the perpetrator, or, in a case such as the Littleton tragedy, when you are trying to gather information about a student's website. Therefore, it is essential to have plans designed to produce those results. (You can find more information on ERPs at the www.soc-um.org site.)

CHAPTER 6

Kids Online in Schools

Schools Online

According to recent government surveys, 89 percent of U.S. public schools had Internet access in 1998, although only 51 percent of U.S. public schools had Internet access in at least one classroom. (Most have Internet access in only their libraries or technology or media centers.) Yet most parents I talk to and most who have responded to our surveys tell us they have no idea how their children's schools are using the Internet or what their children do online at school.

Over the next few years, all U.S. schools will be wired for Internet access. The schools need to recognize that parents are an important part of the team. And if parents don't know what their children's schools are doing, they should be asking these questions and offering their support and help. It's the only way we can make sure that our children are getting the most out of the Internet, safely.

You should understand, though, that the schools haven't found the magic solution either. They are grappling with safety concerns, lack of adequate funding and technology training, and changing technology. There don't appear to be any universal standards. Each school district handles the issue of Internet safety in its own way. Some are using filtering products. (New laws have tied federal funding to schools to their use of filtering products.) Others are sending notices to parents and setting policies for safe use.

Many schools have adopted policies and rules that the parents and students have to sign, before the students are permitted to use the

Internet at school. There is no "one size fits all" here. Solutions need to be customized to take into consideration the school's technology uses and staffing, curriculum, students' needs and behavior, parents' concerns, and community values.

How Do Schools Use the Internet?

Usually the first place a school wires is the library or media center. Children research school projects and often use the Internet for fun, games, sending e-mail, and chatting. Many schools have eliminated chat altogether, since they have learned that chat poses more risks than educational value.

Librarians and library media specialists typically supervise the children while they are surfing. The monitors are frequently positioned so the screen can be seen from the librarian's desk, which helps keep the kids honest. In a typical large high school library, though, more than 150 teenagers may be using the library and more than forty of them may be using computers with Internet access. This makes direct supervision impossible. That's why many schools have implemented filtering in school libraries, as well as relying on acceptable-use policies.

In many schools, classrooms are often wired as well. In the early days of school Internet use, these classroom computers were used as a reward when students finished their classwork. But, as educational programs were developed, many schools built Internet resources into the curriculum.

Does the Internet Improve Educational Levels, or Is It Just Another Toy?

Too often people aren't aware that we have proof of how use of the Internet and computers can improve learning skills and test scores. For example, three third-grade classes at the Logan Elementary School in Baltimore County, Maryland, were selected to participate in a special program. The program began as a challenge by the governor of Maryland to Bell Atlantic to match a program instituted in Union City, New Jersey, to get students linked up.

The program put computers and high-speed Internet access lines into the children's homes and provided the principal and teachers with matching computers and high-speed Internet access. Until the installation of the high-speed telephone lines, many of the children didn't even have phones in their homes. (Logan had a high percentage of lower-income families, since many industries in the area had shut down. A substantial number of the families in the program were under the poverty line, earning less than $10,000 per year.)

Before the project began, only 20 percent of the third grade class was reading at grade level or higher. Within a year, test results disclosed that more than 80 percent were reading at grade level or higher. And the improvements were just beginning.

Standardized test scores indicated that the students' reading grade level increased from 2.6 to 4.1 (sixth month of the second grade to the first month of the fourth grade), an average increase of 1.5, or one year plus 5 months' growth in one year's time. Educators inform me that it is extremely significant for an entire class to advance this far in one year. And standardized testing showed a substantial gain both in reading *and* in math.

An interesting by-product of the program was that children had a 100 percent homework completion rate. (I never came close to getting 100 percent of my homework turned in on time—or even turned in period.) Students in the program also had an increased attendance rate, and the program became a valuable resource for the PIE (Parents Internet Education) program in Baltimore County.

A sad epilogue to this story is that, notwithstanding the overwhelming proof of how much the Internet and use of computers can help children learn, the students' new school, Dundalk Middle School, has decided not to allow the program to continue.

But Bell Atlantic deserves a medal for what it has done for these children. (In fact, Cyberangels gave it the Cyberangels Internet Vision Award for the work it has done with children.)

How the Internet Can Help in Creating Innovative and Effective Projects for Teaching Troubled Kids

Here's a true story of a special program for special children, run by a special woman I know and love, Susan M. Condrey, Ed.D. Susan, who is with the Orange County Department of Education, was awarded the $500,000 Single Gender research grant in 1997, breaking public school tradition by creating single-gender schools. She used to be a principal of the school.

Her program is highly reliant on technology and the Internet and is the pride of Orange County, California. In Susan's own words (the names have been changed to protect the students' privacy):

They came to school in shifts, one gender at a time, sharing the space and the teachers and the curriculum, but not class time. The Single Gender Academies (SGA) in Fountain Valley, CA, began with a two-year research grant, proposed by then governor Pete Wilson, to see if separating students by gender could positively influence them academically, improve attendance, and reduce acts of violence or crime.

The kids at the Fountain Valley School got there after being removed from their neighborhood schools for reasons of expulsion, pre-expulsion intervention, chronic truancy, lack of credits, or because they were transitioning back after incarceration. They came from the surrounding communities, with 85 percent of them from the lowest-performing school districts in the state, from residential areas of high crime, from neighborhoods where multiple families often shared a house or apartment.

Students at SGA may have been streetwise, but they were not sophisticated. They hadn't traveled much or read much. Some had never been to the beach, ten miles away, or to the mountains, an hour's drive. Generally speaking, they were angry, frustrated, and held little hope of realizing the great American dream.

This school was different. Besides separating the boys from the girls, the instructional strategies were technology-based. While there were reading lists and materials, there were no texts. Students spent two hours working independently on individually prescribed lessons, then moved to project-based learning activities that took them virtually and then literally into communities. They learned to think. They did their research first on the Internet and then in the field. They learned to find information, make sense of it, and present it. They videoconferenced with experts and with students from schools throughout the United States often and regularly. The teachers started a mentoring program pairing an adult volunteer with each student. There was the opportunity not only for scheduled activities, but also an e-mail connection to communicate one-on-one. As the doors to the world opened to the classes through the Internet, doors began to open for individual students.

John was living in a motel with his mom and younger sister when she was shot and killed there when John was 12. His dad was in jail. He spent the next several years in and out of incarceration, living in group homes, and changing his appearance from grunge to punk to whatever was shockingly different. Lydia was just bored. Tired of school, she hung out at the mall or stayed home and watched television until going to school seemed too difficult. She missed most of her 8th and 9th grade years. Both of these kids were bright, but behind in credits and in skills, when they were court-ordered to attend school. Neither saw the prospect of much to look forward to.

The single-gender setting provided a certain comfort level, allowing the students to speak out, to risk being wrong, to focus on learning. The Internet provided excitement and experiences previously denied them. Through technology students began to discover, to communicate, to grow, and to learn. John graduated from SGA, is working as a video editor, and hopes to go on to school and maybe work in the entertainment industry. Lydia is doing well and will be transferring back to her neighborhood school this fall. She's saving money from her summer job to buy a personal computer. Their newly acquired assurance shows in their faces.

Cats in India

Teachers are pretty remarkable people. But even the best teachers can learn something from their students once in a while.

Art Wolinsky is very special, even among special teachers. He heads up the New Jersey group of 21st Century Teachers, the White House project designed to bring teachers into the twenty-first century with respect to technology in the classrooms. But thirty years ago, when he first started substitute teaching, he was just beginning to implement his innovative ideas in the classroom.

Art was covering for a teacher who had left a lesson plan. The lesson plan involved a comparison of the telecommunication, health, transportation, educational, and communication infrastructures of the United States with those of developing and emerging markets around the world. Like any good new substitute teacher, Art decided to do it "his" way. So he instructed the students to compare how well the United States and India would each handle an epidemic that killed every cat in their country overnight.

The hands went up immediately. In the United States the president would get on national television and make an announcement about what to do and what not to do, after meeting with his top health advisers. Then arrangements would be made to pick up all the dead cat bodies and dispose of them without causing further health epidemics. People would be taught how to avoid further epidemics and cats could be imported from another epidemic-free country. They would also set up cat grief support centers, and all would be well.

But India, under the students' analysis, didn't fare as well. The lack of a solid infrastructure in the countryside, the students felt, would make the incident a national disaster in India. Cat corpses would be decomposing in the streets, causing epidemics among the human population. The lack of a solid communication system would prevent villagers from understanding what happened, which might result in civilian unrest. All would be horrible in India.

Art used this as one of his core lessons whenever he taught over the following thirty years. And for thirty years the students always came to the same conclusion—India would not handle this situation as well as the United States would. But last year, because of the Internet, one student concluded otherwise.

When Art asked the now age-old question of which country would handle this crisis better, and asked for a show of hands of the students who thought the United States would, all hands went up with the exception of one. When he then asked about India, one hand went up—but it was a very confident hand.

Art started his intellectual probing. "You say India would fare better?" he said, using his most teacherly skeptical tone (we all remember this, don't we?). "Describe and compare the transportation, educational, communication, and health infrastructures in each country for us, please." The student complied, getting it all right.

"Well, then . . . why do you say that India would be better off than the United States?"

The student very simply answered, "Because, according to an article I found online, Bombay has no cats at all."

The Internet has allowed many students to turn the tables on their teachers. And the good teachers are thrilled about this. It means that the students are researching and enjoying learning, not just memorizing facts and dates. Luckily, for his next use of this lesson plan, Art was able to find another emerging market country with a larger cat population—also using the Internet!

Internet Problem Issues for Schools

While the Internet is a terrific educational tool, its use in schools does pose some problems. In addition to the issues parents face with children who access the Internet from home, there are a few issues that are specific to schools. These include what personal information the school may post on its website about the students, use of children's intellectual property and the intellectual property of third parties, and how to judge the difference between a bogus resource and a credible one. They also include hacking, plagiarism, and whether the school can discipline students for what they do on a personal website designed and posted from home. Last but not least, a chain e-mail that circulates among the students can crash a school's entire system.

Children's Pictures and Personal Information

All of us are excited to send Grandma and Grandpa the photo of our child winning the local sports trophy or getting the debate award. Dog-eared clippings from our town paper are cherished and carefully glued into scrapbooks to show our grandchildren. So what's the harm in posting the same photo at the school website?

First of all, a website isn't a local newspaper. It's available to more than 84 million people in the United States alone. And the people who might use this information to reach your children aren't neighbors who are worried about what their neighbors think. They are strangers to your family and your community. (Polly Klaas was targeted from a mailing list compiled for marketing to teenagers in a particular zip code area. Her killer bought this list of girls between certain ages and chose her at random from the list. The list contained her address, name, and age.)

Although the FBI has not yet encountered a case of a child molester targeting a child they found at a school website, they worry (and so do I) that someone will use this information to target a child. Just think for a moment. Children who appear on a school's website are at that school from 8:30 A.M. to 3 P.M. every day. It's easy to find them during those hours and when they are walking to and from school, especially if you know their name and have a printout of their photo in your hand. "Mary, can I talk to you a minute?" How many of our children wouldn't respond to someone who knew their name?

So I recommend that a school use photos of children only after they get the parents' consent, and only in groups of five or more. I also recommend that they not identify the children by name, only by the group: "Ms. Smith's fourth grade class" or the "Volleyball Club," for instance.

This makes perfect sense when you think about it. We'd never let anyone post our child's photo on a highway billboard, would we? We need to think of the Internet as a giant billboard posted on the largest superhighway in the world. If we wouldn't allow something about our children to appear there, we shouldn't allow it to be posted online.

Last year, when I was speaking to a group of parents at a local tech high school, I realized that even bright and well-intentioned teachers don't realize the risks involved in sharing their students' personal contact information online. As I was going through my standard speech on why children shouldn't be posting personal-contact information in online profiles or on their websites, a parent of a teenager timidly raised her hand. "Does that mean that our children shouldn't be completing their assignment of building an autobiographical website, with their e-mail addresses, photos, and hobbies?" Apparently the teacher had assigned the students the task of building a personal website. The teacher had no idea of the risks involved, and immediately changed the assignment, having the teenagers build an autobiographical website without the personal-contact information, and with only first names. It was just as informative, but safer.

More recently, a parent called my office. She was very upset. Her son, an elementary student in Florida, wanted to take part in a class contest to build the best autobiographical website, but she wouldn't permit him to post his e-mail address at the site. Since the teacher required the inclusion of the e-mail address so people could contact the child directly, her son wasn't allowed to compete in the contest.

The school had sent home a permission slip that informed the parents that their children would be designing a website, but didn't mention the fact that their e-mail address would be used on the site. The mother, concerned about her son's and his classmates' safety, had contacted the teacher and the principal but had gotten little help.

When I called the principal, I didn't receive a very warm reception either. (Okay, I'm a lawyer, and I doubt any principal would welcome a call from a lawyer late on a Friday afternoon.) But although his cool reception didn't bother me, his response to my telling him about the potential risks did. He asked me if I could give him proof that a child had been molested by someone who found them at a school website. I asked him if he was willing to allow one of his students to be the first. The conversation went downhill from there, but he agreed to check into it.

The last thing we need is to aggravate a school principal on a Friday afternoon. (They are the only ones scarier than a raging bull when provoked—at least that's how I remember the principal when I was in school.) But it's important that teachers and principals be sensitized to the risks of disclosing personal-contact information about children at a school website. We're all in this together. And we all have the same priority—our children.

Children's Creative Works

Most of us have had the luxury of being able to post our children's original artwork, from their first crayon drawing, on our refrigerator door. As they advance from simple poetry in first grade to orchestral compositions in their senior year, we all think we have the next Pavarotti, Picasso, and Longfellow all rolled into one. Our biases may be showing—they won't be spotted by the next talent scout—but even the simplest and most uninspired creation is still theirs. It belongs to them just as much as if they had registered it with the U.S. Copyright Office in Washington, D.C.

Schools should get parents' and the child's consent before posting the creative works. (So should all sites that post their creative works.) Who knows? Maybe they will be discovered and support us in our old age!

Plagiarism

Kids have always been creative when it comes to avoiding schoolwork. They spend hours avoiding twenty minutes' worth of work. While most of us were limited to finding a smarter older sibling or friend to help us with schoolwork (or better yet, do it for us), our cyberkids can now surf the hundreds of sites that sell term papers to teens online. And they don't even have to retype them; they can just download them, typed and illustrated—ready to go.

Many of the smarter teachers I know have bookmarked these sites so they can routinely compare the student's submitted term papers with those they find online. Since most of these sites provide the term papers only for a fee, check out your credit card statements and make sure you're not subsidizing your children's plagiarism.

Off-School Websites

Just as kids have circulated derogatory jokes and drawings of teachers over the generations, these digital kids circulate their jokes, insults, and drawings using the power of the Web, where they can be viewed by everyone. They then share the URL (Web address) of the site, so fellow classmates can appreciate their work. Often the URL ends up in the hands of a teacher. Teachers and administrators who are the target of the site report it, and threaten to file a lawsuit or to report it to the police. The school then feels compelled to do something. Typically the child is suspended or expelled, or college recommendations are withdrawn.

But several times the ACLU has taken these schools to court for disciplining a child for actions taken off-premises, and in most cases the school has lost the lawsuit. It can be a very costly mistake—a school system may have to pay $50,000 or more in damages when it exceeds its authority in this area.

So what's a school to do? I would suggest they take their lead from a very experienced school superintendent in Bergen County, New Jersey.

A teenager in that high school, after getting angry with certain teachers and administrators, lashed out by posting some pretty vulgar and insulting things about them on a personal website. He wrote the site from home and posted it online. It wasn't posted on the school's server, but was available to everyone with Internet access once they had the URL. URLs of classmates' sites get passed around quickly, and many of the kids in the school accessed the site from the school's computers.

When the word got back to the teachers and administrators, they were understandably furious. They sought help from the police, who threatened to charge the teenager with harassment (but they wouldn't have been able to make that charge stick). Everyone involved seemed to lose their head, but the superintendent managed to keep his. He recognized that this wasn't a school matter, and that the parents needed to be involved. He called in the parents, who were appalled and took this situation as seriously as they should have. Together they worked out a suitable apology and a way to handle the case without blowing it out of proportion.

The press had a field day. This superintendent stood firm against the anger of the teachers and the pressures of the community. He was right.

Months later he shared something with me. He told me that he had met the young teenager at a school event, and the student apologized once again. He also thanked the superintendent for handling the situation with grace. The boy had acted out in anger, and hadn't thought about the consequences of his anger. Eventually, even the teachers came around. I was sorry my children were already out of high school—they would have benefited from attending a school system run by such a patient and wise administrator. We could use many more like him.

Linking to Off-School Sites

If a school links to off-school sites, it needs to review them to make sure they are appropriate for students' use. Many children's sites are now using bridge pages to provide a transition from the protected environment to the Web or off-site sites. PBS Kids and Headbone are two very good examples of how a bridge page can work.

Essentially bridge pages say, "You are now leaving our site. While we have provided certain sites that we think will be of interest to you, you should know before proceeding that these sites are not endorsed by us, may not treat your personal information responsibly, and may have changed since we reviewed them for appropriateness. Once you decide to proceed, you're on your own. So surf safely." (Of course, they do this more artfully, but the essential issues are covered.)

Even if your school decides that a bridge page isn't for them, the school should disclose to parents that children can access nonschool sites, and that although the school reviewed those sites to determine if they were appropriate at the time the links were set up, sites can change, or may no longer be operational, and the school cannot control what happens at those sites. The school has to be sure to tell the parents and kids that use of those sites is at their own risk.

For these reasons, it might be better not to link to off-school sites unless the school intends to maintain those links regularly.

Death Threats/Bomb Threats

Littleton didn't invent bomb threats. Innovative kids have been making school bomb threats for years, especially when the weather is good or they haven't studied enough for a scheduled exam. (When I was young, we used to have someone pull the fire alarm.) But, since the Columbine/Littleton tragedy, bomb threats in schools have increased dramatically.

One county in Maryland was plagued with a bomb threat a day following the Littleton tragedy. Newspapers would repeatedly call me, trying to find ways of locating bomb threats online that threatened a particular school or location. Threats increased during the time the state standardized tests were scheduled in Maryland. (See? these kids aren't so different from us, are they?) And the threats that were specific to Maryland moved like wildfire across the country, becoming threats even to school systems that held their testing at different times. (The game of telephone can be particularly deadly online when rumors spread rapidly across the world, frightening people needlessly.)

Many schools now have well-developed safe-school teams who handle offline risks, like offline bomb threats, weapons brought to school, gangs, violent students, and protests.

Some schools also use online filtering programs that are managed off-premises on third-party proxy servers. These programs provide monthly reports to a school about what sites its students have tried to access from their blocked lists. Typically, their blocked lists include bomb-building sites. Yet none of the schools I talked with review this information and share it with the safe-school team. It would be easy enough for these reports to be shared, then compared with offline information on file with the safe-school teams. Schools need to know who is trying repeatedly to access bomb-building sites, so they can use this information to help handle the offline risks. It's information they already have—but aren't using.

These reports can be used for other safety purposes as well. One of the biggest problems schools face is not knowing when students are making threats online. Students' websites are typically not picked up by the search engines, and finding a site that isn't listed on a search engine, unless you know its domain name, is like finding a needle in the virtual Internet haystack.

When a student builds a controversial or provocative website, usually the only ones who know about it are other students, who use the school computers to access the site. These reports can tell you when there is a sudden popularity of a certain site at a school. They should be regularly reviewed. It's the only way of spotting a student's website early.

It's also one of the few ways a school's administration can use information to prevent violence in schools, because it can identify students who are crying out for help in advance.

Schools can also set up their own reportline, like our KIDReportline (discussed in "Teach . . . Your Children Well.") Or they can let their students know that reportlines like this exist. It's a start.

Restricting Noncurriculum Speech

Schools have an extraordinary amount of freedom in choosing school materials, textbooks, and curriculum programs. This extends to their ability to select materials and restrict speech and free expression in noncurriculum matters as well. The courts have given schools a broad ability to select and censor speech, as long as the well-being and potential safety of the students is at stake.

Although the courts held that a school in the 1960s erred in not permitting students to wear black armbands protesting the Vietnam War (the school defended its decision by saying the armbands could have led to student violence), school administrators have since been permitted to restrict student newspaper stories and student meetings.

But if a school has created an open forum, such as an editorial program or a website that permits community members to express comments, it can't later restrict opinions they don't like. The forum is either closed and easily restricted, or open and outside of the school's ability to regulate.

School systems need to think about the ramifications of opening discussions to community groups, where it impacts their right to control content at their websites.

Pen Pal Programs

One of the best ways of pairing students with other students around the world is through pen pal programs. School-to-school programs are the safest way of allowing students to communicate with strangers online. We need more of these programs, and we can only hope your child's school will help create them.

Unless schools are part of a school-to-school pen pal program, parents should be informed about the pen pal program in the acceptable-use policy, and given the choice of having their children participate. There are many risks relating to nonschool pen pal programs, as I discuss in the pen pal section of Chapter 2.

Resource Credibility: Teaching Our Children Critical Thinking and Media Literacy Skills

It costs thousands of dollars to publish a book. Cable and television programming costs even more. Magazines carefully check facts and universities use peer-review methods to make sure that what is published is accurate and credible. But anyone can publish a website, in a few hours, and say anything they want—often without a credible basis for it. (I often claim online to be tall, thin, blonde, and gorgeous. But no one ever said wishful thinking wasn't allowed online.)

My dress size aside, how can anyone know when they have a real and credible site or just someone's puffery? It's not easy. Online there is no stamp of approval for quality control. A site published by an anti-Semitic group that claims the Holocaust never occurred may look as real and sound as reliable as a scholarly university dissertation. And when our children come across it, it might become the research source for their term paper on World War II.

Schools are facing this issue frequently these days. So teaching children how to evaluate the credibility of a site is an important part of using the Internet in connection with schoolwork. Essentially, it's teaching them to be good information consumers.

Whenever we find a website, we should think about the purpose of the site. Is it designed to sell something? If it's designed by anyone who sells anything, you have to assume that it's designed to at least indirectly promote its products or services. Any site that is designed to sell something should be approached as critically as any offline promotion or advertisement.

Once we understand the site's point of view, we can evaluate what they are saying more effectively. Our children already know, at a young age, the candy bars or hamburgers that are smaller than they appear on television, or the toys that are constructed poorly, or the computer game systems that need optional equipment at additional cost in order to do what is promised. One of the first legal rules our children learn is *caveat emptor*—buyer beware. Teaching them to use critical judgment when reviewing a website is easy.

The information gathered from a website should be accurate and current. And if there is a bias, the website's bias should be obvious, and the authority of its writers should be set forth.

Here are a few things children should be checking when they visit a site to conduct research:

- **Who's the author or website creator, and what's their authority?** Is it written by Nobel Peace Prize Award winners, or by Joe Crackpot? While many won't tell you that they are unqualified to make the statements they make at the site, they leave clues.

    Our children should look first to the credentials offered at the site for the site authors. If the person states that he is a professor at Outer Siberia University, you should check for links to the university. Has the person listed awards? If so, are there links to the entities that gave the awards so you can check? Is this person a published author? If so, does Amazon.com, Barnes & Noble, or Borders have his book listed online?

Search for other sites that reference this person. Not everyone is an award-winning professor and published author, but most good sources are cited elsewhere online.

- **What's the bias of the site? Whose points of view aren't covered?** Bias isn't necessarily bad, as long as it is clear to the site viewer. Remember that everyone has their bias, but some are more significant than others. Is this a site that performs "unbiased" reviews of advertisers? If so, have they disclosed that fact to the readers? Are they a nonprofit entity with a particular mission or purpose? Where was the site created? Is it from an international group that might have a country or culture bias? Is it a U.S. site which might have a U.S. bias?

  Often, you can detect bias by reading closely. The good sites will identify their mission. Think about who is creating the content, whose points of view are included, and whose are excluded. Students should try to achieve balance by including different biases and points of view when they do their research.

- **How current is this information?** Does the page have a "last updated" date notation? Many of the sites I researched for this book, including many on finding credible resources, were last updated in 1996. When I reviewed their content, I took that into consideration. Certain things don't change, such as how to judge credentials, but other things, like branded and approved site lists and what schools are doing, have changed radically. The site I looked to for current information was updated a few months earlier, and gave that date on the front page.

  If the site doesn't contain a "last updated" date, look to see if there's a "recent additions" or "what's new" section of the site, and see how often it is changed. You want to make sure the content is updated often, since it tells you two things: that the site gets regular attention, and that it contains recent information. A good site is updated regularly, preferably at least once monthly, and, with news and hot topical sites, more often than that. Cyberangels (www.cyberangels.org), for example, is updated every week at least once. If you can't tell when a site was last updated, send an e-mail to the webmaster at "webmaster @[the name of the site]." Ask how often the site is updated and the date it was last updated.

- **Is the information stable and consistent?** Is the information consistent within the site? Does everything match the theme of the site and this information? Are they proposing censorship on one page and free speech on another? (I'm not talking about CNN's site, where they seek to present alternate and opposing views.) Is this the only site that espouses this viewpoint, or is there other support for this position? Have you compared it with related resources? Often, a site that appears too good to be true *is* too good to be true. Most good sites, with well-supported positions, will have support from other sites.

- **What have they linked to? Do the links work?** Do they link to credible sites, and do credible sites link to them? Are the links correctly described? Are they current? Who else links to them? Again, is the link information updated and accurate, or do the links not work anymore?

The school and public librarians are the real experts in judging credibility of resources. That's what they do when they select resource and reference books. Talk to them about how they are teaching your children to exercise informed information judgment. They are helping build your children's information literacy skills. If your school hasn't yet adopted an information literacy program, you can point them to a few good sites that might help. I've included these at the Family Guidebook site (www.familyguidebook.com).

Safe Internet Use in Schools

Getting Parents Up to Speed and on Board

The best way for schools to get parents involved is to let them know what's going on. Every survey I have done with parents tells us the same thing: No parents know what's going on at their child's school with the Internet, and many parents don't know what the Internet is or how it works. Yet every school laments the fact that the parents aren't more involved, and parents complain that they're not included. (What we have here is a "failure to communicate.")

Notice and Informed Consent

So the simplest way to get parents involved is by letting them know what's going on (I call that the "notice rule"), getting their consent to anything that has increased risks (I call this the "informed consent rule"), and educating them so they can be a part of the decision making and the solution.

Schools need to tell parents how they are using the Internet at school, what the risks are, and how they are managing the risks. The notice has to be clear and complete, and lay out all the important information in a way even the most computer-illiterate parent can understand. And it should be included in the acceptable-use policy the school prepares and hands out to students and parents.

Whether they filter or not, every school should have an acceptable-use policy, which is a list of the rules pursuant to which children (and others) are permitted to use the Internet. Some school systems like to formalize the process, making it school board policy, with all the formalities that entails (notice, hearings, etc.). Others adopt it on a school-by-school basis as they do most rules, such as no running in the hall, and no smoking on school grounds. But however they do it, every school needs one.

Given all the controversies about safe schools and how schools use the Internet, I am amazed to find how many schools haven't yet adopted acceptable-use policies. I recently spoke before a group of principals from one of the largest cities in the United States. I was shocked when they told me that they had been considering adopting acceptable-use policies for almost two years but hadn't yet done it. That's when schools face legal liability. Waiting two years to set rules about what kids can and can't do online? Why? Once they understand the risks, schools should move quickly to set safety rules and get the parents informed. If the formal process is taking too long, create an informal one, and get the notice out to parents and students.

There's no magic to creating an acceptable-use policy. I've been doing them for years for major corporations, and schools are the same. And, although we cyberspace lawyers hope you will hire us to help us feed our children and pay their college tuitions, you don't even need a lawyer. But the policy does need to tell parents and kids how the Internet is being used and what the rules are, as clearly as possible, as well as what happens if anyone breaks the rules.

Also, most schools freely share their acceptable-use policies, and reading over several and copying what fits your needs is a good place to start. I've put two very good acceptable-use policies in the appendix to review. I've also included, at familyguidebook.com, a list of great acceptable-use policies and where to find them online, as well as some terrific sites that link to acceptable-use policies and teach you how to prepare one.

Setting the Framework

Here's what should be determined in setting the policy and in disclosing it in an acceptable-use policy:

- How is the Internet used at school? Is it in the library only, library/media/tech center only? In the classroom?
- Who supervises Internet use?
- What are the special rules for use at each location?
- What are the risks? Chain e-mails? Chatting? E-mail? Instant messaging? Accessing inappropriate sites? Giving out personal information online? Posting nasty things about others? Copyright infringement? Piracy? Hype and misinformation? Threats of violence? Bomb threats? Doing things that cost money?
- Are filtering software or filtering services used? How do they work? What are the risks of overblocking (innocent sites being blocked) or underblocking (inappropriate sites getting through)? What can be done if a student needs to access a site that is blocked? Are there override mechanisms? Can the site lists be modified to allow a school to add an innocent site to the allowed lists or an inappropriate site to the blocked lists?
- What's the rule about downloading materials? Have the students been warned of the risks of viruses and the seriousness of hacking?
- Are school directories, with telephone numbers and student and parent names, posted on the school website? What about class rosters? School team members and the schedules for games, etc.?
- Can students be disciplined for posting defamatory or provocative information about the school or school personnel on personal websites composed outside of school? (Schools can do this only if they relate to school safety or discipline, unless the students and parents agree otherwise in the policy.) What are the guidelines?
- Where can students report sites that make threats of violence? Is there an anonymous reportline they can use?

- Is the school posting personal information about the student on a website? Do they post student e-mail addresses? Do they post student photographs? Individually or in groups? Are the students identified in those photographs? How are they identified?
- Is the school partnering with third parties on online content and programs? If so, are these programs making personal information about students under the age of thirteen available to these third parties? If they are, parental consent (not just school consent) is required before the information is provided to third parties.
- What information is collected about students' Internet activities? To whom is it disclosed? Is it available to parents upon request?
- Is the school posting student works on a website? Is there a student chatboard or e-mail system? Can students sign up for Web-based chat?
- What happens if the students break the rules? Will there be a warning? Suspension? Check the school disciplinary process on due process and procedural issues.

Once the school knows what the entire system looks like, it should describe it to the students and to the parents. (Remember that the parents may not all understand what the school is talking about, so using familiar terms and not a lot of cyber and techie terms is most effective.)

Tell the students what they are allowed to do and what they aren't. Let them know the consequences of disobeying the rules.

Then explain the risks and get the parents' okay.

Explaining the School's Choices

If the school chooses not to filter, explain this in simple terms. Tell the parents and students why the school decided against filtering, and how it came up with a safety plan that it believes will be effective. For example:

Monroe Middle School has one of the best technology centers in Middletown. Mrs. Richards, Monroe's library media specialist, has just finished her review of available filtering products. She has concluded that they may block more sites than necessary and yet many inappropriate sites get through, and therefore she has set up a special system just for Monroe.

Starting this fall, Mrs. Richards will be teaching a class on online safety, and the social studies classes will be working on a safe-surfing site project and compiling online safety tips. We believe that, given the size of our student body and the number of supervisory personnel at Monroe Elementary School, a combination of online safety education and close supervision of the students online fits our needs best.

In addition, each student will be given an acceptable-use policy that tells them what they are permitted to do and what they are not permitted to do on the school's computer system. This acceptable-use policy will be sent home with each student, and must be reviewed by the student's parents. Mrs. Richards will be available to answer any of the students' or parents' questions and has also posted a list of frequently asked questions and their answers at the school website.

Before a student may be allowed to use the Internet, Mrs. Richards must have a signed consent form back from the parents. The consent form also acknowledges that the parents are responsible for their child's online behavior both at home and at school.

If the school decides to filter:

Monroe Middle School has one of the best technology centers in Middletown. Mrs. Richards, Monroe's library media specialist, has just finished her review of available filtering products. She has concluded that Tough Filter is the best filtering system for our needs. Tough Filter has been selected by five thousand middle schools in our state alone, and is one of the most well respected filtering products, having been out on the school market since 1996. We have reviewed effectiveness studies done by Tough Filter and have concluded that it does a better job of filtering hate and violent content and other content that we deem inappropriate for our students than other competing products.

But, as satisfied as we are about our selection of filtering software, you should know that all filtering software may block innocent sites and allow some inappropriate sites to get through. That's why we want to make sure that our students understand online risks and learn how to use the Internet effectively and safely.

Starting this fall, Mrs. Richards will be teaching a class on online safety, and the social studies classes will be working on a safe-surfing site project and safety tips. We believe that, given the size of our student body and the number of supervisory personnel at Monroe Elementary School, filtering is an important part of our online safety plan and will be used in conjunction with online safety education and close supervision of the students online.

In addition, each student will be given an acceptable-use policy that tells them what they are permitted to do and what they are not permitted to do on the school's computer system. These acceptable-use policies will be sent home with each student, and must be reviewed by the student's parents. Mrs. Richards will be available to answer any of the students' or parents' questions and has also posted a list of frequently asked questions and their answers at the school website.

Before a student may be allowed to use the Internet, Mrs. Richards must have a signed consent form back from the parents. This form also acknowledges that the parents are responsible for their child's online behavior both at home and at school.

If parents are informed, they can decide what risks are appropriate for their children and consent to those risks. If schools merely send home a consent form without the requisite disclosure, that consent form isn't worth the paper it's written on. All consents, to be effective, have to be fully informed consents.

Besides, if a child ends up spending millions at an auction site, schools want the parents, not the school, to be responsible. That's another reason schools should want the acceptable-use policy signed by the parents.

And if the parents won't sign the form, the school should make sure the child doesn't have school Internet access. Otherwise, the school faces potential liability.

Let the Parents Decide

Parents, armed with sufficient accurate information, are the best ones to make decisions about their children's safety. Is there a dispute over when a child's photograph can be posted at the school's website? Let the parents decide. Tell them what the controversy is—some parents and students want the fame and attention, while others are worried that this could fuel a pedophile's attempts to contact the children. Lay out all the risks. And give the parents the choice.

If the school wants to make sure it is absolved of the risks and claims relating to those risks, a waiver alone isn't sufficient, since students themselves have claims that cannot be waived by the parents. An indemnification from the parent is the only way the school can make sure it is covered. However, when parents agree to indemnify and hold the school harmless from any such claims, the parents have to bear the risks of their child suing after reaching the age of majority—as long as the school fully disclosed the risks to the parents.

For example:

We are very proud of our students. And we often celebrate their academic successes and sporting wins by publicizing their photos and stories of their feats in our school newspaper. These are often also covered by our community newspapers. It is a natural transition to post these same articles and photos on our school website.

But many online safety experts have warned against posting minors' photos online. They believe that certain people could use this information to locate and perhaps hurt your child offline. They indicate that the posting of this information on the Web is different from posting it in a school newspaper or the community newspapers, largely because the Internet is composed of more than 84 million people in the United States alone, far more than the number of readers of the school newspaper or community newspapers. They also point out that the people who might abuse this information may not be local neighbors who are concerned about the well-being of children in our community, but strangers who have no ties to the community.

Yet, to date, law enforcement tells us that they have not traced any offline molestation or abductions to a school website's disclosure of information about their students.

That's why we have decided to leave the choice up to the parents. While our school policy will be that our students may be shown only in group photos, identifying the group and not individually identifying the students by name, parents may give written consent to having their child's photo and name posted at the site when the photo and name appear in the school's newspaper. We will make this consent form available to the students upon request. Parents need to make sure that they understand the risks involved and are bearing responsibility for any adverse consequences of that decision. The consent form will provide that parents waive all risks and indemnify the school and the school board from any claims relating to having posted the photo and name.

We also want to hear from parents about this and other Internet-related issues. Please call Mrs. Richards with any questions, or log on to the school's website at _____. Our school is very special as a result of our close working relationship with our parents and community. We will face these exciting and challenging times together.

How Can Parents Get Involved?

The Best Parent Is an Informed Parent

In December 1997, at the first White House Summit on Online Safety for Children, while I was signing copies of *A Parents' Guide to the Internet*, a tall, slender, and very attractive woman shyly approached me. (I, of course, hated her on sight!) She introduced herself as Della Curtis, explaining that she was a library media specialist and headed the Office of Information Technology for the Baltimore County School System. She then handed me her book—a thick handbook of school Internet polices, which included sexual harassment policies, website development and posting policies, acceptable-use policies, personnel-use policies, and more. She explained that she had researched the area of technology and Internet risk management in schools, and would be honored to have me look over what she had done.

She took a signed copy of my book, shook my hand, and left. Two hours later, she returned. By then I had read her policies, and she had read my book, cover to cover. (I told you she was a librarian! No one can read better or faster than a librarian.) By the end of that same two hours I knew that I would be working with this extraordinarily talented woman. I had to. She was too much of a find to let go. Luckily, she felt the same about me. (She's now one of my dearest friends, and heads up the Wired Kids task force advisory committee for schools, libraries, and community access.)

Together, with an equally extraordinary group of library media specialists from the Baltimore County School System, we developed a program for parents called P.I.E. (Parents Internet Education). P.I.E. included an hour-long cable television special I hosted that aired on COMCAST (one of the sponsors of the P.I.E. project) and a weekend

Internet fair that included panel discussions and courses on how to use the Internet.

But the real jewel of the program was the Internet education classes developed for parents. These classes were given at the local school level, and parents could attend where their children attended school. It became the largest and most successful program in the country (and probably the world) to teach parents about the Internet.

The entire P.I.E. program can be found online at the Baltimore County Public School site, at www.bcplonline.org/centers/education/LibraryWeb/pie.

Build a Solid Team of Parents, Friends, Librarians, and Schools

As more and more schools and libraries are getting online, teachers and librarians are getting wired, too. (No, that doesn't mean that they are doing anything they shouldn't be doing—it means that they're getting online.) They're a great resource for parents. They have a chance to get to know our kids and our neighbors' kids, know what they're doing when you're not looking, and know what wonderful resources there are online.

Ask them to set up a program to try to get parents involved. Do what you can to help; they deserve our support and admiration. (I've said it before—librarians are our most underestimated natural resource. And I've been lucky enough to know some really sensational ones.) You should also check out the American Library Association's website (www.ala.org). It's a wealth of resources and tips.

For example, the ALA features a great site called KidsConnect (www.ala.org/ICONN/kidscom.html), which is run by the American Association of School Librarians, a division of the ALA. Through e-mail submitted at the site, kids can send inquiries to the librarians online, and within a couple days get help in locating resources that respond to their inquiries. The kids are then referred to their school library media specialist. KidsConnect helps build teams.

If you want help, after you've finished this book and have had a chance to surf around for a while, you may be able to contribute meaningfully to the plans to get your schools and libraries online. Share the wealth. Let them know what you've learned and let them teach you what they know.

Look over the school's proposed acceptable-use policies and see if there's something you can suggest to improve them. Volunteer to help teach other parents and share resources and sites you've found. Share keywords (the words used in sites you want to filter or block) that you've discovered if they use filtering software.

The only way we can truly protect our children in cyberspace is to build a solid team of parents, friends, librarians, and schools.

Team-Building Tips

Here are a few tips to think about when you're looking for places to help and build teams:

- What are other kids accessing?
- How much do other parents know about the Internet?
- What kinds of use policies have been set up?
- Coordinate with other parents, and agree on a common policy for when your children are computing at friends' houses.
- Enforce the joint policy with other parents and respect their values.
- Share new ideas and family website finds with others.
- Are other parents using filtering software or tools? If so, what software are they using?
- How can you get the best out of the software they chose?
- Plan a few community projects, like a cyber–scavenger hunt.
- Use your library's tech resources.
- Make sure your librarian and library media specialist are important parts of the team.

The best acceptable-use policies I have found come from libraries, and the "cream of the crop" seem to come from school libraries. Check with your school librarian or library media specialist and see what they're using. I've listed many resources for acceptable-use policies at familyguidebook.com, and two here in the appendix, Baltimore County's Student Acceptable-Use Policy and the Trevor Day School's Policy (a private school in Manhattan that has developed some very special programs for students using laptop computers). Both policies are among the best I've seen and among the earliest. If you know of a good policy, let me know so I can share it with others at the www.familyguidebook.com and www.wiredkids.org sites.

Stay Tuned for the Following Editorial Message . . .

I get e-mail from teachers all the time. They want me to recommend course materials and classroom resources on online safety. They want my opinion on Web-filtering products, closed-systems services, and their acceptable-use policies. But, most significantly, they want to know what liability they face, personally, if kids get into trouble online while under their supervision.

How sad that teachers—who are already overworked, underpaid, and without adequate support from us parents—feel they face legal liability for information our children might access. How schools are dealing with the whole Internet access issue might be at the core of this fear.

Keeping our children safe requires a team effort. Schools, libraries, and parents have to join forces if we are going to make sure that all children will be safe and get the full benefit of the Internet. But many schools are either ignoring the problem, thinking that filtering software alone is the solution, or are making decisions behind closed doors. This is a community issue, and everyone has to take part and understand what the schools are doing online.

When teachers face twenty-five to thirty children in their class, and someone now installs one computer in the back of the room, what are they supposed to do? Who will be training them? How is the computer supposed to be used—for recess or for learning? When the computer goes down, how are they supposed to fix it? (Most are now relying on talented "techie" students to repair the computers and debug the software.)

The answers won't come all at once, and there is no single set of answers for all classrooms and schools. Arriving at them will take time, patience, and flexibility on the part of educators and parents alike. Schools have to sit down with parents and teachers and design a program that works for them.

Teachers should be able to sleep at night without worrying that irate parents will try to sue them for what their children do online. (However, I just learned that more than one lawsuit has been commenced against a school system for that very reason.)

As a cyberspace lawyer, I see more than my share of adversarial situations. Let's make sure that our teachers are not afraid to use this wonderful technology. Let's support them so they can lead our children into the next millennium. To help in this effort, Wired Kids (www.wiredkids.org) will be designing a new area just for schools and teachers, where we will discuss acceptable-use policies and the legal issues involved.

I welcome ideas and comments from teachers. I want to make sure that we show our support for all the hard work they do, and to thank them for all they've done for our children. I especially welcome anyone who wants to join us as a volunteer in the Wired Kids project. I'll be heading it up. We'll also be looking for model acceptable-use policies. We'll use them as examples, good and bad. You can contact me at parry@aftab.com.

CHAPTER 7

Teach . . . Your Children Well

Of all the tools and tips I share with you, the most important one, more important than any software or hardware device you can buy, is that the first and best line of defense is Internet education. You have to teach your children to be aware and careful in cyberspace.

Even if you use every technology protection available, unless your children know what to expect and how to react when they run into something less than perfect online, they are at risk.

We can't filter life. So arming them well means teaching them well. (Now, all together—with my apologies to Crosby, Stills, Nash & Young— "Teach . . . your children well. . . . ")

Who's Teaching Whom?

Let Your Children Teach You: Learning to Listen

Throughout their lives, children are being taught and lectured to by adults. Teachers, parents, and family members all know more, and are constantly proving that to children. Guess what? Most of our kids know far more about computers than we do. Proficient with computer games of problem-solving mazes with dragons and spaceships that boggle our minds, they spend hours honing their skills. Few adults have the hand-eye coordination necessary to kill off the monsters and retrieve the treasures. But our children do. They can point and click with the best of them.

Give them a chance to level the playing field. Armed with this book, so you won't appear too ignorant, sit down in a comfortable chair and let your children show you around the family computer.

If they are already online, ask them to show you their favorite online forums, chatrooms, and sites. Check them out. In addition to helping you understand your child better, and giving you a good simple tour of the online world, it will help you begin to understand how to balance your values and your children's preferences.

Even if you're an experienced websurfer, let your child lead the tour. Let them talk and teach you for a change. Make it an "us" afternoon or evening. This exercise will help you to see the computer as something that brings you together instead of something that pulls you apart.

Aside from surfing together, feign interest in the newest computer game to capture your child's imagination. (Many of you have been waiting for an excuse to play these games anyway, so grab the opportunity. That way, when you are found playing the football game, NFL 2000, for twenty consecutive hours, you can blame me and this book.)

You'll be amazed at your children's skill. Although there are plenty of space and sports games for simple enjoyment, there are far more problem-solving games in which your children must break through levels of the game by solving problems and discovering clues.

Take the joystick when it's offered. This will be one game that you won't have to let them win. You don't stand a chance against the new generation of computer-savvy kids we're raising.

When you look at their faces while they are teaching you, and their extraordinary patience with your ineptitude, you'll understand why I suggested this in the first place.

In addition, if you use parental-control software, and your children want to visit sites blocked by the software or not yet rated by a PICS-compatible service (I'll explain that later, don't worry), take the time to visit those sites with them. It will help build trust between you.

Educate Your Children About the Dangers in Cyberspace

The buck stops here.

Teaching your children to be aware and careful in cyberspace is more important than any software or hardware device you can buy. But for some reason, the moment anyone mentions the word "computer" or the "Internet," everyone panics. I don't know why. All the normal advice applies exactly the same in cyberspace. Use the same lectures your parents gave you . . . the same ones their parents gave them. . . .

We can use the basic rules and just translate them into cybertalk. Let me show you how easy it is.

The Same Old Thing—in a New and Improved Package

- Don't talk to or accept anything from strangers. (See? Familiar territory. . . . Repeat after me. . . .)
- I need to meet your friends.
- Come straight home.
- Don't say nasty things about other people.
- Don't take things that aren't yours.
- Be polite to and respectful of others.
- Don't tell people personal things about yourself.
- Don't tell people personal things about your family.

I told you that you already know this stuff but just needed someone to translate it into cyberspace terms. Here's the translation:

- **Don't talk to or accept anything from strangers.** Who's a stranger online? Everyone is! Yet we talk online in chatrooms and discussion groups all the time. It's one of the most entertaining things we can do online. So how does this advice work online? Teach your children that anyone they don't know offline is a stranger. You can chat with them, but never tell them anything that you would tell a friend. Remember, chat with them—but don't confide in them. Talk about movies, or music, or sports—nothing personal. A teenager put it best; she said, "Remember that the people you chat with online are not your friends, they are just people you chat with."

But this is the hardest thing for our children to remember. As I told you before, one of the biggest problems with cyberpredators is that they function in your home. Our kids feel safe with us seated nearby. Their stranger danger reflexes are not engaged.

There is a sense of intimacy online that cyberpredators

count on. They need to convince your children that they are not strangers at all. They hope to convince them that the standard rules don't apply. You need to remind your children that these people *are* strangers and that the standard rules always apply.

- **I need to meet your friends.** We all heard this from our parents, and have said this to our own children. You'd never let your children spend time with real-life friends you hadn't met, would you? Why should it be any different in cyberspace? You should get to know the people they are frequently talking to online: who is influencing them, is the friendship appropriate, and are they the kind of children you want your child associated with. While you don't have to know everyone they run into in cyberspace, you should find out whom they are chatting with regularly.

  There are some special reasons to find out whom they are friends with online that don't exist in real-life friendships. In real life our kids can spot the adults. In cyberspace they can't. Most of the predators who are out to meet your child offline— and who have something other than friendship on their minds— pretend to be children to get past their "stranger danger" radar screen. (You can read more about how they operate in "Anatomy of a Cyberpredator—Protecting Your Children from Molesters in Cyberspace" section in Chapter 4.) Sometimes parents can tell an adult online better than a child can, and might be able to spot an adult who is posing as a teenager or young child to fool your kids.

- **Come straight home.** When I was young, I was famous for wandering around after school. Friends always invited me home with them, or something interesting was going on. My mother would panic and I would get the same lecture day after day.

  Wandering aimlessly online isn't any different from my wandering around after school. My mother needed to know I was safe, and that I was doing something productive, like homework. Allowing your children to spend unlimited time online, surfing aimlessly, is asking for trouble.

  Make sure there's a reason they're surfing. If they are just surfing randomly, set a time limit. You want them to come home after they're done, to human interaction and family activities (and homework).

- **Don't say nasty things about other people.** Saying nasty things about other people in cyberspace is called "flaming." It often violates the "terms of service" of your online service provider and will certainly get a reaction from other people online.

Flaming matches can be long and extended battles, moving from a chatroom or discussion group to e-mail quickly. If your child feels that someone is flaming them, they should tell you and the sysop (system operator, pronounced "sis-op") or moderator in charge right away.

- **Don't take things that aren't yours.** Kids are surfing and doing their homework. They are surfing and building their own websites. While surfing, they often "borrow" things that others have written, and photos and graphics belonging to someone else. For the most part, they are breaking the law. They are stealing someone else's property.

  Many people think that attribution (giving credit to the source) is enough when you copy something. But they are wrong. There is something called "fair use," which I've mentioned elsewhere in this book. But using a graphic at your site, or using a whole poem or story, isn't fair use. While it's unlikely that anyone will sue your children for copyright infringement based on a term paper or school report, more and more people are being targeted by entertainment industry members for websites and public postings that violate their intellectual property rights.

- **Be polite and respectful of others.** There are rules for proper behavior everywhere. The online world is no exception. Many online areas have their own rules of correct behavior—sometimes called channel rules or codes of conduct. Learn the rules first.

  Chatrooms each have their own rules, too. Don't barge in and start talking until you've had a chance to see what everyone's discussing. Read the discussion thread for a while, instead of asking everyone what they were talking about. And be respectful of others and their opinions.

  Don't post the same message over and over. Other people's time is valuable, and they don't want to have to weed through the same messages you posted in tons of places. If someone helps you, say "thank you." Courtesy goes a long way in cyberspace. It all comes down to respecting others.

- **Don't tell people personal things about yourself.** And don't tell personal things about your family. You never really know whom you're talking to. And even if you think you know whom you are talking to, there could be strangers lurking and reading without letting you know that they are there. It's like writing your personal diary on a postcard.

With children especially, sharing personal information puts them at risk. Make sure your children understand what you consider personal information, and agree to keep it confidential online and everywhere else. Practice asking them questions about themselves they may encounter in a chatroom. We teach our children to be polite, not to ignore people or tell them something is none of their business. We also tell them not to talk to strangers. This sometimes creates confusion, and confusion puts kids at risk. Whenever they don't understand the clear rules, they may wing it. When it comes to sharing personal information online, you never want your kids to wing it.

Prepare Your Children for the Unexpected . . . and People Who May Not Have Their Best Interests at Heart

Most of our children are taught, at a very early age, how to call 911 and what information they need to provide. They are taught to find a police officer when they need help. We teach them their name, our names, and our address when they can barely talk, in case they are separated from us. Most children are taught what information they can give out on the phone when a stranger calls, and what not to say. They are taught never to say an adult is not home. Instead, they are to tell the person on the phone that you can't come to the phone right now. We practice this with them . . . "Okay, now, Sally, what do we say when someone calls and asks you where you live? What about if you are home alone?" And we practice with them until they get it right. We have learned that practice makes perfect. And we want our children's safety skills to be perfect.

But how well are we teaching them to handle online emergencies and dangerous situations? Not very well at all. Some of us are uncomfortable discussing pedophilia with children. Good touch and bad touch aside (which I recommend all parents discuss with their children), telling children that they may be considered sexual prey to some evil and sick people isn't our idea of a pleasant afternoon discussion.

Luckily, a six-year-old I met while doing a safety program for Microsoft in Seattle gave us a solution to this problem. When I asked about safety tips, he raised his hand quickly and informed me that you should never share personal information with others online. When I asked why, he proudly smiled and said that burglars are always looking for this information so they can come to your house and rob you. As horrible as burglaries may sound, they sound a lot less dire than pedophiles. And making the house and material things the target of the criminal is a lot easier to handle than making your child the target. In addition, it works!

So how do we teach them? We discuss possible online scenarios. Practice he said/you say conversations with them: "If they say this . . . what will you say?" (I've included some suggestions in my Safe Surfing Club Quiz at www.familyguidebook.com, which will have many more suggestions, updated frequently, many of which are suggested by parents.) Then practice online with them.

Go online from work or another location when your child is in a chatroom. (Warn them first—trust is an important factor here, remember.) Then chat away, asking them questions when you think they are off guard. See how well they handle themselves.

You can check on them from time to time once you think they have the rules down, but let them know you might. Make it a contest of sorts. See if you can "fool" them, or if they are too savvy to be "fooled." Kids love to beat their parents in games—so make this a game. (This works best with younger kids, twelve and under.)

Meeting Online Friends in Real Life

Before we start, you need to recognize that the *only* way to stay truly safe in meeting someone offline is *not to do it*, period! Never do it or allow your children to do it. I intentionally placed this chapter after the cyberpredator chapter, hoping that you might still be frightened enough never to allow your teenagers to meet someone offline.

Even teenagers recognize the risks involved. The problems result from the conflicts between raging hormones and romanticism, and being smart and careful. They often think "this couldn't happen to me" and take unnecessary risks gambling that their luck will hold. Not every offline meeting ends in disaster, but many end in disappointment and enough end in disaster that our teenagers should be cautioned not to take needless risks.

When teenagers worked with me to write online safety tips for younger kids, they recommended that no one under the age of eleven meet anyone in real life they met online, *even with* a parent present. While they wavered a bit when teenagers were involved, they understood the seriousness of the situation.

But teens will be teens, and that means their main purpose in life is breaking the rules and taking risks. Here are some basic rules if you are either going to allow your teenagers to meet online friends in real life, or you know that they will ignore our no-meeting rule and do it anyway. (One of my elite Teenangels group is the offline chaperone for her girlfriend when she regularly meets online friends offline. The worst, so far, they have encountered is someone masquerading as a jock when he clearly wasn't—instead he had multiple body piercings and was "kinda weird.")

But think about it, and make sure your teenagers think about it seriously, too. This is where the bad stuff happens.

Remember my motto? Information doesn't hurt people, people hurt people. This is the only real way people can hurt your children . . . by meeting them in person.

Now, I know many of your teenagers will ignore me, and although I am not condoning ignoring the firm rule of *never* doing it, I'll point out some tips that will help limit the risks . . . not eliminate them! (These are good tips for parents who might consider cyberdating too—but note that there are more rules that apply there. Check out the www.cyberangels.org site for cyberdating safety tips for adults.)

Meeting cyberfriends (especially if there is any romantic interest, and there usually is when teenagers are involved) is a bit different from meeting anyone else for the first time. When you first meet a cyberfriend in person, offline, you feel as though you know them—the normal first-meeting precautions are often tossed to the wind. You know their favorite actors, rock groups, sports teams, authors, and foods.

What your children need to realize is that while they think they know these things about the other person, they really only know what they have been *told*—and that the other person may not have been telling them the truth. They don't *really* know the other person. So teach your teenager to treat their online friend as a stranger, using all the normal precautions they should use with any stranger.

In addition, people aren't always truthful online, even when they don't actively want to deceive you. You can be anyone you want to be online—shy teens can be outgoing, heavy ones can be thin, scholars can be athletes, and athletes can be scholars. Adult women tend to lie about their weight or age, while men tend to lie about their income, level of baldness, and athletic condition. Teenagers pretend to be older than they are, and sometimes even pretend to be of the other gender. The one rule you can count on is that everyone lies a little. (And some lie a lot!) So keep an open mind and prepare your teenagers for the likely shock and surprise of reality versus fantasy.

That photo they sent your teenager may be old or heavily doctored up with Photoshop. It could be from when they used to be a teenager, when they had better skin or were thinner, or it could be of someone else altogether. The best thing about the Internet is also the most dangerous: a person's personality can show through—what you are inside gets a chance to shine without getting overpowered by what you are outside. But the cues we use in life, such as body language, dress, personal hygiene, tone of voice—the way we judge the truth of statements—are lost in cyberspace.

Please don't let your teens rush into any offline meeting. As I said, I recommend that they never do it at all. If you are going to let them ignore me, make sure they use their head and are careful! Here are some tips you should heed and warn your teens about:

1. **Don't believe everything you read online**

   You can be anything or anyone you want to be online. I keep trying to get people to believe that I'm tall, blonde, and gorgeous. (So far, no takers.) That cute brunette sixteen-year-old guy may not be cute, may not be sixteen, and most important, may not be a guy. There is no truth-in-advertising protection when you meet someone you know online, offline.

2. **Take your time, don't rush into things, and get a little help from your friends**

   Take your time to try to get to know the person online first. Everyone can put their best cyberfoot forward in the first few e-mails. Being consistent is tougher. Make sure you keep the old e-mails to compare the information they give you. In one e-mail, he might tell you that he works for the GAP, and in another that he is a student, so make sure you check out these inconsistencies. He could be taking night classes, or he could just as easily be lying. Trust your gut. When you start feeling uncomfortable with what you're hearing, you're usually right.

   Don't be rushed, and don't rush the other person. Let the relationship develop online until you are comfortable with each other. Take your time.

   Ask your friends to look over the e-mail. Sometimes

they aren't blinded by the same rose-colored glasses you might be. What you considered cute might ring differently to them. It helps you keep perspective.

Especially when we've been hurt before or are lonely, we think that we have now figured out a checklist for a perfect relationship (which may be the exact opposite of our *last* relationship). When we see these points in the other person, we forget to explore the other points. Life is more than satisfying a "how tall are they, where do they live (are they 'geographically desirable'), what clothing do they wear, what music do they listen to, what sports do they play, and whether they like MTV, Jewel, and romantic movies . . ." checklist. Values, experience, and all the emotional baggage we carry (yup—even teenagers carry emotional baggage— just think back . . .) need to be explored, and this takes time. Give it the time it deserves.

3. **Honesty is the best policy**

Okay, maybe you aren't as thin, tall, or athletic as you want to be. Maybe you haven't been at the head of your class. Maybe you are afraid that if you tell them the truth about you, no one will want you.

But, if you start out lying, you'll be caught eventually. If you want to shave a few pounds off, or use a doctored picture, okay. But confess once you think the person might be more than a casual e-mail. Don't bait and switch—that's the surest way to end a friendship or budding romance.

4. **Start with a phone call**

You should move from e-mail and chatting online to a phone call before you meet offline in person. The safest way to do this is by using a public phone. Set up a time for the call, and give the other person the telephone number of the public phone. Once you are comfortable enough, you can share real phone numbers.

I recommend that you get their number and call, but make sure you use your call block option (usually *67). That way you can block their access to your telephone number. Lots of personal information can be gotten online once someone has your telephone number. Reverse searches are possible, too; these provide your address and name if they input your telephone number.

But if the other person reads this, too, and knows not to give our their number either, someone will have to be the first one giving out their telephone number. So if you have to, give out your number, but *only* if you have caller ID. If things go sour, you can always block their calls. It also lets you know what their number really is. If they block your caller ID, don't accept their calls.

5. **When you meet, do it with a couple of friends or, preferably, your parent (I can dream, can't I?) and only in a very public place**

The first time you meet in person, bring a couple of friends. (I would much prefer that they bring a parent, too, but I'm being realistic here.) Meet in a mall or fast-food restaurant not very close to your home. Plan for a short first-time get-together—coffee or a soda. Tell them in advance that it will just be for a few minutes, so they will understand. If they insist on meeting you alone, don't go.

Then compare what this person told you about themselves online. Does it match reality? If not, forget them—remember the honesty thing. (I'm not talking about a few extra pounds, or a worse complexion.) Ask your friends what they think; this is one time that they might have a better sense of the person, since you are blinded by online propaganda. Use your head. No matter how lonely you are, you're still safe.

6. **Tell a friend and leave a note**

Make sure someone else knows whom you are meeting, where you are going, and when you're coming back (someone other than the person you take with you). Store all the e-mails, and let your friends know where to find them. If anything goes wrong, they will be the source of information on how to locate the person you have been chatting with. A mother I met shared her tips about this: When her adult son meets an adult woman (at least he hopes she is a woman) he met online, offline, he puts all the details in an envelope and gives it to his mother, in case anything bad happens. That way, if all goes right, his privacy is preserved. And if it doesn't, she can quickly access the information she needs to report it.

7. **Never leave with them or go home with them**

If the meeting goes on longer than you planned, make sure

you stay in a public place. *Public* is the operative word here. Remember when your mother told you never to get in a car with a stranger? Don't get in a car with them or follow them home or to a private place of any kind. Also, contact the people who know the details of your meeting, and let them know of any change in your plans. If this is a date, you should still take it slow, even if you're not used to taking dating slow—this is different. Also, don't leave at the same time, and make sure you are not followed home. The best way to do this is not to go home directly. Go to a friend's house or another public place instead.

8. **Report any attacks or threats to law enforcement**
   If things go wrong, whether you followed my rules or not, don't be embarrassed to go to the police. Give them all the facts. If you don't report them, in all likelihood they will do it again. You are allowed to say "no" and have it respected. If anything goes wrong, remember it's not your fault!

9. **Don't be embarrassed to insist on following these rules**
   Your safety is the most important thing. Anyone who cares about you will respect you for being careful. It's like defensive driving: Even if you are the best driver in the whole wide world, there are all those other drivers out there to worry about. This is defensive cyberfriendship. And it's just plain smart!

10. **Don't be provocative online—it provokes many things you may not be prepared to handle**
    Try not to make your online comments or profiles provocative. Cyberflirtation escalates quickly—and it's almost impossible to step back to a less amorous and tamer level. If someone makes you uncomfortable, report it right away. Make a copy of the e-mail, and keep copies of anything you found offensive so that it can be checked out.

11. **If you are being cyberstalked or harassed by this person after you decide not to see them anymore, get help**
    Read about cyberstalking and harassment in this book, and online at sites such as www.cyberangels.org. Don't try to handle a stalker yourself, without help. (Cyberangels has teams to assist cyberstalking victims.) Don't respond when the stalker contacts you. Just ignore them, and most of the

time they go away. Never share a photo with anyone online you wouldn't want broadcast to 200 million people all over the world. Often cyberflirtations end in one party cyberstalking the other and posting personal information (and photos) online with sexually suggestive messages, like "Jennifer is looking for a hot time!"

Don't give them any ammunition. When the old-fashioned "For a good time, call Sally" is posted on one bathroom wall, the results can be horrible; when it's posted on the Internet's cyberwall of sexual usenet groups and chats, it can be very, *very* dangerous!

And, if you're sixteen or under, and anyone posts anything like that online, know that there are federal laws that protect you. (You can read more about this in "And Now for the Really Boring Stuff: The Law.") So report it right away.

Clues We Give Away—Shannon, Now Known as "Tiffany"

Most kids know not to share personal information online, but certain kinds of information come out during the course of conversation—things that, on their own, don't pose many risks, but when put with other bits of information allow someone to find your child.

These are facts that our kids wouldn't think twice about sharing. The best example of this is contained in a story I found on the Web. I found it three years ago, at a site that had gotten it from another source. Apparently it's been circling the Internet for the last three or four years, being sent by e-mail from teen to teen and posted on many personal websites.

Since I couldn't figure out who owned it to get permission to republish it, I had to write my own interpretation. (If you want to read the original, visit www.fantasyrealm.com, and if you own it or know who does, please contact me at parry@aftab.com.)

Tiffany Peterson grabbed her backpack from the bench, tossed her mitt into it, and turned and waved to her teammates. She rushed off, hoping to catch Timbo5 before he had to get offline for dinner. She turned the key in the lock and rushed through the door, and it slammed behind her. "Mom! I'm home!" she shouted as she took the stairs two at a time. She had only five minutes before she knew he had to get offline.

Just another minute as she signed on as "Shortstopteen"—there he was! Right where he always was—in their favorite teen chatroom, Teen Sports.

• • •

Shortstopteen: Hi Timbo. Guess what? We won!

Timbo5: Hi Shortstop. What was the score?

Shortstopteen: 9 to 7! I caught the last ball! The tying runs were on base! It puts us into the play-offs.

Timbo5: kewl. Who do you play next week?

Shortstopteen: Randolph Township, the Tiggers. They were the state champs last year. It'll be a tough game.

Timbo5: Are you still playing second base?

Shortstopteen: Nope. I convinced the coach to let me play short-stop. ;-) [You'll understand this when you get to the "Netiquette" section.]

Timbo5: What happened to the last shortstop?

Shortstopteen: She moved to Texas. And the coach said that his best shortstops have all been blonde. So I got it! ;-)

Timbo5: Great! Congrats. Gotta go. Mom's calling me for dinner. See ya tomorrow.

Shortstopteen: k. CU L8R ["Okay. . . . see you later," for you newbies out there.]

Tiffany chatted with a few other friends for a while and then logged off. Timbo5 was her favorite online friend. He was fourteen, just like Tiffany, and lived in Virginia. He played baseball, too. He played first base, though. He also wanted to play for the major leagues when he grew up. Tiffany hoped that by the time she grew up, women could play for the major leagues, too.

Although she didn't even know his real name, and he didn't know hers, she knew lots about him. He was much more fun than most of the other kids in the chatroom. He knew everything about baseball. She wished he lived closer to New Jersey, so they could go to Yankee games together.

And Timbo5 really cared about her, always warning her not to tell anyone her real name or address. It was nice that he cared, but Tiffany already knew not to share any personal information. Her parents and her teachers had all discussed this with her and the other kids. She was very careful never to give out anything that could help anyone find her in "rl" (real life, offline).

Her mother called her, and she ran down the stairs to dinner to share the good news with her family about the playoffs and her lucky catch.

The following week, Tiffany had practice every day. Somehow things didn't feel right, though. It was as though someone was following her. She kept looking over her shoulder when she walked home, and it was starting to get dark earlier. She found herself picking up her pace, and was winded when she arrived home. She unlocked the door quickly and looked around. Although she didn't see anyone, she was very uncomfortable. She didn't even shout "Hello" to her Mom, and just ran up the stairs to her computer.

Shortstopteen: Hi Timbo . . .

Timbo5: Hi Shortstop, what's up?

Shortstopteen: I was nervous today. Must be the pre-playoff excitement. Thought someone was watching me on the way home.

Timbo5: Did you see anyone following you?

Shortstopteen: Nope. But it felt weird. Like I could feel someone watching me . . . but no one was there anytime I looked.

Timbo5: Are your parents home?

Shortstopteen: Yup. It's okay. Probably just pre-game jitters. ;-)

Timbo5: You haven't told anyone online where you live or your real name or anything, have you?

Shortstopteen: You know that I'm very careful. You lecture me all the time! You're starting to sound like my parents! ;->

Timbo5: oh!oh! Gotta stop that!

Shortstopteen: LOL [laughing out loud]

Timbo5: ROFLOL . . . [rolling on the floor laughing out loud]

Tiffany forgot her fear and chatted until dinner was ready.

The next day was the big game. Tiffany played really well, hit the only home run, and the team won, advancing to the finals. When she got home that night, she logged on and told Timbo5 about her big win, and complained that they had practice the next day.

When Tiffany was warming up, tossing the baseball around on

the field at the next day's practice, she looked up at the stands and saw a man sitting there looking right at her. She felt the same fear and discomfort she had when walking home a few nights before. She glanced up at him from time to time, but soon forgot him when practice got going. When practice was over, she remembered the man, but looked up to find him gone. She took a deep breath and started the long walk home.

This time, she was sure someone was following her. She kept looking around, and although she didn't see anyone, she was really scared. She took the long way home, because it was busier and better lit, but wished she were already safe and sound in her home. Once, when she looked in the storefront window, she saw a reflection of someone she thought might be the man in the stands, but when she turned around no one was there. But she was sure she had recognized him. At one point she even heard footsteps.

As she neared her block, she broke into a run. It sounded like the footsteps were speeding up, too, and she ran even faster. She unlocked the door and slammed it shut. Her mother, alarmed at the noise, walked into the living room from the kitchen. "Are you okay, Tiff?" she asked. "You look upset." Tiffany caught her breath, and said that she was just in a rush to get home.

When she took the stairs this time, she took them slowly, thinking while she climbed. She really had to talk to Timbo5. She was very scared. But when she logged on, Timbo5 wasn't in the chatroom. She sent him an instant message, and saw that he wasn't even online. Just when she really needed him the most!

The doorbell rang. She heard her mother get it and heard a male voice. A few minutes later, her mother and father called her down. She was still trying to figure out how to tell her parents about her fear without alarming them. She was so afraid that they might take her computer away if they thought she might have given out personal-contact information online. When she climbed down the stairs, her thoughts were elsewhere.

Her parents were seated in the living room with a man—the one whom she had seen in the bleachers. She started to worry. "Tiffany, please sit down. This is Sergeant Thompson of the state police." Tiffany looked at her parents' worried faces.

"Hi, Shortstopteen," said the sergeant. Tiffany couldn't figure out how he knew her chatroom name. "I'm Timbo5," he said. She couldn't believe her ears. Timbo5? This police officer? Timbo5 was only fourteen, and lived in Virginia.

"Let me explain," he said, and proceeded to tell her that he worked undercover in chatrooms trying to protect children from online predators. "But how did you find me?" Tiffany asked. "I never gave you my real name or any real information."

"Even though you never gave me your name, *per se,* you gave me lots of other information about you. You gave me the name of the team you were playing this week for the playoffs. It was simple enough for me to check and see which state had baseball champs from Randolph Township named the Tiggers. Then I called the Randolph Township school and found out which team they were playing this week in the play-offs. Then I checked the roster in the local paper and got your name as the team shortstop and confirmed that it was you by checking your name as the home run hitter at the final season game. I looked up all the Petersons online in the White Pages directory, and found your address and telephone number. I called your parents and told them what I had planned."

Tiffany was stunned. How could this forty-year-old man sitting in front of her be her friend Timbo5? Besides, the police officer said he was from New Jersey, too. How could that be when Timbo5 was from Virginia?

She knew who Timbo5 was because he told her things about himself. And she didn't take his word for it, she checked him out. He had an online profile she checked that said he loved baseball, was fourteen years old, and lived in Virginia. That was written proof!

But Tiffany started paying attention when Sergeant Thompson explained how he had written his profile just to help convince her of his false identity. He then explained that he had followed her home, after spotting her on the field, as the blonde shortstop.

"I did this to help you," he said. "A friend of mine had a fourteen-year-old daughter who gave out too much information to a stranger who showed up at her house one day and killed her. Since then I've vowed to teach others how to make sure they don't give away information without realizing it."

Tiffany now realized that she had fallen into the same trap as Sergeant Thompson's friend's daughter. She thought about all the little details she had given away that allowed her to be found in real life. Sergeant Thompson looked at her. "Will you help me help other kids and teach them what you just learned?" Tiffany gave her word that she would. And she and her parents were overwhelmed with gratitude that Tiffany had avoided tragedy and learned this lesson the "easy" way.

Using an Alias: Are We Teaching Our Children to Protect Themselves or to Lie?

To prevent children from giving away personal information, I have advised parents to teach their children to use a special online name, rather than their real one.

No child on earth (and, frankly, no adult either) thinks that their parent gave them the right name. Susans want to be Taylors, and Taylors want to be Jennifers. It's a no-win situation for parents. Allowing the kids to choose their own special "online name" lets them correct their parents' worst and first mistake—it lets them name themselves what you should have named them in the first place.

Many kids make up a special online persona entirely, finding a fake school, home address, even a fake sports team. They post this information in their profiles, too. That way when someone asks them for personal information, they don't worry about whether they have to tell them that they "can't tell them" (and admit they aren't in full control of their life) or tell them that they won't give out that information and risk seeming rude. It's not a judgment call. They can just give their special online name. That way they can always tell their real offline friends from their online friends. Offline friends know their real name, and online friends know only their online name.

My Teenangels disagree with me here. They say it teaches children to lie, and might be confusing. And since confusion might lead to children disclosing things they shouldn't, this might be more dangerous rather than safer. So think about what will work with your child, and be consistent. I still like the online name part, but I think that entire online personas may be going overboard.

Kids Will Be Kids: Teaching Them Accountability

Teaching our children to be accountable for their actions is a natural continuation of the discussion about aliases. When people can be anyone they want to be online, does this create a problem with accountability?

If you could do whatever you want, and not get caught, would you break the law? Insult your mother-in-law? Cheat on your taxes? Eat two desserts? That's what our kids face online. They think that they are anonymous and can't get caught.

What Kids Tell Us About
Pretending to Be Someone Else

These are a few of the responses we received from teenage girls, when we surveyed them about whether they pretended to be someone else online. Here's what they said, in their own words:

- "I've pretended to be a few celebrities and the people have fallen for it, but I do tell the people that I am not that real celeb, because these girls get a little tooooo trusting and start giving out REALLY personal info, and they should be glad that I'm just making a joke out of it, and not some psychopath killer!! You know. Gosh, sometimes girls can be so freaking stupid to give out their personal info!"

- "Yes, I have talked with many people from different parts of the world, and I, like many other people I'm sure have made up nice lil' stories about 'myself.' Like for instance, I live in Hawaii, I'm 5'7, 108lbs, with long beautiful hair and I'm a runway model. OH, I WISH THAT WERE TRUE! See, it's easy to pretend to be someone else for a little while. Admit it!! It's pretty fun sometimes! Just watch so that you don't get yourself into trouble. It's all about using the motor that God put in your head!"

- "I used to change my personality on the Internet. I didn't know who I was inside, and this messed me up. I used to pretend that I was perfect, and was friends with everyone. It made me feel better about myself. The Internet was a perfect place for me to be, and I excluded myself from the outside world."

- "Yeah I always pretend to be an 18/f [an eighteen-year-old female] who weighs 120lbs and is 5'9, cause . . . well . . . I'd love to be thin."

- "Yes, [I pretend to be] someone older and prettier."

- "I invented a whole new life—where I live, my age, my looks, my character."

- "Yes, I pretend to be a big slut . . . I don't get guys in real life, so I cyber [have cybersex] and be all suggestive and flirty."

- "No, I am always myself. I think if people don't like me for myself, [they] aren't worth talking to!"

- "Of course I've pretended. Everyone does. You pretend to be older . . . or you pretend to be a guy . . . or you just pretend to be whomever you wanna be."

- "Yes, I just changed myself to be someone I wasn't because I wanted to get a different reaction from people. It gave me a way to see myself as who I wanted to be, but by doing it I realized that that is not who I want to be and that I just want to be me."

- "I haven't. I like being myself—how I actually am. At home and school no one knows the real me because I have to act differently. I'm more free talking with people on the Internet. They know the real me and they don't judge me by the way I look."

- "No. I don't like to hide my personality. I think it's important to be yourself."

- "Yes. If I am ever in a chatroom I always make up things about myself. This is why I say don't trust anyone because everybody else does the same thing."

- "Since nobody seems to be eager to talk to a 15 year old, I always pretended I was 18 year old female. However, that sometimes attracted bad attention from guys."

No One Can Find Me Online . . .

Part of the problem is that they don't understand they *aren't* anonymous online. Even with aliases, they need to understand that they leave a trail of electronic bread crumbs wherever they surf.

I've told you about e-mail bomb threats and death threats made by kids. Is this really any different from what we did when we were growing up? When I was young, we would do different kinds of things when we got into trouble, but we still got into trouble.

My friends and I would call up the local pizza parlor and order pizzas with extra anchovies (which was the most disgusting thing we could dream up) for the cranky old woman down the street who always complained about our walking on her property and making too much noise.

Then we would sit in the dark, looking out of the carefully parted curtain to see the delivery truck pull up, and the woman arguing with the delivery boy. We would laugh hysterically and be secure in knowing that we had gotten some kind of revenge. (Now, as a lawyer, I can confess this knowing that the requisite statute of limitations has expired and I cannot be charged with my juvenile delinquency—although I still got a serious lecture from my mother when she heard about this a few years ago. Luckily, my children are prevented from following in their mother's pizza-crime-spree footsteps by the advent of caller ID.)

Many of us remember similar stunts we performed as kids, and may even shrug them off (using "kids will be kids" reasoning). But we need to recognize that a death threat sent by a teenager looks exactly like one sent by a crazed adult really intent on killing you. These are credible threats, and we as parents and educators need to understand how serious they are.

This is an important time to teach accountability. Our children have to be held accountable for their actions. And, following the recent tragedies and mass killings at schools, there is now a zero-tolerance policy where online threats are concerned.

Telling Boastful Fun from Serious Threats

Deciding when a threat is real and when it's just "kids being kids" has become a real problem since the Littleton tragedy. Hundreds of copycat websites have been set up. Words associated with the Littleton tragedy, such as the "trench coat mafia" and others, have proliferated in search engines and in personal profiles online.

Students in North Carolina put up a detailed map of their high school, showing the locations where they said they would be placing bombs. Others posted bomb threats in chatrooms and rumors abounded. A fifth-grader in New Jersey sent threatening e-mail to classmates. The FBI showed up a few days later with a search warrant, and she was detained. (An FBI agent shared with me the fact that he never thought he would ever have to serve a search warrant on an eleven-year-old.)

Schools have been dealing with bomb threats for years. (Sadly, children have been committing murders in schools for years as well. But the issue of children killing children in large numbers is new.) Unfortunately, this means that kids no longer have the luxury of "being kids" by making blind and groundless threats without being held accountable for them.

How Do We Teach Our Children to Be Accountable?

When my son was young and got into trouble at school, he could count on my arriving at the school armed to defend him. But, when I was growing up, my mother would have arrived at the same school ready to kill me. I think as we have become more sensitive about our children's feelings, we have forgotten that they have to be held accountable for their own actions and face consequences. For this they need us to be more consistent, and to be better role models.

Yet, when they need them the most, so many of the people they would traditionally have turned to have let them down. We tend to be preoccupied, and we may not teach our children to be accountable for their actions. And others they might look to as role models aren't the kind of role models our children need these days.

The traditional family unit is the exception, not the rule. Following a breakup, parents too often forget that divorcing their spouse doesn't also mean divorcing their children. The family courts are filled with parents who refuse to support their children and live up to their responsibilities. Families ignore their aging family members, who live alone and are forgotten.

And sports figures, movie and television stars, rock musicians, and elected officials are too frequently better known for their failings than their leadership and role-model characteristics. Drug abuse, alcoholism, violence, and disregard for the truth and ethics are terms that describe too many celebrities these days.

So when our children seek role models and can't easily find them, what do we do? Good role models today are hard to find. Is this what we tell our children? I hope not.

We have to try to be their role models and help them find others, too. We need to find heroes in everyday life, people who give back to their communities, who understand the responsibilities that come along with the celebrity, who live the golden rule—the kind of people our children can look up to to teach them how to succeed, while also showing them, by example, how to be "good people."

Hopefully, we can teach our children that they can and should expect more from us and others, and we can and should expect more from them.

Avoiding Witch Hunts

Okay, we have to balance the fact that kids will be kids with teaching them to be accountable for their actions. But what do we do about threats that children make? Given the fact that some kids do take violent action after building a website threatening such action, no one can afford to ignore threatening websites anymore. But there is a fine line between being vigilant and conducting a witch hunt. And it's one we have to walk very carefully.

Following the Littleton tragedy and the copycat events that succeeded it, everyone seemed to join one of two camps. Either you wanted to ban bomb-building sites and censor hate or violent sites constructed by kids, or you wanted to teach tolerance and ignore content posted by kids online threatening violence. But neither extreme works.

We need to do two things. We need to teach our children that they are accountable for their actions, and we also need to listen better and give kids a place where they can report situations that they believe to be dangerous, without the fear of retaliation.

Is Tattling Allowed?

When the Littleton tragedy occurred, parent and school administrators worried about how they could spot troubled and potentially dangerous children and teens before tragedies happen. All we need to do is ask our kids. The kids have always known the troubled ones in their group, and more important, the ones who are dangerous to themselves and others. They may even be seriously afraid of some of these kids, but are unwilling to "tell."

Kids and teens tell me that they don't like to "tattle" but would do so about potentially serious situations if they could do so anonymously. Fearing reprisals, they feel uncomfortable telling a school administrator, counselor, or teacher, and many think that an anonymous tipline works best.

KIDReportline: The Background

I gave an interview to the *Wall Street Journal* immediately after the Littleton tragedy, saying that if we searched out websites written by teenagers, taking their threats seriously, half of the teens online would be in jail. I protested that kids act out fantasies online—it's one of the best things about the Internet, being able to pretend.

The article appeared the next morning, and I couldn't sleep. *Someone* had to do something. If Cyberangels said it can't help in this situation, who can? Were we turning our backs on our responsibility to help others in need online? Was there a way to balance privacy and free speech with spotting troubled kids who were speaking out in advance of acting out their violence against themselves or others?

I felt that I had to come up with something, and KIDReportline was born. It was designed to give kids a place to report what they think are serious threats without fear of reprisal.

How Does It Work?

There are several important conditions to our accepting a

KIDReportline tip. The person sending us the tip must be a child. The person whose site is being reported must be a fellow classmate and be considered a threat to themselves or others by the person reporting the site. Finally, the site must display violence or threats of some kind. These are our rules:

1. We take tips only from classmates of the students whose sites are being reported. Adults, whether teachers or parents, can report their suspicions to the school, family members, or law-enforcement authorities. Classmates often feel they have no place to turn. They are afraid of reporting anything to the school administration. They may fear reprisals, or be embarrassed to "tell." But classmates are often the only ones who can fully appreciate the risks posed by some of their classmates. They are also usually the only ones who know of fellow classmates' websites.

2. We take tips only about students' websites. If the student is threatening violence using another medium, we will advise the classmate sending us the tip to report it to their school, parents, or elsewhere. Having the violence or threats communicated online allows us to evaluate those sites directly. Our expertise is Internet-related. Other situations will have to be handled by other advocacy groups. Cyberangels can handle only Internet-related risks.

Cyberangels doesn't use any database or data-collection mechanism for these tips. To the extent permitted by law, we also keep the identity of the reporting party confidential. Sometimes the reporting classmate just needs someone to listen to their fears. We try to be that someone.

We also use the least intrusive measures we believe are advisable. When someone sends us a site that communicates what we think is a credible threat of violence to the student who composed the site, or to others, we report it to either the school or to law enforcement. Sometimes, if we think it is advisable, we reach out to the student who composed the site himself, offering help.

Why Do We Do It?

This is the only way we can see to balance the free-speech concerns with our desire to help avoid another tragedy because no one listened to the threats. More than anything else, we hope to be a place where kids can find someone to listen to their fears and problems.

We hope that by using Cyberangels' website's popularity to communicate this service, and by using our extensive experience with judging the credibility of Internet speech and our contact with the Internet communities online, we can provide a place that will help without using gestapo tactics.

Further, we don't seek out any sites, and we respond only to credible reports sent by classmates, of Internet sites. It's our way of doing more than talking.

Many schools have contacted us, asking if they can share our site and the KIDReportline e-mail address with their students. Others have indicated that they are going to start a similar service of their own.

The more schools do to help kids communicate their concerns, and the more they and parents listen to what kids are saying, the better off we'll all be. This is one innovation we hope will be copied by anyone who cares about kids. Give your kids and their school our e-mail address: "reportline@cyberangels.org."

We hope they never need it.

Defensive Parenting: Avoiding Problems Before They Happen

Forewarned Is Forearmed: The Parent's Creed

When children are armed with the ability to decode passwords, scramble our files, and locate our credit card information on our computer systems, it's hard to control them. It's even harder to figure out what they might do next, in order to stay one step ahead of them.

But who said parenting was easy? Parenting is always learning on the fly, having to address the unexpected, having your kids leave a chocolate bar on your sofa cushion in June or leave dirty handprints on your outfit just as you are leaving for work. Why should your kids' computer activities be the exception?

I've already taught you how many things can go wrong and where the risks are. Here are a few extra things to consider when you're trying to stay one step ahead of them:

- **Passwords.** Don't share your passwords or store them where they can be found: Remember that those who control the passwords control the world. Choose a password you can remember easily, but one that's not so obvious that your children can figure it out. (And, no—don't put it on a Post-it and stick it on your computer's monitor.)

Also, change your password frequently. When you type it in, don't let them look over your shoulder. Never store it on your hard drive, or preprogram it into your sign-on screen. This may cost you a few seconds when you go online, but it may save you plenty of heartaches.

You should also remember that some services, such as America Online, will allow you to charge certain purchases to your account. Since most AOL members have their bills automatically charged to a credit card, or deducted from their checking account each month, this is a more convenient way of purchasing something online than having to type in your credit card information each time. That's another reason to guard your password: It identifies you as the account holder.

- **Protecting your children when they're not home.** Make sure that you and the parents of your children's friends are in agreement about monitoring the children's activities online, and that you use similar tools to enforce your choices. If not, circumventing your parental controls is as simple as your children walking next door and computing at a friend's house. If you can't agree on a joint policy, make sure the other parents honor your wishes and keep your children off their computer while visiting. It's a matter of respecting your role as a parent. Make sure you do the same for them.

- **Back-up or password-protect your files.** Don't leave important files on your computer without a backup and password protection if your kids are using the computer unsupervised.

  Even the most innocent and experienced computer user may push the wrong keys at the wrong time. I've done it myself (far more often than I care to admit). Important speeches or articles are lost with a click of the mouse. The outline for my first book, carefully prepared on my new laptop during a trip to Moscow, Russia, was lost completely. The computer shut down, without provocation (I swear I didn't do anything), and the automatic backup didn't work. Jet-lagged and exhausted, I had to start from scratch.

  So, if you have something important, make a backup copy on a floppy disk. Or better yet, password-protect your files on the computer, in addition to saving important files to a zip disk (a special device that stores copies of your files in special condensed disks) or floppy. That way, it's less likely that your children will be tempted to snoop through your personal files. Many software programs allow you to password-protect certain information. It's easy and will avoid a myriad of problems.

- **Credit cards.** Don't store your credit card information on your computer. As inconvenient as it might be to have to access it from somewhere else, it creates too much of a temptation for computer-savvy kids and their friends.

- **Keep the computer in a central family location, not in your child's room.** Make sure that the computer with online access is located wherever the family hangs out together. It's harder for our children to get into trouble right under our noses (not impossible, however, just harder). Your children's friends who may be provoking the situation would also have problems provoking it with you around: Provocation requires too much energy to be done quietly. You'd notice something is up. This one tip has become the most repeated one. When I appeared on a televised town meeting with Tom Brokaw and Jane Pauley, Jane waved to me (I was amazed she knew who I was) and said that she didn't have the room in her kitchen to put her family's computer there. Now, as amazed as I was that she knew who I was, I was even more amazed that she had reviewed my safety tips.

- **Let your kids know that many people are not what they seem.** I remember a comedy skit where a middle-aged beer-bellied man in his underwear was pretending to be a young teenage girl while chatting online with a teenage football jock, who was really a middle-aged woman in curlers and a housedress.

  While my kids laughed at the skit, it also brought the issue home. People online are not always what they say they are. Many kids are lured online by adults masquerading as kids. As disillusioning as it might seem, warning them about this risk now may protect them from serious danger later.

- **Make sure you can see what's on the monitor.** Let your children know you look at the monitor from time to time. Kids can get into trouble under our noses, but knowing that you can see what they're doing, whenever you want to, keeps them on the straight and narrow.

  One parent who attended a parent event at a school asked

me how they can see what's on their kid's computer screen when they shut it down as soon as the parent is within viewing range. If your child hid anything they were doing as soon as you entered the room, what would you as a parent do? You'd look in the drawer they just shoved things into, right? Why is using the computer any different. You are still the parent! Repeat after me: "I am still the parent! . . . I am still the parent!" I'll show you how to check what they had on their screen before they shut it down at familyguidebook.com (it's called checking the history files), but I'd suggest you sit down next to them and ask them. When all else fails, talking to our kids isn't a bad option.

- **Check your hard drive and floppy disks every once in a while.** Look for downloaded images stored on your hard drive or on floppy disks. They are easily spotted, because they generally end with either ".jpg" or ".gif."

    Let your kids know you're checking downloaded materials.

- **Cover your own tracks.** If you visit sites you don't want your children to see, check your hard drive for wayward graphics and make sure your bookmarks don't lead them to those sites.

    One of the reasons the First Amendment exists is to let you see what you want to without having to worry about whether it's appropriate for children. But be careful about naming your bookmarks, and make sure you haven't stored anything you don't want your kids to see on your hard drive or on an accessible disk.

- **Don't send them out there alone until they're ready.** Screen e-mail when your kids are younger and sit with them while they're in any non–child unsupervised chatrooms. Make sure they know the chatroom rules, too, and where to report violations and things that make them feel uncomfortable. Knowing the basic rules will help them surf more safely. Remember, one of my mottoes is "Information doesn't hurt children—people hurt children." Therefore, the two most important rules, in my opinion, are:

1. Make sure your child knows what information can be shared and what cannot be shared with others online. You never want them giving out personal information that would allow a stranger to find them offline.
2. Make sure your child knows never to meet an online "friend" in person.

- **Play an active and interested part in your children's online life and don't overreact.** Get to know your children's online friends and correspondents. Your children shouldn't be afraid to tell you anything, so don't criticize them when something goes wrong. Encourage your children to come to you when they are uncomfortable or receive a message that violates your rules or makes them uncomfortable. Secrets can be dangerous. Be the one your children share their secrets with, and be worthy of that valuable trust.

    Don't rely on software to prevent your children from getting into trouble. Even with all the software devices and tools we have on the market to protect our kids and to keep them from getting into trouble online, there are many ways a computer-savvy kid can still get into trouble. The tools are imperfect. Several of them let many sites through that you may not want your children to see. Some don't prevent your child from sending their personal-contact information to others. Don't rely on technology to protect your children—that's your job.

- **You need to know if your kids can be trusted to follow your rules and not to hurt others online.** Educate them on the risks of hacking and other improper computer and online behavior. Teach them good Netiquette. Then, if they still can't be trusted, lock your computer and take the key with you. There may be no other way of keeping them out of trouble.

The Basic Rules—Quick and Simple

Some basic rules for you to remember as a parent—your parental cheat sheet. (I've designed it to fit neatly on your inner wrist in case you want to talk to your kids and have problems remembering these rules. That's the big difference between being a parent and being a high school student: You can use a "cheat sheet" as a parent and not be suspended.)

- Make sure your child doesn't spend an inordinate amount of time on the computer.
- People, not computers, should be their friends and companions.
- Keep the computer in the family room, kitchen, or living room, not in your child's bedroom.

- Learn enough about computers so you can enjoy them with your kids.
- Watch your children when they're online and see where they go.
- Make sure that your children feel comfortable coming to you with questions.
- Keep kids out of chatrooms or IRCs unless they are monitored.
- Encourage discussions between you and your child about what they enjoy online.
- Help them find a balance between computing and other activities.
- Get to know their "online friends" just as you get to know all of their real-life friends.
- Warn them that people may not be what they seem to be.
- Teach them to exercise their judgment in cyberspace, just as they do offline.
- Don't overreact when they come to you with problems they encounter online. You want to encourage them to tell you things, not scare them off.
- Discuss these rules, get your children to agree to adhere to them, and post them near the computer as a reminder.
- Remember to monitor their compliance with these rules, especially when it comes to the amount of time your children spend on the computer.

Get to Know Your Kids, and Create a Workable "Safe-Surfing Contract" for Them

How Much Do You Really Know About Your Kids?

Take this quiz. I bet you'll be surprised how little you know about your child or your teen.

What are their best friends' full names?

What are their best friends' telephone numbers?

What's their favorite television program? Movie? Rock group? Radio station? Magazine?

What are their teachers' names?

What subjects are they studying in school?

What's their favorite subject in school?

Who's their favorite teacher?

Is there a school bully they are afraid of?

Are they part of a clique? Picked on by other cliques?

What's their favorite book? Author? Kind of book?

Do they have a diary or journal they keep?

Unless you are really extraordinary, you'll miss one, some, or all of these questions. Use this as a time to get to know your child better.

Find out what your children's interests are. What do they read? What do they watch on television? If they're already on the Internet, what do they access?

Even without an ulterior motive, it's a wonderful way to get to know your children. Too often we talk *at* our children, rather than listen *to* them. And they have wonderful things to tell us if we just listen . . . really listen.

Ask them to show you around the Internet. Access their bookmarks with them. Don't ambush them and make it look like you're spying on them. Take this opportunity to share some of their interests. You might be pleasantly surprised to learn some of the things that interest them.

For instance, how do they find their way around the Internet? Do they rely on hyperlinks (links to other sites), or do they use a search engine? If so, which one? Ask them why they prefer one over the other, and how they formulate their searches.

Once you have a better idea about how your children use the Internet, you can start developing a set of rules to govern their behavior online and to guide them into safer waters. Your rules should be designed to help them understand proper Netiquette, know what to expect from others online, how to behave when something unexpected occurs, and how to protect themselves and you from getting hurt in cyberspace. That's a "Safe-Surfing Contract."

These rules are mutual rules, and they should be constructed with input from both parent and child. They shouldn't be forced upon your children. Part of what makes the rules work is the communication between you and your children when the rules are being designed. Some kids respond well to a written policy signed by both the parents and the child; others would prefer a list to be posted near the computer, as a reminder. You should do what makes you both comfortable. After all, you know your children best.

Points to Consider in Setting Your Own Rules and Drafting Your Own Safe-Surfing Contract

I have given you some basic rules to help you come up with your own family safe-surfing contract, and you should feel free to change them to suit both your and your child's needs. In the list below, I've tried to sum up the most important tips to remember. Consider it your cheat sheet in advising your child. (It also fits neatly on your inner wrist: That way you can keep the parental cheat sheet on one wrist and this on the other—a matched set!)

- People on the Internet can pretend to be anyone or anything they want. Don't let them fool you.
- Don't use bad language.
- Don't get into arguments with or answer anyone who uses bad language.
- Don't answer if someone says something that makes you feel uncomfortable or that you feel is "bad."
- If someone is doing something that makes you uncomfortable, you should tell your parents right away. But don't turn off the computer or log out of the area where the person is doing something "bad." (The adult can then find the person and report his activities as a terms of service violation.)
- Use a fun name when you're online, not your real name (not even your real first name and not a provocative name like "teen girl").
- Don't spend all your time online.
- Never give your real name, address, ICQ number, school, parents' names, friends' names, where your parents work, your sports team names, your scout troop information, anyone else's e-mail address, or any telephone number to anyone.
- If anyone asks you for this information, don't answer them, and tell your parents or the adult in charge of the chatroom. (If you are using a special secret cyberspace name, you can give them that instead.)
- Never talk to anyone you met online over the phone, send them anything, or accept anything from them or agree to meet with them unless your parents agree and/or are with you.
- Never show your picture online or send it to someone without your parents' consent.

- Don't put any real information in your online service profile without your parents' consent. Don't say things in your profile that you know will make others angry or that will provoke "bad" communications.
- There are places on the Internet where people talk about and show pictures of things we don't agree with. If you see something like that, click the Back button and tell your parents.
- Don't do anything online that costs money unless your parents say it's okay.
- Never give out your password, even to your best friend.
- Never give out your or your parents' credit card information.
- Don't copy other people's material and pretend that it's yours.
- Don't rely on strangers you meet in a chatroom for important advice.

Formalizing the Rules

I've included a sample safe-surfing contract in Appendix 3. I'll tell you what I tell my legal clients when they ask me if they should use a form agreement. If it fits all your needs, use it. Otherwise, you should use it as a guide in writing your own.

Sometimes parents think I'm being overly legalistic in suggesting drafting a written policy. It's not a legally enforceable contract, it's a guide.

If you discuss these issues with your kids, you never have to write one out. You want to make sure that you've really discussed each point, that they understand what you've discussed, and that they have agreed to follow the rules. Once you do that . . . there's no need for a written policy.

Kids are the ones who like them, though—it makes them feel part of the decision-making. But remember that the issue here is communication, not your ability to sue your children for breach of contract.

Netiquette: Teaching Your Children How to Behave Properly in Cyberspace

Origins of Netiquette

To understand Netiquette, you need to understand the Net. The Net was populated by techies who believed in free expression, the golden rule, and generosity (at least that's how they tell it). Commercialism was always frowned upon (and actually violated the terms of service of the National Science Foundation's original Internet network).

But even with the changes brought by Web business to the original spirit of the Internet, some of the old rules still apply. These are called "Netiquette" (etiquette for the Internet). It's always good to know the rules before you set forth in a new environment, and the Net is the newest environment of all.

Remember, too, that in addition to the rules of the online world, there are different rules for people all around the real-life world. On the Internet people from many countries will be sharing ideas, and what is normal and correct for them may be strange to you. So the rule of the game is RESPECT.

There's a lot to learn, but don't worry about having to learn all this new stuff at once. We were all newbies once, and you'll soon be a seasoned veteran, laughing at all the inside Net jokes.

Ms. Parry's Rules for Correct Internet Behavior

We all teach our children how to behave properly. Although we rarely see it ourselves, once in a while we hear from other families that our children are actually polite. Online manners are no different. There are rules for proper behavior in cyberspace called "Netiquette."

And it's a good thing we have them, because people do outrageous things when they get behind a keyboard—things they would ordinarily never do in real space. Somehow, whether it's the fact that they think they're anonymous, or that the Net brings out the daredevil in us, I don't know. But please don't let your kids fall into the trap of saying and doing things online that they know shouldn't be said or done.

We need to teach them that they can be traced, and that nothing is ever truly anonymous online. Everything they say should be said with the understanding that others will know, sooner or later, that they said it.

There are some other basic pointers you should know and teach your children if you want them to be good "netizens":

- **Get to know the rules before you say or do anything online.** Some discussion boards and chatrooms have special rules about what you can and can't say or do. Since some people can be very critical to those who break the rules, knowing the rules first may save you and your child needless heartache.

- **Think before you type.** Make sure that what you say is appropriate, won't result in flaming, and puts your best cyberfoot forward. The one thing you can count on is that everything you say online can come back to haunt you.
- **Don't be critical of others, especially newbies, even if they break the rules.** If you need to help or correct someone, do it by e-mail, not in a public forum like a chatroom or newsgroup. Remember, everyone was a newbie once.
- **Don't waste others' time or bandwidth.** Don't send chain e-mail, pass cyber rumors or hoaxes, or spam others (posting a message in many places at once). Don't carbon copy (cc:) people just because you can. Copy only those who need to read something.
- **Protect the privacy of others.** Don't openly list someone's e-mail address in a large cc: without their permission. Instead, use a bcc: to protect their privacy. Don't use anyone's password without their permission.
- **Don't take things without paying for them, like shareware.**

These things are bad Netiquette, too:

- Using ALL CAPITAL LETTERS—it's considered shouting and is hard on the eyes.
- Flaming—inciting or provoking an argument.
- Posting false or rude information about someone else.
- Sending a large attachment without asking if it's okay first.
- Referring to someone by their real name in a chatroom or channel.
- Sending e-mail to people you don't know, advertising something. (It's another kind of spam.)
- Talking about something off-topic in a special topic chatroom.
- Not waiting your turn or following the chatroom or channel rules in a special online event.

These are all no-nos. Remember that just because you're hiding out behind a computer monitor, you aren't exempt from correct and thoughtful communications.

Emoticons: Laughter in Cyberspace

Some of you may be seasoned veterans, but many of you are new to both online services and the Internet. To help, I put together a list of emoticons (sometimes called "smileys"), which are shortcut terms that allow the reader to understand subtleties in your online communications. This is just a quick sampling, but you can find many more at www.familyguidebook.com and at www.cnet.com.

Since people cannot communicate sarcasm, teasing, humor, or other emotions online (after all, typing is typing), people who use the Internet have developed emotion indicators. They are called "smileys" or emoticons.

<g>	a grin
<G>	a big grin
:-)	a smiley face
:->	very smiley face
;-) or ;->	a wink
:-(	a frown
:-P	sticking out your tongue
@----->---	a cyber rose
<):-)	a clown
(:-0	someone who is surprised
:D	happy and loud
:ox	shhh! It's a secret!

If you don't understand why these emoticons mean what I say they do, turn the book sideways. (If you still don't get it, turn it the other sideways. <G>)

Balance: When Do You Know if They've Had Enough?

One of the biggest challenges parents face is making sure their children don't become consumed with computers and websurfing. We all recognize the benefits of teaching our children to use computers, but we also need to recognize the risks associated with letting them spend every waking hour hiding behind a computer monitor.

A cyber–pen pal is a poor substitute for a real live friend. And fingers limbered by typing are poor substitutes for those limbered by throwing a baseball or playing Chopin on the piano. Clouds in the sky look different from clouds on a Windows 95 screensaver. Any parent faced with kids who enjoy video games—and the impossible task of trying to distract them from the video screen—understands how addictive interactivity can be. Yet knowing how to use and enjoy computers and cyberspace is an important part of our children's development. How can we help our kids maintain a healthy balance?

Set rules about how often, and for how long, your children can be online. My Teenangels group says that we need to be flexible about setting time limits, since school assignments may require more online research on some days than others. As a general guideline, we all agreed that limiting their surfing to an hour and a half daily is about right, assuming they don't have a research assignment.

While you should try to teach your children to follow your rules on their own, some software products limit the time, or may even set the hours the computer can be used and the Internet can be accessed. (These products can be used to limit the time spent playing computer games, too.) A few parents who are particularly savvy about this try to drop by their children's favorite chatrooms from their work Internet access to see if their kids are online. It's the tech equivalent of knocking on their door to remind them to get off the phone and do their homework.

When Is Your Child Old Enough to Use a Computer?

Too often parents get caught up in measuring their children against other children: who is speaking first, walking first, the first out of diapers. I am often asked when children should be introduced to a computer and how to tell when they are ready. I always give the same lawyerly answer: "It depends." It depends on you as well as on your child.

Most children are introduced to computing while seated in our laps, watching us "play" with our computers. My niece, Danielle, would play with a spare keyboard when she was ten months old. She would bang away perfectly safe, far from the computer itself. As she got a little older, she would wander over from time to time to get a peek at the flashing colors and sounds of the monitor. If her mom or dad ignored her for the computer for too long, she would scramble into their laps, needing once again to be the center of attention. (My goddaughter recites the alphabet in the "qwerty" format of a keyboard.)

As Danielle got used to the computer, her hand would be guided on the mouse, and she soon learned, at eighteen months, that moving the mouse moved the cursor. She would giggle while the cursor played wildly around the screen.

Software designed for young children made different sounds every time she struck a different key on the keyboard. (My sister used a Mac program called KeyWack.) Danielle was learning that the computer could be fun for her, as well as for her parents. By the time she was two and a half years old, she could sit and play her favorite programs, still learning how to control the mouse cursor. By her third birthday, she could manage the mouse with the best of them.

A few days after her third birthday, in receipt of a new CD-ROM featuring her favorite character, Arthur, she surprised all of us. While my sister was on the phone, she heard the computer whirring to start-up. Danielle was seated in front of the computer, having loaded the new CD-ROM, and had begun playing the program. It was the first time she had ever used the computer alone.

Are all children ready to use the computer by themselves at three? Of course not. (Some start at two!) It depends on the family, how often the child sees family members using the computer, and the child herself. When parents play sports, children are interested in sports. When parents cook, children like to cook. When we enjoy computers . . . children follow our lead, excited about what makes us excited.

So let your children sit in your lap and touch the keyboard and mouse. (This is called lap surfing.) Find a few programs that use characters your children enjoy and find a few family sites with their favorite characters, too. Often books can be coupled with interactive programs, fostering an interest in reading at the same time they're becoming familiar with the computer. (Check out Kid-Space, a wonderful site for really young children—www.kid-space.org—where they can make music online even before they can read.)

Guide their hands when using adult-size accessories. You may want to check out what child-size accessories are available for your computer. (Actually, I was surprised how few gadgets there are for young children. I expected to find more products geared for a child's hand and lots of other gadgets.) The right-size accessories can be much more comfortable. They fit the child's hands better and are usually peanut butter–proof. They're also more colorful than their adult counterparts. (Grandparents may find them more comfortable than some smaller devices themselves, especially those who suffer with arthritis.) I've listed some products I like at the familyguidebook.com site in the section called "Parry's Picks."

As delighted as I am that my genius niece has followed in the family technology footsteps, I do not recommend that she be unleashed unsupervised with my sister's expensive Power Mac. Right as I was writing *A Parents' Guide to the Internet,* we learned that my cherubic niece had deleted file after file from my sister's computer since she could drag and drop files into the trash can, and Oscar the Grouch would praise her each time she deleted a file. Talk about timely advice!

But remember that this isn't a competition. Your children should use a computer when they want to, and advance at their own pace. (Just keep an eye on those files . . . and Oscar the Grouch!)

Online activity is less important for younger children than for children who have learned to read and can follow online directions— generally those six and older. Even then, online family and children's sites should be visited only with a parent or another adult family member. It's a great way to spend time together and share your values and thoughts with them.

Your children shouldn't be allowed online unsupervised until you are sure that they know the rules and will follow them. Fancy child-protection software shouldn't be used as a substitute for parental supervision.

You also need to set the rules and administer your own test, one designed just for your child and your family. Only you can make sure your child is ready.

So . . . when is a child ready? When her Internet-savvy parent thinks so.

CHAPTER 8

Making and Implementing Your Choices

Finding a Fit That's Right for You and Your Kids

Okay, now you know the risks. I've even given you some tips on teaching your children how to handle information and be smart information consumers. Now what? Where do you go from here?

What will you do with your children? Will you rely on trust and education? Will you get some help from filtering tools? The choice is yours. But before you make your choice, I thought I'd share with you what other families are doing.

What Are Other Families Doing?

AOL tells me that 80 percent of the parents with younger children use their parental controls.

A national survey of parents in computer households was conducted by the Annenberg Public Policy Center of the University of Pennsylvania (http://appcpenn.org/internet). The results were released in May 1999. (I was one of the panelists at a conference held in conjunction with the release of their survey results.) It was a small study of 1,100 households with children from ages eight to seventeen who had computers in the home. About 60 percent of these households also had Internet access at home.

The Annenberg study suggested that roughly one-third of households with home Internet access are using some type of filtering tool. (This is a much higher percentage than what my less formal inquiries from parent groups and kids disclose.) The study also showed that parents were of two minds where the Internet was concerned. A vast majority, 78 percent, said that they were "strongly" or "somewhat" concerned that their children might give away personal information on the Internet, and fear that their children might view sexually explicit material. Yet a substantial majority, 59 percent, also believe that children without Internet access are at a disadvantage when compared to their peers, and more than 70 percent say that the Internet allows children to discover fascinating, useful things and get help with their schoolwork.

Joseph Turow, Ph.D., who authored the report, put it best when he said, "Parents are juggling the dream and the nightmare of the Internet at the same time."

I think the study is most helpful where it shows what parents who have Internet access are doing. The parents surveyed overwhelmingly said that they set rules about their children's Internet use, and "keep an eye on" what their children are doing online. Of the households with online access at home, and with children between the ages of eight and twelve, the Annenberg study reflects:

- Eighty-four percent of parents set rules about the sites their children visit.
- Eighty-four percent of parents set rules about the time of day or night children are allowed to go online.
- Seventy-eight percent of parents set rules about the kind of activities children perform online.
- Sixty-three percent of parents set rules about the amount of time spent online.
- Seventy-three percent of parents set rules requiring that their children go online only with an adult, whether at home or outside the home.
- Forty-nine percent of parents set rules restricting their children to home online use.
- Thirty percent of parents set rules restricting their children to online use that is relevant for schoolwork.

As the children get older, the rules become less restrictive. For their teenagers between ages thirteen and seventeen:

- Seventy-one percent of parents set rules about the sites their children visit.

- Sixty-eight percent of parents set rules about the time of day or night the children are allowed to go online.
- Seventy percent of parents set rules about the kind of activities their children perform online.
- Fifty-five percent of parents set rules about the amount of time spent online.
- Twenty-nine percent of parents set rules requiring that their children go online only with an adult, whether at home or outside the home.
- Thirty-five percent of parents set rules restricting their children to home online use.
- Twenty-one percent of parents set rules restricting their children to online use that is relevant for schoolwork.

The parents who had Internet access at home said that they use the following ways to keep their kids out of trouble online:

- Eighty-six percent of the parents of children between eight and twelve years of age, and eighty percent of the parents with teenagers, set rules that their children need to follow when online.
- Eighty-eight percent of the parents of children between eight and twelve, and seventy-three percent of the parents of teenagers, keep an eye on what their children are doing online.
- Sixty-seven percent of the parents of children between eight and twelve, and twenty-nine percent of the parents of teenagers, do not allow their children to go online except with a parent present.
- Thirty-five percent of the parents of children between eight and twelve, and twenty-seven percent of the parents with teenagers, use protective software such as Net Nanny that guards children's access to sites.
- Twenty-four percent of the parents of children between eight and twelve, and seventeen percent of the parents of teenagers, deny children online access at home.

But by now, you should know what I'm going to say: Although it's nice to know what other parents are doing, it's irrelevant when it comes to making the right choice for your family.

What Are the Choices?

When I first wrote *A Parents' Guide to the Internet* two years ago, other than the traditional multifeatured filtering and blocking products, parents didn't have much in the way of options or choices. Since then, the big four parental-control filtering and blocking products have become the big six, AOL has added several new levels of parental controls, and a few new types of monitoring products have been developed. But the most exciting changes are in the area of safe harbors—closed or semiclosed environments built for kids or preteens or teens. These are sites we as parents like, but more important, our children love!

While some parents want their children to be shielded from anything they find objectionable (which may be different from what you find objectionable), others want their children exposed to everything to be able to learn from it. Some couldn't care less about overblocking information, and others think that's the only issue. Others want to use a filtered or kids-friendly search engine, but no other filtering. That's your right as a parent—to set the rules for your family. You can raise your children on sprouts and tofu, or McDonald's every night. In the same way, you can decide what your children should be allowed to do online and where they can go.

But to make a choice, you need to know what's out there. There is now lots of terrific, safe, and entertaining content online for younger kids, preteens, and teens. Most of it's free, and a few have low monthly subscription fees. There are filtered search engines, kid-friendly Web browsers, and safe-site lists galore.

Yet, whether you elect to use a filtering and blocking product, join a kids-safe subscription service, rely on free safe-harbor sites, or a combination of the above, remember that educating your children about online safety has to be the primary defense. Don't rely on any product or sites to do your job, which is to make sure your children are safe and able to exercise responsible judgment. Adding technology is like using a seat belt and adding an airbag. Your first defense is being a good and careful driver. The airbag and seat belt add protection if the unexpected occurs, or other drivers aren't as careful as you are.

Our children need to be taught to handle different content and difficult situations, to judge credibility and decide what is worth their attention and what isn't. Only education can do that. They need to understand their own family's values in exercising that judgment. And only you can teach your family's values to your children. Filtering may be a big help in many cases, especially when the children are young. But remember, you can't filter life. (Repeat after me. . . .)

And if you are interested in learning more about using technological tools to help you enforce your choices, there are more than one hundred different software programs and methods that have been developed to restrict and monitor access to, and rate the content contained in, certain sites on the Internet. Many also restrict information being sent from or being sent to your children on the Internet and online services. While some parents may find these tools helpful, they aren't a substitute for good parenting. When they are used, they should always be coupled with education and good communication.

Yes, Virginia . . . There Is a Good Side to the Internet!

Just as you were ready to give up, having "had it up to here!" with the bad stuff online and the dark side of the Internet . . . tah-dah! Welcome, ladies and gentlemen, to the good side of the Internet!

A few years ago, there weren't many options available to parents who wanted to limit their children's exposure to non–child appropriate content. You could filter, or limit their surfing to rated or preapproved sites, but these methods were very restrictive. The industry responded to the need parents had identified for quality and fun content for kids. And the more great sites and services we have for kids, the less likely that they will wander off into the kind of content you might find inappropriate.

Now we have a wide range of choices of fun and valuable content—and that are safe, too!

There are now many good kids-friendly search engines, hyperlinked good-site lists compiled by teachers, librarians, and community groups (which you can click on to be whisked away to the site), lots of great kids sites for all ages, safe-harbor sites designed for children and preteens (which are safe playgrounds for kids on the Web), and subscription clubs for kids (subscription closed destination sites containing kid-friendly content).

I discuss a few of my favorites here, but make sure you keep checking back at www.familyguidebook.com for new ones as they are released. This is an area of serious growth as companies try to develop quality edutainment (educational/entertainment) content, services, and products. They've finally figured out that providing what parents need and kids want is good business.

Finding Kid-Friendly Content

Filtered Search Engines

There are two different kinds of filtered search engines: those that were designed from the bottom up to be kid-friendly and those that filter search results from major search engines. Most of the largest search engines have a "clean site" search option now, which screens the sites for content appropriate for children and searches only those sites. Anyone who has tried to search for "girl" sites or "toy" sites and found far more than they had expected will appreciate the filtered search engines.

I've listed my favorite ones below. We've tested all of these and are confident that they have done their homework in prescreening the sites and banner advertisers (those ads that appear at the top of a Web page) to be child-appropriate. If you use another one, I suggest you run it through its paces first.

Kid-Friendly Search Engines

With these search engines, you are ready for a safe and kid-friendly search as soon as you get to their sites—and no registration is required:

AOL's NetFind Kids Only

www.aol.com/netfind/kids

AOL's NetFind Kids Only searches sites that AOL considers safe for kids. It's a webwide extension of its well-loved Kids Only section of AOL, available to AOL and all Web users alike.

Ask Jeeves for Kids!

www.ajkids.com

Ask Jeeves for Kids! is also an offspring of a very popular search engine, Ask Jeeves. Ask Jeeves for Kids! works differently from other standard search engines, since instead of using Boolean logic (keywords linked together by +'s and −'s), they let you use simple questions. So instead of searching for blue+sky+why, you can search for "why is the sky blue." It also has a very helpful feature that catches common spelling errors, asking you if you really meant to spell New York "New Yook" (although whenever I search for "Parry Aftab," they *insist* that I'm misspelling something). It also shows you what other kids are searching for right now, which gives your child good ideas of what kinds of questions to ask.

DIG
www.dig.com
Disney's kid-friendly search engine searches only Disney's websites, but there are so many terrific activities, games, and stories at the Disney sites that your kids may not miss the rest of the Web. Of course, I'm a bit prejudiced, but you might want to check out http://disney.go.com/home/channels/liveevents/today/html/index.htmlsection5 to read a safety chat I did with Mr. Toad.

KidsClick
http://sunsite.berkeley.edu/KidsClick
KidsClick is a search engine created just for kids by the librarians at the Ramapo Catskill Library System in New York. (I had the honor of speaking to this talented group last year about online safety.) They started with the American Library Association's Great Site list and worked their way up from there. In addition to its being a wonderful resource for children and educators everywhere, the creators of this great search engine are warm, caring, and talented people.

Yahooligans!
www.yahooligans.com
Yahooligans! was the first child-friendly search engine, launched several years ago. Yahooligans! is a special service offered by Yahoo!, one of the most popular search engines/directories, and has many wonderful categories of sites and services for kids. But it's more than a miniaturized version of Yahoo!—it has lots of great activities for kids, too, like their downloader page, which has sounds, videos, and pictures. Kids love to use them in their reports and on their websites. Yahooligans! also has a random feature that lets your children surf random kid-friendly sites.

Regular Search Engines with Kid-Friendly Options
With these search engines, you first have to go to the regular site, then select or register for the safe-surfing filters they offer.

Family Filter from Altavista
http://image.altavista.com/cgi-bin/globalff
Altavista's Family Filter allows parents to filter out all images, videos, and audio search results. It also allows parents to filter all searches, in-

cluding searches of websites. The filter features can be set search by search or password-protected so parents can set their children's search options one time for whenever they search on Altavista.

SearchGuard from Lycos
http://my.lycos.com/safetynet/safetynet.asp
SearchGuard is a safe-surfing option available at the Lycos site that filters search results for adult, hate, and racist content. Registered users can easily turn SearchGuard on and off by entering their password. SearchGuard also has an optional feature that allows parents to block access to chat, e-mail, and message boards.

Approved-Site Lists

Too often we focus on the bad stuff. We lecture our children on where they shouldn't be going online. We tell them what not to do. But we need to think back a bit, to when they were toddlers. Every time we said "No!" we needed to give them a "Yes!" alternative, or they would be right back where we told them not to be. These approved site lists are a great place to start.

American Library Association
The American Library Association has several terrific good-site lists. When it comes to the Internet, no one understands it as well or can guide children better than librarians and library media specialists.

ALA's Cool Sites for Kids
http://www.ala.org/alsc/children_links.html

ALA's 700+ Great Sites: Amazing, Spectacular, Mysterious, Wonderful Web Sites for Kids and the Adults Who Care About Them
http://www.ala.org/parentspage/greatsites/

ALA's Internet Guide for Teens
http://ala8.ala.org/teenhoopla/links.html

Cyberangels
I know I'm biased, but Cyberangels' volunteer group of moms, Cyberangels' CyberMoms, has reviewed hundreds of valuable and safe sites

for kids in many categories, like science and homework helpers, giving them our seal of approval. We reviewed them also to make sure they post privacy policies, and have helped many great sites develop safe-surfing and privacy policies in order to qualify for our site list. Interested in helping? Our CAST (Cyberangels Approved Site Team) director can always use more caring help. (Send her an e-mail at CAST@cyberangels.org or Cybermoms@cyberangels.org.)

Cyberangels' Cybermoms' Approved-Site List
http://www.cyberangels.org/cybermoms/links.htm

The Children's Partnership
When I look for leadership and guidance in child advocacy issues, I look no further than the talented and caring people at The Children's Partnership, and Laurie Lipper and Wendy Lazarus are very special people who put children first. They were the first to understand the issue of online safety for children, and The Children's Partnership is the leader in the area of Internet advocacy for children, health issues and children, and equitable access to education and technology resources for all children.

Their site is a wealth of information, too, including their new Parents' Online Resource Center in English and in Spanish, their ground-breaking *The Parents' Guide to the Information Superhighway*, and their *Keeping Kids Safe Online: Tips & Tools for Parents*. (I was honored to have my first book included in both of these guides.)

The Children's Partnership
Parents Online: Things You Can Do With Your Children and Teens
http://www.childrenspartnership.org

Other Great Site Lists
from Trusted Companies
SurfMonkey Kids' Channel Cool Sites
http://www.surfmonkey.com/directory/Coolsites/default.asp

Yahooligans! The Web Guide for Kids
http://www.yahooligans.com/

Lycos Directory of Internet Kids' Sites
http://dir.lycos.com/Home/Kids/

Webcrawler Kids & Family Channel, with Children's Television Workshop Family Workshop Website Guide
http://webcrawler.com/ctw/

Netscape Kids' Directory
http://directory.netscape.com/Home/Kids/

Relying on Tried-and-True Brand Names

There are certain names we have always trusted where our children are concerned. These include Children's Television Workshop, PBS, Disney, Nickelodeon, *Sports Illustrated for Kids*, *Time for Kids*, *National Geographic*, The Discovery Channel, and others. These have managed to translate their offline entertaining and educational content to the new medium of the Internet. And, rather than suffer by the translation, their content has become even more entertaining as children have become involved with their interactive content.

> The Children's Television Workshop—www.ctw.org
> Public Broadcasting System's PBS Kids Online—www.pbs.org/kids
> Disney—www.disney.com
> Nickelodeon: www.nick.com
> *Sports Illustrated for Kids*—www.sikids.com
> *Time for Kids*—http:/pathfinder.com/TFK/
> *National Geographic for Kids*—www.nationalgeographic.com/kids/
> The Discovery Channel for Kids—www.discoverykids.com

Also, some well-known corporations who aren't involved with media or entertainment have decided to jump on the Internet-for-kids bandwagon, too. These include names that are trusted in the real world, and their credibility is important to them, online and offline. This shows in their sites.

Fleet
Fleet Kids (built in conjunction with Headbone, one of the leading websites for children and preteens)
http://www.fleetkids.com
Fleet Kids was designed to promote learning for K–6-graders on money matters, learning how to work together in teams, and becoming active

citizens. It was really done as a public service; there's no link to your local Fleet branch. Fleet, by putting the kids first, is building brand loyalty the old-fashioned way—they are earning it! If you want to know what they teach children at the site and how it works, check out http://www.fleet.com/fleetkids.

Chevron
Chevron Kids
http://www.chevronkids.com/
This is a great site, and aside from the fact that cars are involved and are tangentially connected to Chevron's products, it doesn't promote the company. It promotes what kids love instead. They have lots of free stuff, fun activities, and a terrific online privacy and safety policy that has been used as a model by many industry groups, including CARU. They are getting the level of respect they have gotten by doing it better than so many others.

You should let them know that you appreciate their efforts in helping build fun and valuable sites for your children. Unlike other companies that get a direct benefit from providing content to children online, these are doing it for goodwill value.

Special Safe-Harbor Sites

Many of the newer websites for kids satisfy parents' desires for quality content for children, but more important, they also satisfy the kids' desires for fun and entertaining content. These names aren't familiar to the offline parent, but they control the kids market online. They are especially attractive to preteens, who are too old for the kiddie sites but too young for full exposure to everything the Web has to offer.

The following are a few of my favorites and the kids' favorites:

Bonus (www.bonus.com) is a kids website designed for children and preteens (for ages three to thirteen, with some content appropriate for lap-surfing prereaders, as well as some for "advanced" teens to age sixteen). Bonus describes itself as a theme park for kids with kid-safe rides and attractions. And kids see it the same way. Bonus doesn't have chat, but it does have games—lots of them. They have teacher and parent sections, too. They are also active supporters of the Wired Kids project, creating online safety games for kids and surveying kids to see how they use the Internet. Last but not least, Bonus and I have launched an online safety column for Bonus, written by me, where I answer kids' online safety questions (with some help from my friends).

Freezone (www.freezone.com) is a website community designed for kids ages eight to fourteen. It takes the term *community* very seriously, and provides all the tools preteens need to build their own. They have safe and monitored chat, discussion boards, home pages, and postcards. It is often cited by preteens as their favorite place to chat and has some of the most comprehensive safety-screening procedures online. Parents can take a preview tour of what their kids can do online.

Headbone (www.headbone.com) is a website community for preteens and children ages eight to fourteen. It is "the leading content-based, community-oriented kids destination site" online. And it provides more of its own original content than do the other leading kids sites. Headbone has online profiles, buddy lists, and chat, all monitored and available to kids under thirteen only with prior parental consent. They take safety very seriously. They are also partnering to bring Headbone to television and to newspapers around the world.

KidsCom (www.kidscom.com) is one of the original kids sites, catering since 1995 to kids ages four to fifteen. KidsCom has monitored chat, international pen pal programs, and lots of games. While kids love the site, what really makes KidsCom unique is their ParentTalk site, which provides a community for parents to teach their children about the Internet and keeps them closely involved with their children's surfing activities.

Lycos Zone (www.lycoszone.com) is a safe haven on the web designed for kindergarten through eighth grade kids. It has a "fun & games" zone with separate areas for different age groups, a "homework" zone and a "new & cool" zone. It even has an area for parents and teachers. It has some great links to other sites for kids, too. When kids visit the site, Lycos' search guard filter is automatically enabled.

Mamamedia (www.mamamedia.com) was formed by educators, rather than media and entertainment experts. It targets kids between the ages of five and twelve. While many of the other sites rely on building communities and content, Mamamedia relies on having kids build their own content by engaging in activities online. Everything revolves around their mission, to teach children how to eXplore, eXpress themselves, and eXchange their ideas. They have unique tools that help children create their own stories, characters, and content, too. Mamamedia is consistently identified by educators as one of the most valuable sites for children online.

Zeeks (www.zeeks.com) is a newcomer to the kids destination site pack. It also has games, free e-mail (a special proprietary one designed for safety), and chat (currently outsourced to Freezone). It also has lots of original content and has many activities and creative tools for kids to use to create their own content. Kids can also create their own calendars online. The site is designed for kids from six to thirteen. It also offers a free filtering software, called ZeekSafe, that works with your browser.

A new service should be available by the time this book is released. It's run by people I love and trust, so it is worth mentioning here. Surf Monkey, one of my favorite products (you'll learn about it later in this chapter) is creating a kids and preteen portal. It can be found at www.surfmonkey.com.

Special Online Services for Kids and Teens

Many parents don't want their children on the Web itself. Instead they want a safe place their children can go to, but not be able to use to get to other sites. I call these kids club or destination sites. Your children dial into them, as you do with AOL, and can surf around their online playground without your having to worry that they are surfing in non-approved areas. Parents are willing to pay for their children to use these sites.

Junior Net

Junior Net is a subscription-based service just for kids and preteens from three to twelve years. It costs $9.95 per month and is advertisement-free. It's often referred to as a "kids Internet." Many great kid-friendly content providers, like *Sports Illustrated for Kids*, *Highlights for Children*, *Ranger Rick*, the *Weekly Reader*, and Jim Henson's *Bear in the Big Blue House*, have joined forces with Junior Net and provided their content for use in a closed environment. Junior Net then adds some interactivity to tried-and-true favorites, like *Highlights'* Hidden Pictures. Junior Net adds it own special content also, while keeping children off the Internet itself and in its protected environment.

Disney's Club Blast
(www.disneyblast.com)

Disney's Club Blast is a special subscription service within Disney.com that provides families access to exclusive premium content in a parent-trusted environment. Members enjoy a range of activities, including communication tools like "D-Mail," Disney's BlastPad instant messaging, chat within the gaming environments, message boards, clubs, and auditorium chats with kid-friendly celebrities. There are over a hundred interactive games, activities, stories, and comics, including multiplayer games supporting up to twenty-four guests simultaneously. In addition, Disney's Club Blast includes parental controls that let parents manage their children's online communication. Membership to Disney's Club Blast is $5.95 a month or $39.95 a year (members also receive a 10 percent discount on all merchandise offered at The Disney Store Online).

And More Coming Up . . .

Cyberspace Kids (www.cyberspacekids.com) is a newly launched closed system that uses the Crayon Crawler kids' browser. Noodles (www.noodles.com) and Nickelodeon (www.nick.com) are also building free closed systems for kids and preteens. At the time of this writing, these weren't available for my review. But the caliber of the people behind them guarantees that they will be fun for kids and approved by parents.

One from Column A, Two from Column B

Using Technology to Help Implement and Enforce Your Choices

There are several methods currently in use to allow parents to control their children's access to certain information and sites on the Internet. Parents can filter out certain inappropriate sites and content. They can also filter incoming information that children receive and outgoing information that they send to others. (Different categories of content, such as drugs, alcohol, sex, hate, and violence, among others, can be selected by the parent to limit filtering and blocking to customized categories of offensive material.)

The blocking features can also block sites that have been previewed and are known to contain inappropriate content, as well as block incoming e-mail, instant messaging and attachments, and areas of the Internet, like newsgroups, FTP, and IRC.

Parents can use parental controls or special software. They can use website ratings provided by third-party rating groups. They can sub-scribe to a filtered Internet service provider (which filters all access for parents and children) or a subscription-based closed system for pre-cleared "clean" content.

The technology allows parents to monitor and track their children's access, and even report every word they type or receive online. There are ways of using the tools to limit their children's surfing to certain preselected "safe" sites. And they may be able to use one or more of these in combination to make sure that they find the best fit for their child.

To Filter or Not to Filter— That Is the Question

A few years ago, parents had two choices when it came to using technology to help control their children's surfing. They could use a filtering/blocking software, or they could unplug their computers. But all that has changed.

Over the last couple of years, many new and innovative products and services have been developed to expand parents' online safety tech-arsenal. There are now many multifeatured filtering and blocking pro-ducts. You can use all of their features, or just whichever ones match your family's (or child-by-child) needs. There are products that monitor your children's surfing and everything they say and do online, then give you a blow-by-blow account or generalized report. Other products give your children their own customized child-friendly desktop, which can also filter Internet access and restrict certain activities, like e-mail. There are even products for home use that use smart cards to permit or limit access, child by child.

The best thing about all these choices is that if you can't find one product that does what you need it to, you may be able to choose one from column A and two from column B, combining good content options also, to create a truly customized solution. (Just make sure the software products you choose are compatible with each other.) But remember—before you even start looking at software helpers, you have to educate your child about online safety and how to exercise responsible judg-ment and use critical thinking. That way they can handle the things that get through the software.

While you might decide that using tech helpers isn't what you want or need, you should be familiar enough with what they offer to make an informed choice.

The Controversy

Using technology to help protect our children from *abuses* of technology—hmmm, it sounds like a horror movie of robots run wild, doesn't it? And many people see the use of technology to help manage children's online access as another horror story.

I have been amazed at the level of controversy the issue of *parents* using filtering products to help enforce *their* online choices for *their* children has wrought. I don't get it. (There are special First Amendment issues that apply when libraries filter, but that's for another book.)

The arguments that are usually raised against filtering in the home are:

- The products overblock by blocking "innocent" sites.
- The products underblock by letting certain sites through that are supposed to be blocked.
- Children should be taught how to handle inappropriate information, not be fitted with "blinders."
- Parents rely too heavily on these products and fail to take other precautions, thinking that these are the single solution.
- The people who select the filtering criteria have biases that are reflected in their selection.
- These biases may not be clear to those using the product or service.
- The people who select the sites for blocking are untrained or unsupervised, and may not perform their jobs properly.
- Certain content, like information about parental drug or alcohol abuse, or incest, should be freely available to children without their parents' knowing that it is being accessed by the child.
- Kids can get around the software easily.
- Children should have unlimited access to all legal information—they have free speech rights, too.
- Once we allow any kind of filtering, we risk starting down the "slippery slope" that leads to governmental censorship.

The first thing you need to understand is that kids can't get around the new generation of filtering products. A skilled hacker can (usually, but not always better skilled than your preteen). But most of the products shout with their last dying tech-equivalent of a breath, flashing on the screen or shutting down entirely, that they've been tampered with. Then you need to look no further than your local resident hacker wanna-be to find the culprit.

Skilled computer programmers can do just about anything with any software. But you should know that I offered three high school skilled computer-hacker types $100 each to crack the big four products Cyber Patrol, CYBERsitter, Net Nanny, and SurfWatch. No one collected a dime.

As far as I'm concerned, that's definitive proof. (It's been scientifically proven that teens will do everything in their power to earn $100.) So if you're putting off looking at parental-control software because you're afraid your kids can get around it, don't. It's old news, and not true anymore.

Most of these other issues are very valid. We should be critical of products that don't deliver what they promise. We should also make sure that parents understand the strengths and weaknesses of each product and any biases. That's why we reviewed the big four with these questions in mind. When I get to the section on the products themselves, I'll show you what questions you need to ask when you're looking at any other products, to be able to make an informed choice.

I also agree, and think most of you would agree, that we should always be on the lookout for governmental censorship and be protecting free speech everywhere. But parents deciding what their kids can see and can't see isn't a free speech issue. It's a parenting issue!

For parents who need extra help, and those who might otherwise keep their kids offline entirely, there's no question that these products can be very helpful.

But filtering in the home is a family-by-family choice. It's also a child-by-child choice. What works for one child in the family may not work for another. The operative word here is choice. It's the parent's choice, not free speech groups', advocacy groups', or the government's choice. No one should feel pressured to filter or not to filter. Yet some parents are feeling pressured.

I can see it now . . . (I have a sick imagination, I should let you know in advance.) A mother walks through the park, and she is approached by someone lurking in a trench coat. He opens it to display a bunch of watches on one side and on the other lots of CD-ROMs sewn into the lining. "Pssst . . . lady, I got some Net Nanny here. No questions asked!"

And, remember, it's a child-by-child fit. What works for the younger child in the family who breaks every rule in the book may not be the right fit for an older sibling who has never stepped out of line in her lifetime. That's why some programs are customizable for more than one child in the family—so that your six-year-old can be treated differently from your sixteen-year-old.

Hey, guys, I wrote this book to empower you, remember? You don't have to answer to others about other parenting choices, do you? No one says anything about how you dress your children or what you feed them (at least not to your face). Homemade chocolate-chip cookies warm from the oven, or stale Chips Ahoy from the cabinet—that's your choice. You should be making the choices that make you comfortable. (But if I'm coming over, the warm cookie thing is a nice idea!)

Parental-Control Software: Added Protection

Child computer safety products fall into several categories. They either block "bad sites" or allow you to access only "good sites." These are typically called filtering and blocking software. They include familiar names such as Net Nanny and Cyber Patrol. But newer types of products provide children with special kids-friendly desktops, which do more than just control where they surf. These include Edmark's KidDesk and Surf Monkey. Some products are free; others have to be purchased. But most are very affordable, typically under $30.

What Kinds of Things Can Technological Tools Do?

A Quick Overview of Features

There is a lot of variety in what the technology can do these days. (It's moving so quickly that we will update this section frequently online at www.familyguidebook.com.)

Most blocking products or features work by classifying sites. They review sites and include them in either a good or white/clean site list (which contains kid-friendly sites) or a bad or black/banned site list (which have been reviewed and found to be inappropriate for children based on certain criteria). Children can be limited to only the good sites, or prevented from going to the bad ones.

But since the Web is growing by more than 200,000 registered sites a month, no bad-site list can hope to keep up. That's why most products also filter words and phrases, and some even filter them in context to prevent blocking innocent phrases. (The difference between blocking and filtering is this—blocked sites are reviewed and categorized in advance, and filtered sites are reviewed as they are accessed by the child.)

When children attempt to access a site that is blocked or filtered, they can't access it. Some products tell you why you can't access it. They provide announcements or "alerts," informing the child that the site is "blocked by ———— [name of product]." Others work in stealth mode. That means that they don't tell you they're blocking (and may not even tell your child that they are working). When a site is blocked in stealth mode, you merely get an error message.

Many products monitor and report on online use: where the children have been, how long they were there, and what they did online. (Some even take periodic snapshots of their screens or give you a log of everything your child said or your child heard online.) Certain products can also monitor offline computer usage as well, such as how many hours (and which hours) the child spends on the computer or playing computer games, and can restrict them from using certain software offline.

A few online services (such as America Online) provide their own proprietary products that work only on their systems. These are provided without charge to members. Some of the other software products can be used with online services (such as AOL and CompuServe), and others are designed only for the Internet and work with ISPs (such as AT&T, Mindspring, and MCI/Worldcom). Many ISPs are making free software available for their members as well.

You can also use software to block certain incoming information (such as e-mail and instant messaging) entirely, to filter incoming information (to block those irritating pornography links contained in the e-mail), or to prevent certain information from being sent by your children to others (such as their names and your telephone number). Online searches can be blocked as well, or limited to preapproved kid-friendly search engines.

The programs are either customizable or preset by the manufacturer of the software. The more they can be customized, the more time they take to install and set up. Some allow you to set different levels of protection for different children, so you can set more restrictions for your younger children than for their teenage sibling. Many of the better systems combine these various options, giving you the greatest protection and maximum flexibility.

Filtering, Blocking, and Monitoring—Oh, My!!

I've included below a detailed description of the kinds of protection technologically available. Later in this chapter, you'll find a chart comparing the features of each of the leading programs we've reviewed and our reviews of the products. We also give you the results of our tests, where we ran these products through their paces. These will be frequently updated at the www.familyguidebook.com site, too, and we're interested in hearing what you have to say. Drop me an e-mail with your thoughts at parry@aftab.com.

How They Work

Bad-Site Lists

There are products that block certain sites determined (by either the company or the parent) to be undesirable. These types of software have lists of "bad sites" (updated on a regular basis) compiled by the software company, and access to anything on these lists is automatically blocked. Some also allow you to add or delete names from that list, so you can customize it for your child.

You should know, though, that most software companies don't allow you to see their blocked-site list. Net Nanny deserves a special mention here, since they allow you to see everything they block and modify it any way you want. That means that *you* decide what your child should see and not see, not the filtering product companies.

With the purchase of a product, you usually get a subscription for updated lists for a certain period of time. The cost of updates after the subscription period has expired varies, as do the frequency and ease of installing updates. Given how rapidly websites are being added to the Web (about 200,000 per month), the more frequent the updates the better. (And, needless to say, getting something for free is better than having to pay for it.)

Before you jump on the "bad site" blocking bandwagon, however, you should know that there has been substantial controversy over how the "bad sites" are selected. Inconsistent determinations, improperly trained or untrained reviewers, and lack of real quality-control can result in an unreliable list, limiting either too many sites or not enough.

Some companies use technology to scan for "inappropriate language" used in certain sites. Then they have human reviewers check and see which of those sites should be blocked.

But many innocent and valuable sites are still blocked, either intentionally or inadvertently. For example, my sister (yes, the one who wrote for *A Parents' Guide* the "totally unbiased recommendation of my sister's book") is KidDoc, the pediatrician for *Parenting Magazine* online, which is found at www.parenttime.com (Time Warner's parenting site). She answers questions about children's medical problems online. In one of her chats, she discussed an infection a toddler had on her labia. Many products block her chat because of the inclusion of that word. Is that the kind of site parents want blocked? Whether it is or not, parents need to understand that sites like that are often blocked. I suspect that many health-related sites will have similar problems.

Ask the filtering company you are looking at to provide their criteria for reviewing sites for their bad-site lists and their good-site lists. I've included the criteria used by Cyber Patrol, CYBERsitter, Net Nanny, and SurfWatch at familyguidebook.com. Make sure you agree with their criteria, because when you use a bad-site list product, you're really buying their judgment. Any company that is rating or selecting content for your children should match your own values. If you can, with open lists like Net Nanny, you may want to check out the sites and see if you agree with their classification. If not, make sure you can add and delete sites from that list as often as you want to.

Even if you don't review their criteria, or the list itself, often children need to access a site for schoolwork and find it blocked for various reasons. You want a product that will allow you to unblock a site if you find it okay for your child. Otherwise, you would have to turn off the filter to allow your child to access the site.

Look at the bad-site lists for sites you think are valuable but that might be blocked, like Planned Parenthood or National Organization of Women, or AIDS information sites. These lists can be very long, but skimming them can give you a good sense of the product and any biases. Remember that there are no good or bad blocking criteria, just one that agrees with your values or doesn't.

The following are things to think about when reviewing a bad-site-list blocking product or feature:

- How many sites do they have on the list?
- How do they select these sites? What are their criteria? Are they open about it? Who reviews the sites? What kind of training do they receive? What quality controls exist?
- Can you see what's on the list? Can you add and delete sites from the bad-site list? Do they block innocent sites just because they might be controversial?
- Can you select certain categories to block or to unblock?
- How often is it updated? How is it updated? Are there charges for updates? How long is the free-upgrade subscription period?

Access Only to Preapproved "Good" Sites

Some manufacturers, recognizing that they can never keep up with all the new sites being published on the Web, have opted for a list of preapproved, prescreened sites that are considered child-friendly. Each manufacturer screens the sites based on its own criteria, and while a site may be on one manufacturer's good list, it may not be on another's.

While using an approved list addresses the problem with bad site blocking, not being able to view sites that have not yet been approved may limit your child's access to terrific new sites. This option makes most sense with a young child, usually under ten. But this is less of a problem than it used to be, since these good-site lists have been expanded to include thousands of child-friendly sites.

One valuable feature on some good site list software is the ability to add entire white or clean site lists. (You can get some ideas about where to find lists of good sites at "Yes, Virginia . . . There Is a Good Side to the Internet!")

These programs also include a subscription to the approved list, which the manufacturers frequently update. As with the bad site software, there is often a charge for updates after the subscription period has ended, and the frequency of updates varies product by product. The problem with quality control of bad-site screening also exists with the good-site screening, since sites may not be included in the approved list based on inconsistent standards and the application of these standards by often improperly trained or untrained individuals.

Here are some things to think about when reviewing a good-site list product or feature. The things to consider are the same as with a bad-site list, except here the number of sites is very important if you are limiting your children to only those sites on the good list. Also, the site selection criteria are particularly important if your child won't have access to any sites outside of their list. Make sure there is no hidden political agenda.

- How many sites do they have on the list?
- How do they select these sites? What are their criteria? Are they open about it? Who reviews the sites? What kind of training do they receive? What quality controls exist?
- Can you see what's on the list? Can you add and delete sites from the site list? Do they limit sites to those with a particular

political or religious viewpoint? If so, is it your political or religious viewpoint, and are you comfortable restricting your child to that limited viewpoint?

- How often is it updated? How is it updated? Are there charges for updates? How long is the free-upgrade subscription period?

Rated Sites

While the good-site and bad-site lists are rated, in effect, by qualifying them as either appropriate or inappropriate for children, there are many services that rate sites based on a wider range of criteria. The criteria allow the sites to be rated and sorted into categories, which might include age appropriateness or type of content.

The sites are either self-rated based on certain preset criteria, or are rated by third-party rating services. The sites then carry a computer code. While this code is invisible to us, it is read by your browser and allows or denies access to the site, depending on the rating criteria set in your browser.

While all rating services use PICS (the Platform for Internet Content Selection) technology to allow their rating codes to be universally read by the major Web browsers, like Microsoft Internet Explorer and Netscape Navigator, PICS is not a rating service. The major rating services are RSACi (now administered by ICRA, the Internet Content Rating Association) and Safe Surf.

Ratings allow good-site accessibility and bad-site blocking (at whatever level you select on your browser). In addition, using them with your Web browser gives you use of the rating system without charge.

Unfortunately, blocking out the "adult" and other inappropriate classifications doesn't help very much, since so few of the adult and other inappropriate sites have any ratings at all. That means that the only safe way to use it to select rating content is by setting it to block any unrated site as well as those that don't match your selected rating level. That means your children can access only the rated good sites.

Since only 120,000 sites are currently rated by RSACi, limiting access to only rated sites may err on the side of being overly protective of your children's access to content on the Internet.

Until more sites are rated (an effort we support), we recommend using another parental-control system—hopefully, one that supports PICS-compatible ratings. We've included this information on our software comparison chart.

Keywords and Phrases
(Either in Context or Not)

Certain words tend to be used in most of the sites that have content you want to screen or block. The technology allows you to block access to any sites that contain these words—"keywords." (Some products allow you to add or delete words from the keyword list.)

One of the biggest problems with filtering is that innocent sites may be blocked inadvertently because they contain a keyword. That's why many software programs filter only sites that use a keyword in context or are used in a phrase with other keywords.

One of my favorite inadvertent blocking stories was shared by an Internet father, the codesigner of the Kids of the Web site (www.kidsoftheweb.com). When they moved their website to a new ISP, www.hooked.net, they found that most of the parental-control software programs blocked it, since the site was a subdomain (that means it was located after the "/" following the top-level domain www.hooked.net/), and "hooked" was blocked as a drug term.

Some of the words typically chosen as keywords are "tobacco," "smoking," "wine," "drugs," "sex," "breasts," various vulgarities, and other descriptive terms and slang terms for sexual activities and organs. Unfortunately, unless your software has been programmed to block these words only when they are used in context with certain other trigger words, you may find it to be overly restrictive. Let me show you what happens (I made up these examples):

Blocked: "John, a young slave, looked down the *tobacco* road, wondering why he didn't have the freedom to keep walking until he found where he wanted to be."

Blocked: "Jim Carrey's movie *The Mask* proves that he's really *smoking*!"

Blocked: "Welcome to France . . . Enjoy this site and your tour of the *wine* country."

Blocked: "Parents of *sex*tuplets have problems coping with the workload."

Blocked: "Perdue's fresh roasted chicken *breasts* make preparing dinner much easier for working couples."

Blocked: "You can buy this comic book at your local *drug*store."

That's why you want a software that screens keywords only in context. That means the keywords are blocked only when they are used in combination with other words. (They also block using algorithms, but I won't bore you with an explanation of how that works. Just trust me.)

You should know, however, that certain adult sites have learned how the keyword blocking works and have started misspelling words commonly blocked by the filtering companies and parents. They'll use words like "penus," and begin words that correctly begin with an f with a ph. They may also add an extra k at the end of certain words. It's hard to argue that certain adult-site operators aren't seeking a younger audience along with the adult audience when they do things like this. (Of course, the explanation may be as simple as the fact that they just can't spell.)

Filtering graphics, sometimes the most inappropriate content for kids, isn't very easy, though. Unless the site also uses some of the filtered keywords, many sites with horrible graphics, such as child pornography, aren't filtered at all. Although the filtering companies are working on this, there aren't many satisfactory options yet. That's another reason that educating your children about what they should be viewing and what they shouldn't be viewing is so important.

Alerts

Some of the software lets you know when they're working by posting a notice when sites are blocked. Other programs block access but don't tell you that's why you can't access the site. I don't like that "stealth" feature.

Make sure your kids know what steps you're taking. The Internet is still too finicky for users to know that the reason they can't load the site is the software, rather than a problem on the Net. Your kids will spend lots of time trying to get it to work. Why frustrate them unnecessarily?

It's also a good lesson to them about what content is being blocked and why it might be blocked (another good opportunity to discuss values). If they still want to see whatever was blocked, first view the site alone, and if it's okay, let them access it, too.

Monitoring Access, with or without Blocking

Some of these programs keep track of where your kids have been. They give you a report of the sites your kids visit (and may also block access, depending on the product). It's the "fly on the wall" parents always wished they had.

Some products monitor everything, giving you a report of offending sites and language. Others do random snapshots of the screen. Some even let you know what your children say and do, word for word, as well as what is said to them.

Again, make sure your children know they're being monitored. It's a matter of respecting them and earning their trust.

Software That Works with
a Certain Online Service

Some blocking software works only with a specific online service (like AOL), while others work with all online services. Even though the most popular online services have their own parental controls (most use or are based on Cyber Patrol technology), you may want to customize the parental controls beyond what is offered by your online service. If you use ISP direct access, rather than an online service provider, you don't need this feature.

Software That Works Only
on an Internet Service

Many of the programs work only on an Internet service, like AT&T or Mindspring, but not on online services like AOL. Don't buy a program that is Internet-service-only if you use AOL.

Software That Works to Restrict Both
Online and Offline Computer Usage

Some programs control the amount of time and the hours of the day your child can access the Internet. These programs also often allow you to restrict how much time and the hours during which your child can play computer games or access certain files or computer drives. This can be a godsend for working parents who don't have child care for those few hours the children are home after school. It keeps them offline until a parent is around to supervise them. It may also keep them out of your financial programs and your personal files, as well.

Software That Is Customizable for
More Than One Child at a Time

Some products allow you to make different settings for different children in your household. Otherwise, you're back to your one-size-fits-all setting, where your fourteen-year-old has to live with the same controls as your six-year-old. The secret to successfully using parental controls is finding a fit for each child. If you have more than one child in the household, get a product that allows you to use different settings for each child.

Incoming Screening

This is an important feature. Many of the dangers are being home-delivered these days. E-mail messages can have HTML coding that links you directly to adult sites, and people who you don't want to reach your children can send them e-mail and other messages that you don't want them to receive. Incoming screening screens all inbound information, including e-mail, ICQs, and instant messaging. Once your kids are using e-mail on their own, this may be an important tool to help screen out undesirable information, like spam, and filter out certain e-mail senders or messages.

Outgoing Screening

If I had to choose one feature that is the most important feature to keeping children safe, this would be it. Outgoing screening prevents your children from sending anyone your telephone number, address, real name, or anything else you decide to block. It's particularly helpful when you are dealing with younger children, who might be fooled into disclosing the personal information you agreed shouldn't be disclosed. It also keeps them from being able to fill out most of the registration and survey forms that children's sites want them to complete. They'll need you to help them do that, which gives you control over what information these sites have about you and your children.

Actually, these work by adding your personal information to a key-word list. You have to be smart when you add the info to the list, and remember to list your phone number as both (111) 123-4567, 111-123-4567, and any other variation that your kids might use. But you should know that a child who wants to give out this information can circumvent this by telling someone in the chat that when they use the number "6" they really mean the number "4," and then convert their telephone number accordingly. If you think your child is likely to try this and you're worried about their trying to meet strangers from the Internet, consider a product that monitors everything they say online, such as Cyber Snoop or Disk Tracy.

Server-Level Blocking

Server blocking or filtering is when the parental controls are installed at the ISP or online service company level, not on your computer.

That way, you're blocking or filtering at the source. With server-level blocking, parents don't have to worry about updating lists or setting up the software either. Most server blockers, however, aren't customizable.

Bess

Bess is a server-based filter that is installed at your Internet access server. They claim to be used by more schools than any other filtering tool. Bess is purchased by your ISP and offered as the parental control, or is sold to schools or community access centers, which then run all Internet access through Bess's proxy servers. It doesn't require any installation, but it can't be customized by parents. It filters incoming and outgoing e-mail and newsgroups and prevents all access to chatrooms. It is the easiest of all the products to use, since, like parental controls on AOL, you need only to turn it on and it's working. There's nothing to configure.

Also, Bess is updated automatically, which allows Bess staff to update blocking for all its users quickly.

Filtered ISPs

Some Internet services offer only filtered access. Many are created by religious and special-interest groups. This is fine as long as you understand their biases and filtering criteria. Mayberry U.S.A. (www.mayberryusa.com) is a nonpartisan filtered ISP. I'll include a list of other filtered ISPs at familyguidebook.com.

Parental Controls from Your Online Services

Each of the online service providers offers some type of parental control feature for no additional cost. These range from children and teen-only areas and the ability to block e-mail and instant messaging features to providing Cyber Patrol (or its technology) for their members' use.

Kids Only and AOL's Parental Control

America Online (AOL) parents can restrict their children to their "Kids Only" forum or a teen's level of access, with prescreened content and monitored chatrooms. Parents can also prevent their children from receiving e-mail or instant messages, and may prevent them from entering chatrooms or accessing the Web. AOL also provides its members with Cyber Patrol technology at no additional cost. (Given how many families use AOL, I've included a description of their parental controls in Appendix 4.)

Strict terms-of-service enforcement has also helped AOL maintain a safer environment. (Remember when my account was closed for my daughter's friends' flaming match?)

Prodigy's Parental Control

Prodigy provides parents with the option of controlling access to its individual bulletin boards, chat areas, or newsgroups. Parents can also block complete access to the Web for certain users.

Prodigy offers kids and teens their own chatrooms, as well as special Web areas exclusively for them. Prodigy also makes Cyber Patrol available to its members. Within Prodigy's monitored chatrooms and public forums, users are prevented from posting items deemed unacceptable for children.

Prodigy's kids' online area is located at http://kids.prodigy.net. (Don't all rush there. It's viewable only by Prodigy members.) Prodigy has designed its kids area to appeal to kids of all ages.

MSN Child Protection

The Microsoft Network uses RSACi ratings. When you open your account, you can enable their "Content Adviser" to set a rating level.

MSN is a strong proponent of RSACi ratings, and uses them as a default setting in their Internet Explorer releases 3.0 and higher.

MSN doesn't have any special areas restricted only for children. But it does prescreen certain newsgroups based on their hard-core sexual content or the fact that they promote criminal activities, such as computer piracy or pedophilia.

A Little About Some Special Products

We selected four of the most popular brands of parent-control software currently on the market to review: Cyber Patrol, CYBERsitter, Net Nanny, and SurfWatch. We've also separately reviewed some special products—

those that just monitor activity online, and Web browsers and special desktops for children that also screen content or limit access to sites.

KidDesk Internet Safe

Edmark is a leader in the kids educational software. KidDesk is a special desktop that uses all the expertise Edmark has to offer children. Children can only send e-mail to people in the same house, such as siblings and parents. They can choose the look of their desktops, too. Parents can allow children to surf preapproved sites and to add sites to that list. Kids love it and parents trust it. That's a great combination. They have a free KidDesk lite, too. You can reach KidDesk and download their free KidDesk Lite at www.edmark.com/prod/kdis/download.

Surf Monkey

I love Surf Monkey, and so do kids. It has a special e-mail feature that allows parents to preview the e-mail before releasing it to their children. It can filter all but certain preapproved sites. Younger kids especially appreciate the Surf Monkey, an animated character that reads their e-mail out loud if they are unable or unwilling to read it themselves.

Some early problems arose because Surf Monkey was ahead of its time. You need a powerful computer to be able to use it without problems. They recommend a Pentium 133 or higher, but I recommend a Pentium 200 MMX or higher. But, if you have the power, there are few products like it. And families who try it agree, uniformly.

But I can talk all I want. The real reviews have to come from the "parents in the field" and their kids. Here are some examples:

> *Age 10½—boy:* "I liked using Surf Monkey. I have my own e-mail address with it. I like where you can vote for your favorite stuff. This week they had you vote for your favorite Pokemon. I can get to lots of great sites using this."
>
> *Age 7½—boy:* "I like the monkey talking to me. He helps me to know what to do. I can visit lots of cool places and find lots of fun things to do using this."
>
> *Age 9—girl:* "I love the monkey. He even can read my e-mail to me. I have my own special screen that is a launch pad, and very cool. I can chat, too, and my mom and dad let me chat there. But the reason I really like this is that it's just for me, just my size, and my parents let me use it all I want."
>
> *Mom:* "This browser is very good for young people just

learning to surf the net. Surf Monkey is there to help the children learn how to use the browser and Cybot is there to help the parents with the supervisor controls. They have lots of fun activities for the children on the home page, as well as allowing the child to get their own Surf Monkey e-mail address. Incoming and outgoing e-mails are screened for profanity. The parent can decide whether the child can receive e-mail or chat or not. This program will definitely stay on my computer until my youngest is old enough to move on to a regular browser."

What else it there to add? Only two things. You can download the product at www.surfmonkey.com, and believe it or not . . . it's free!

Surf Monkey has a new product—Surf Monkey "light." It's called the Surf Monkey Bar and, like Surf Monkey, it is free and available online. It's a toolbar, rather than a desktop and browser. It takes much less memory and power than regular Surf Monkey (and solves that power problem I mentioned). And it works with your existing Microsoft Internet Explorer 5.0. It can also be downloaded in just a couple minutes (if you've ever waited the eternity of software downloading, you know how terrific that is). It stays resident on the desktop, and can be set up to work for everyone or just the kids.

But, whether you choose the browser or the toolbar (or even their new kids website service), I have one thing to say. *Try it . . . you'll like it!* (With my apologies to Mikey. . . .)

ZeekSafe

ZeekSafe has a toolbar product, too. It resides on your desktop and filters out inappropriate sites using a proprietary software program. Approximately 100,000 sites are blocked by ZeekSafe. It's also free and easy to install. You can download it from www.zeeks.com.

ClickChoice myFilter

ClickChoice offers a new filtering product called myFilter. This free, downloadable software claims to monitor approximately 100 million Web pages and rates them as accessible to children (through age twelve), teens (through age seventeen), and adults, with an Adult(+) rating that gives full Internet access.

ClickChoice prescreens the webpages using filtering technology to discover webpages that contain possibly objectionable terms. Then their site reviewers (which they claim to number in the thousands) read the pages to properly rate their content.

The ClickChoice rating categories include pornography, profanity, pyrotechnics, hate speech/promotion, tobacco, alcohol, drugs, gambling, violence, and cult activity. This product can be downloaded for free (after supplying some demographic information) at clickchoice.com.

What's Coming Up?

Other new free and filtered browsers are being introduced after the writing of this book. One we think is promising is Crayon Crawler, which can be downloaded for free at www.crayoncrawler.com.

The Fly on the Wall: Monitoring Software

Disk Tracy, Kids Cam, and Cyber Snoop

These three products monitor everything your child says online. While two of the Big Four (CYBERsitter and Net Nanny) provide a monitoring feature giving a report of the sites your child has visited, these products give you a word-for-word report.

Disk Tracy and Cyber Snoop also have other features, like blocking and filtering.

Kids Cam works a bit differently. It takes a snapshot of the screen at certain intervals, giving that information to parents. While these products can give you information about what your kids are saying, most people I talk to feel they are overkill.

The 800-Pound Gorillas: The Big Four Multifeatured Products

Comparing the Products

The big four products are Cyber Patrol, CYBERsitter, Net Nanny, and SurfWatch. We thought you needed to know how well these products stacked up against each other and our test sites. So, we ran them through their paces.

How We Conducted Our Review and Testing of the Software

Throughout this book I have tried not to sound like a lawyer, but unfortunately I need to put my lawyer hat on for a moment or two. (I've

	Program	Cyber Patrol 4	CYBERsitter 99	Net Nanny 4	SurfWatch 3.0
Filter Updates	Frequency	Weekly	Weekly	Daily	Daily
	Ease	Automatic	Automatic	Automatic	One-button click
	Cost	3 mo. free	Free	Lifetime free	6 mo. free
Program	Security Features	2-level password	2-level password	3-level password	1 password
	Modes	Stealth or alert	Stealth only	Stealth or alert	Alert only
	Number of different users	9	1	12	1
Filtering Methods	Library categories	•Alcohol & tobacco •Questionable/ illegal and gambling •Sex education •Militant/extremist •Drug/drug culture •Satanic/cult •Violence/profanity •Partial nudity •Full nudity •Sexual acts graphics and text •Gross depictions •Intolerance	•Adult/sexually oriented •PICS ratings adult/violence •Hate/intolerance •Tobacco/alcohol •Guns/violence •Cults/occults •Gay/lesbian topics •Violent games •Gambling sites •Illegal activities/ drugs *CYBERsitter also offers optional filtering in an additional 14 categories.*	•Adult material •Gambling •Drugs/alcohol •Violence •Hate •Criminal acts •Pedophilia •Child pornography	•Drugs/ alcohol/tobacco •Gambling •Hate speech •Sexually explicit •Violence *SurfWatch also offers optional filtering in an additional 15 categories.*
	Outgoing information	✔	✔	✔	✘
Blocks and Filters	Website/URL/IP	✔	✔	✔	✔
	Keywords/phrases	✘	✔	✔	✔
	Word patterns	✘	✔	✔	✔
	Search engines	✔	✔	✔	✔
	Newsgroups	✔	✔	✔	✔
	Chat applications	✘ (except for IRC)	✔	✔	✔
	PIC ratings capable	✔	✔	✔	✔
	ICQ/IM	✘	✔ filters language or blocks entire program	✔ filters language or blocks entire program	✘
	E-mail	✘	✔ filters all text	✔ filters all text	✘
Other	Monitoring child's use	✘	✔	✔	✘
	Time controls	duration and certain hours	duration and certain hours	duration and certain hours	✘

always wondered what a lawyer's hat is supposed to look like—one of those wigs barristers wear on TV series imported from England?)

I want you to understand what the review and testing represents and what it doesn't. In order to do this, I've described the test settings and how results were obtained. Your experience may differ from ours.

Which Software We
Selected for Which Testing

We selected four different brands of child-protection software for the site-blocking and full-feature tests: Cyber Patrol (version 4.0), CYBERsitter 99, Net Nanny (version 4.0), and SurfWatch (version 3.0). All other products mentioned in the book have been tested and reviewed for the purposes mentioned in the book. (For example, if we talked about how well a monitoring software tracked usage, that feature was reviewed.)

We tried to select the most popular products, although many companies refused to disclose annual sales or sales to date. As far as we can judge, Cyber Patrol, CYBERsitter, Net Nanny, and SurfWatch are among the most popular. Of the four, Net Nanny has been on the market longest. It shipped its first product in January 1995. SurfWatch shipped its first product a few months later. SurfWatch claims the most users (approximately 3.5 times as many as its nearest competitor). Cyber Patrol, though, seems to have captured the online service market and is catching on with certain ISPs. SurfWatch seems to be doing the same with the kids market—filtered search engines and safe harbors and closed systems. Net Nanny's new product was just launched, although reviewed in advance for this book. It is so much better than its previous version that I suspect its sales figures to increase dramatically, and that it will cut into Cyber Patrol's and SurfWatch's industry markets.

How We Conducted Our Testing

In order to test each software product, we installed them according to the manufacturer's instructions and used the default settings (the ones that came with the software), rather than customizing the programs. Each was tested on the same Pentium 200 MMX machine, with 32 MB RAM and a 28.8 kbps modem. (Some product tests were double-checked on a Pentium 133 machine, with 24 RAM and a 28.8 kbps modem.) The computers all used Windows 95 as the operating system. The programs were installed one at a time, and uninstalled when the test was completed and before the next product was installed.

The same person conducted all the tests, with the exception of running some of the programs through the site lists to see which they blocked and which they didn't. Each software was tested against sites we selected at random based on their content. Eight categories of sites were preselected, which included a list of good sites that used certain trigger words like "sex," "drugs," et cetera, and seven categories of problematic content, like bomb building, alcohol, tobacco, hate, violence, sexually explicit, and satanic and cult. (A list of the sites used has been provided to the software manufacturers so that they can review those sites and take any action that they feel appropriate to either add them to their blocked-site lists or remove them from the blocked-site lists. I will also supply the list to any reader who requests a copy, in writing, and includes a self-addressed stamped envelope. All requests should be mailed to my attention, c/o McGraw-Hill, 11 West 19th Street, New York, NY 10011.)

In addition, random testing was done with each product, searching for offensive sites (including topics other than sexual content claimed to be blocked or filtered, using the default settings, like drugs and alcohol). We surfed using each software, testing its effectiveness with sites and links from those sites. The actual effectiveness rankings, however, were done only with the test sites.

Drumroll, Please!!! The Test Results: How the Big Four Performed

One of the biggest criticisms we hear about filtering and blocking software is that they block innocent sites—that is, they over-block. We tested the programs against a list of "good sites," to see how often they blocked innocent sites. All the products tested surprisingly well. Some didn't block any sites. Cyber Patrol blocked four, but two of these were the Go Ask Alice sites from Columbia University that were recommended by the American Library Association but were the subject of some controversy because of the language and subject matter of their frank sexual and drug-use discussions. These were probably blocked as a result of complaints received after the controversy arose.

It was especially interesting to me that two years ago, when I tested the same products (different versions, of course), they blocked a much higher percentage of innocent sites.

Of the four, Net Nanny and SurfWatch performed best, and didn't block any "good sites." CYBERsitter came in next, blocking only one (a drug-education site). Cyber Patrol blocked four, three on health education and one on drug education. But of the forty-five sites tested, very few were blocked.

I think their performance is indicative of the length of time they have been on the market and the breadth of experience they have. The longer they have been on the market, the higher up they have climbed on the learning curve. They've had more chance to interact with schools, librarians, and parents, and their ability not to block innocent sites is a direct product of their extensive experience. When filtering and blocking is concerned, it's less a matter of technology and more a matter of experience. And these are the most experienced products out there.

Next the products were tested to see how many "bad sites" in various categories were blocked. We tested them against a sample of bomb-building sites, alcohol sites, tobacco-product sites, hate sites, violence sites, sexually explicit sites, and satanic and cult sites. (And if the site had been removed prior to all products being tested against it, which occurred occasionally, it was removed from the sample for all purposes.) Here's how they performed in each of those categories (with the shaded statistics reflecting the best performance):

	CYBERsitter 99	Cyber Patrol Version 4.0	Net Nanny Version 4.0	SurfWatch Version 3.0
Bomb Building	5 out of 20	12 out of 20	7 out of 20	12 out of 20
Alcohol	0 out of 18	15 out of 18	0 out of 18	17 out of 18
Tobacco	2 out of 18	2 out of 18	0 out of 18	10 out of 18
Hate	6 out of 18	12 out of 18	11 out of 18	13 out of 18
Violence	4 out of 12	4 out of 12	6 out of 12	5 out of 12
Sexually Explicit	18 out of 19	17 out of 19	17 out of 19	15 out of 19
Satanic and Cult	5 out of 14	4 out of 14	7 out of 14	4 out of 14

What Does This Mean?

We selected a very small sample of sites to test the products against. We began with a sample of about twenty sites for each category, but several sites were either inaccessible or shut down between the time the sample was compiled and the testing was completed for all products.

This may not be indicative of how the products will perform on an

Internet-wide basis, but it is a good indication of which types of sites they block best. SurfWatch blocked the most sites in more categories than the others did. (Interestingly enough, SurfWatch blocked best in our tests two years ago for *A Parents' Guide to the Internet*, too.)

This testing is only a small sampling and may or may not be indicative of the results of a larger sampling. Other groups have conducted testing, and you might want to review those tests. Cyberangels has a list of approved filtering products—and their reviews of those products—at their site, www.cyberangels.org. We also have a very extensive list of products and our review of those products at www.familyguidebook.com and www.wiredkids.org.

But don't base your decision on our test results alone. All of the companies will provide a demo version, and we've listed all their web-sites (as well as linking to them) at www.familyguidebook.com. Try them out and decide for yourself.

Be careful, though, since both Cyber Patrol and CYBERsitter have informed us that their products do not work properly when installed on a computer that has another filtering product installed, even if only one is turned on. (Their product instructions, however, do not warn of such a problem. I have suggested that they add that warning.) That's why we conducted our tests by installing and uninstalling the products one at a time. We recommend that you do the same with your demos, if you want to shop around.

Choosing Your Comfort Level

Throughout this section, I've given you lots of information about your options, from straightforward parenting to technological fixes, and everything in between. In increasing levels of control, I've done a quick review of the types of protection parents can offer their children—from relying on trusting them and educating them to never letting them use a computer. As you gain more control, you need to realize that you also limit more information your children can access, both good and bad, and rely less on trust. In addition, the more you limit access to certain sites or services, the more choice you give up to third parties. (So it's important to make sure you agree with their choices.) That's the balance you'll need to strike. And it's your choice. But know that it's not engraved in stone, and you can and should make changes as your children get older, earn your trust, and have greater needs to access broader content for school.

In a nutshell, here are your choices.

Levels of Control and Protection
(in increasing levels of control and protection)

- Trust and education
- Home safe-surfing agreement (see Appendix 3)
- Encouraging use of child-friendly sites and supervising their surfing
- Tracking use and duration using software
- Filtered search engines
- Filtering and blocking at your desktop
- Server-level blocking, parental controls on online services, or a filtered ISP
- Limiting your children to child-friendly safe playgrounds online
- Limiting your children to child-friendly subscription services
- Locking the computer (or using a product that prevents online access) when you're not home
- Living in a computerless home and community

Note that there is no way to make sure your children are 100 percent protected—unless you choose to live computerless and make sure that your child's school, friends, and library don't have computers either. Since that is highly unlikely, and even more highly undesirable, recognize that everyone should be accepting some level of responsibility for safe surfing and sometimes things will get through that you wish hadn't. It's a risk we have to learn to live with—to minimize, but learn to live with nonetheless.

CHAPTER 9

And Now a Word from the Real Experts—The Teens and Kids

I speak to groups of students every week, and have been for three years now. As most of you parents and teachers can attest, whenever you talk (and listen) to kids, you're bound to learn something. Sometimes you can even learn something good.

I've included this chapter in the book to share some of what teenagers and kids have taught me. You might hear your child's voice in here, or the voice of one of their friends. To be able to craft an online safety solution for your family, you need to know what they are thinking. The best way to do that is to talk (and listen) to your own children. Reading this over with them might help them open up a bit.

This chapter is divided into four sections. The first section, "The Rules Don't Apply to Me," shows you what real teenagers have told us about what they do online, and the risks they take. These are from the survey we did with *Seventeen Magazine* online of almost eleven thousand teenage girls. The second section is "They Could Write This Book for Me." I'll share the safety tips the same eleven thousand teenage girls we surveyed gave us. The third section, "'Dear Mr. President,'" shares some thoughts from inner-city high school students about the Internet, and violence in schools and in the media. They might surprise you—they surprised me. The last section, my favorite, "The Teenangels," is about my Teenangels, a special group of teenagers who are being trained in online safety to act as ambassadors to schools around the country, to create online safety programs and train local teenagers to be online safety guides for their schools. They have shared their thoughts and their very own safety tips for teens, kids under ten years of age, and parents. Some of our younger "angels in training" have written their own abbreviated tips for children ten and under (in their own words, grammar glitches and all).

"The Rules Don't Apply to Me"

We did our first survey of students and families with the Baltimore County PTA, polling roughly six thousand families. We then followed up with a survey of the middle school students, asking them to share what they do and what they know about online safety. We also asked them to share the three safety tips they would give to a friend who hadn't yet been online. It was eye-opening, since by comparing their answers with what they tell others, we realized that they set different rules for others than they do for themselves.

One survey response, in particular, always comes to mind. Students were asked to write an essay telling a younger child important safety rules for using the Internet. Most students wrote that keeping one's name, address, and phone number private were important.

One seventh-grader wrote:

I think there are some rules you should know about:
(1) When you go into a chat room never ever give that person your name, address, or phone number *unless you feel safe.*
(2) Never ever agree to meet a person *unless you know their personal history.*
(3) Never ever, ever, ever, ever, ever, ever, ever, *go out of town* with a person that makes you feel you are in danger.

I added the italics to emphasize how kids look for loopholes. (I think they are all future lawyers in training.) And you might be interested to know that this particular seventh-grader said she had given out her *full* name, address, and phone number online.

The People Behind the Survey

In late 1998 I met (I actually only *virtually* met them, since we haven't met face-to-face but only online) two remarkable academics from the University of Southern Florida, Dr. Michael Berson and Dr. Ilene Berson. They, too, are experts in the field of online safety, and have written many of the leading articles and performed many leading studies in this area. We decided to collaborate on a series of surveys of teenagers themselves, and approached *Seventeen Magazine* online to host the survey for us. The results were remarkable, although they mirrored what I had been hearing for years.

The *Seventeen Magazine* Survey

About half of the group surveyed reported that they were fourteen or fifteen years old, and in ninth or tenth grade. A further 32 percent were evenly split between thirteen-year-old eighth graders and sixteen-year-old eleventh graders. All of them said they were girls. This is what we learned:

- Sixty percent have filled out a questionnaire or form online and given out personal information (name, address, date of birth, phone number, or school name).
- Twelve percent have agreed to meet in person with someone they have met online.
- Forty-five percent have told someone they met online personal information, such as their real name, age or date of birth, address, phone number, or school name.
- Sixty-one percent have received pictures from someone online.
- Twenty-three percent have sent pictures to someone that they have met on the Internet.
- Fifteen percent have received suggestive or threatening e-mail messages that have made them feel uncomfortable.
- Three percent have sent suggestive or threatening e-mail messages that have made them feel uncomfortable.
- Thirty percent have been in a chatroom where the discussion made them feel uncomfortable.
- Two percent have explored a bomb-building site on the Web.
- Thirty percent have read hateful messages on the Web.
- Fifteen percent have read messages on the Web that have threatened violence.

A vast majority said that their parents had discussed online safety with them (70 percent), with the next-largest percentage representing the number of teenagers who said that their teachers discussed online safety with them (35 percent). And about half the teenagers said that their parents sit with them occasionally when they are surfing, and check their screen occasionally or always, to see where they are surfing. About 60 percent of the teenagers reported that their parents, caretakers, or teachers discuss their online activities always or occasionally. One of the most interesting early correlations we discovered is that teens whose parents spent time surfing with them didn't engage in cybersex, while almost 60 percent of the teenagers in general reported engaging in cybersex (without defining what that means).

Also, 65 percent of the teens reported that their parents haven't installed filtering software, and another 20 percent didn't know if their parents had or not. More than 70 percent said their parents used the Internet at home.

More teens reported using instant messaging most (over 60 percent), with the closest other activity being surfing for new things (at 12 percent). (Only 1.5 percent reporting visiting game sites as what they did most, but a survey of boys probably would have disclosed a much higher percentage of gaming activities.)

When we asked them to explain if they had done anything online that they wouldn't have done in person, here's what they said (in their own words):

- "Yes, obviously people are more bold and outgoing on the Internet when they don't have to deal with the consequences of their actions."

- "Of course! All people do. A computer with a phone line is like a mask to the world. You can do or say anything and you won't ever have to meet this person. For instance, my little brother is 13 and he tells people he's 16 or older. He's a sweet guy and has a very high respect for females. Online, however, he says very cruel and suggestive things to and about them. He acts like a monster. It's disgraceful . . . and a little scary."

- "Yes, of course . . . our usual boundaries and personal walls are down and we can act more carefree and outspoken if we feel like. At least this is true for me . . . you can act like a goddess."

- "I have cursed out a lot of ppl [people], and when my bud comes over, we go into places like the African American room and yell "KKK ALL THE WAY" or go to the Jewish room and say "HEIL HITLER," but I haven't done that since I started going back to church and was saved by Jesus Christ. We were just joking, we weren't really racist."

- "Yes, but I'd rather not describe what I did. Instead, I'll just say that online, you can be absolutely ANYONE you want to be, which is why a lot of people do things that they would not normally do. In real life, people everywhere judge you based on your looks, actions, and who knows what else, but online, all that really matters is your attitude and personality."

- "Uh well, I tried cyber sex before and I wouldn't ever do that in real life. Sex period. I don't believe in premarital sex. I think that is a great gift you give your husband. I once told someone off because he/she was being perverted and talking nasty to me and I didn't like it."

- "Well, once I told this guy I met in a chat room all about me and, like, my phone number and stuff. I now realize that this was really stupid of me and will never do anything like it again cause although it's not likely, he could be a psycho or something."

- "I feel I can speak more freely to someone online about my problems because most of them don't go to my school or even the same state. I can ask them advice and they would probably give me the best because they aren't in favor of a certain person. I can introduce myself and meet new people because it isn't as uncomfortable to look into their eyes and if you become really uncomfortable I can just get out of it by blocking them or getting offline."

- "I have had cyber sex . . . that's something I never have done and never will do until I'm married in real life."

- "I am much more bold online than in real life. I am VERY shy and I say things on the Internet that I normally wouldn't say in public."

- "I have lied for no reason. Actually, I told a guy I couldn't give him my number cause my mom doesn't want guys calling me cause it was during the school year. My mom doesn't really care who calls me I just didn't know what to say."

- "Yeah, I wouldn't flirt with people I just met in person, unlike on the Internet."

- "Flirt more easily, say things I wouldn't say in person, not bad things, just more honest things."

- "Yeah, because it's a lot easier to talk and get to 'know' someone online because you can't see their face. I never have done anything bad but I've been a lot more easy going and free for what I'd say online then in a live situation which in someways have helped me to be more comfortable talking to new guys in person."

- "Well, honestly . . . yes. I had cyber sex! I will never have real sex until I am married, after I engaged in cybering, I totally felt grossed out, like I know I was doing something wrong! I will not make that mistake again."

When we asked them if they ever pretend to be someone else in cyberspace, here's what they answered (in their own words):

- "Of course I've pretended. Everyone does. You pretend to be older . . . or you pretend to be a guy . . . or you just pretend to be whoever you wanna be."

- "Yes, I just changed myself to be someone I wasn't because I wanted to get a different reaction from people. It gave me a way to see myself as who I wanted to be but by doing it I realized that that is not who I want to be and that I just want to be me."

- "Yes. If I am ever in a chatroom I always make up things about myself. This is why I say don't trust anyone because everybody else does the same thing."

- "Since nobody seems to be eager to talk to a 15 year old, I always pretended I was 18 year old female. However, that sometimes attracted bad attention from guys."

- "Yes. I pretended to be anyone from Leonardo DiCaprio to a serial killer."

- "I once pretended to be a 16 year old girl. I wanted to talk to my boyfriend to see if he would agree to meet her in person. He did and I told him who I really was and we broke up."

- "Yes, I've pretended to be so many people. It's fun and safe and because nobody knows who you really are."

- "Well we've ALL pretended to be older or have a different name or something. Who doesn't? It's part of the fun about being online . . . you can be whoever you want to be for a little while."

- "Yes, I pretended to be someone that I wish I could be like a popular person."

- "I haven't pretended to be someone else, but I have pretended to be a couple of years older than I am, because not many people my age are online to talk to, and if they are, they must be lying about their age, too."

- "No, I think it is wrong to lie to other people about who you are. I wouldn't want someone to do it to me so I don't do it to them."

When we asked them if they had ever been in a situation online that frightened them, here's what they said:

- "My friend agreed to meet a guy she met online when he came to our hometown, and she wanted some of us to come along to keep them company. I told my parents but luckily the guy's game got canceled. I wouldn't have gone and I would not support her decision to meet anyone in real life. She kinda felt betrayed but at least she's still alive."

- "Once I was scared because this guy kept telling me all this stuff about me, like my name, address, friends' names, etc. he said he knew where I lived and stuff, and I better watch out. It ended up being a joke from a friend of a friend, but I was still scared, and I was very angry at the friend who gave the person the info just to scare me. It wasn't funny."

- "Once I was on ICQ talking to a bunch of my friends when this guy I had been chatting with sent me a file. Unknowingly, I opened it and then I realized that the person had hacked into my system. Suddenly, my CD-ROM drive started opening and closing and annoying (but not threatening) messages started appearing on my screen. Soon after my mouse buttons switched functions. I had just finished a big assignment, so I was afraid the hacker would do something to wreck it. I shut down my computer and that was about all I did about it. One of my friends had a similar experience, only hers was scary and threatening. When she got hacked, pictures of a dead girl with her face smashed in appeared on her screen, along with threatening messages and sound clips."

- "I know this is normal in fact it doesn't bother me I just laugh. Most kids are always exposed to this stuff not just on the Internet so its no big deal in fact sometimes it makes it interesting. But one time this dude got really mad at me and he knew my parents were out of the state and he could have called one of my friends and found my address but instead he kept calling every 5 minutes. . . ."

- "There was one time, when I got online to check my e-mail. I ended up going into my regular chatroom, and when I arrived, some guy started giving out my personal information. I don't know how he knew anything personal about me, but he was telling everyone in there about the frightening and terrible things that were done to me as a child. My best friend doesn't even know what happened to me when I was little. All I did was, denied all of what he said and logged off. I cried all week long."

- "This guy IM'd [instant messaged] me and my best friend and he knew all this information about us . . . and we hadn't even talked to him before. He knew who we were, where we lived and everything and he kept playing with our minds trying to tell us that we started IMing him first and so on. I told my parents about it but they didn't really care. So this went on for an hour and a half. I had friends try to get him to stop. He told us where he worked and he kept insisting that we go places with him like out to lunch or dinner and he would buy us x-mas and b-day presents even though we had never met him. He would leave them on his car at work for us to come and get, we would go get them and just smash them all over the ground . . . thinking he would get the point. He was convinced that him and my best friend were dating then I came along and I'm the one who stopped it all. No one could get this guy to stop. We changed our screen names plenty of times but he had already hacked into our account so he could always find us. Well he hacked into mine. Well in December we got a new computer and we both changed our screen names and he hasn't been able to find us since."

- "[A]bout a year ago I met a guy online and I told him my phone # and found out he lived about 5 minutes away from me we talked 4 about a week then he asked me out and I agreed. We met up at the mall he was totally normal 15 year old guy. He wasn't some psycho or anything but I got in a lot of trouble from my parents and I will never give out any personal information again. It's not safe and its a stupid idea. If anyone who reads this is thinking about giving out info to someone on the net PLEASE think twice about it you could get yourself into a lot of trouble."

- "I received a threatening E-mail from someone on my E-mail address. I immediately changed my password, and made sure that I didn't have information on my profile. I never E-mailed the person back, since that is what lets them know your account is active and they can find out more about you. Then, I decided to make sure about it, and stopped checking my E-mail account. I just got a new one."

- "I was in a chat room once and this person was threatening to kill themselves, and I find that scary. So I IM'd them not to do it, and I chatted with them for a while, and made them feel better about themselves, and promise not to do anything drastic. And they did promise."

- "I told these people to leave this foreign guy alone because they were making fun of him. They were calling him names and mocking everything he said. The people I got smart with told me I better watch my back because they could find out where I lived. That's why I left."

It would be interesting to ask your children to reply to the same questions. You might learn something about your children you didn't know.

They Could Write This Book For Me . . .

Most teenagers and even younger children know most of the online safety rules.

Here's a list written by my little angels in training, who are nine and ten years old, Alyssa, Lauren, and Maggie.

Alyssa's, Lauren's, and Maggie's Safety Tips (in their own [uncensored] words)

1. Always ask your parents before you use the Internet.
2. Never give out your information or your name, address, phone number, school, or parent's name.
3. Don't lie about your age so you can go to a site on the Internet.
4. Don't buy anything without your parent's permission or if they are not there.
5. Never use bad language or you could get kicked off the Internet and never be able to go on again.

6. Don't ever open or answer any e-mail from people you don't know.

7. Never send a picture on the Internet to anyone you don't know.

8. Never ask to meet a person in real life you met on the Internet.

9. If somebody says he is a manager of 'N Sync and you get free tickets and signed stuff and asked you if you wanted it say "no" because it could be a lie or maybe he could be a scum bag.

10. If someone says there is a sale at the GAP and they need your address and phone number always say no.

11. Be careful of bad people on the Internet or you definitely will get hurt.

12. If someone is disobeying the rules, ignore them!

13. Never believe anyone if they tell you how old they are. Even if you think you can ask them questions only a kid would know the answers to, it doesn't prove they're really a kid.

14. Tell your parents if anything goes wrong.

Maggie's Advice

Maggie also wanted parents to know how she feels about them snooping into kids' e-mail and invading their privacy.

1. If you have your child's password, don't snoop around in their e-mail.

2. If you want to check their e-mail go through it *with* them.

She also wrote a letter on behalf of all kids to their parents that she wanted to share.

Dear Mom and Dad:
I know all of the rules for safety online. I know that there are people out there who might want to hurt me. But don't worry, they won't catch me off-guard. Safety is important but I don't feel comfortable with you reading my mail unless you tell me first. I also want you to know that I know a lot of the rules for online safety. Here are some of the ones I would tell a friend that

has never been online before: Don't talk to strangers. Don't download anything without your parents permission, it might have a virus. Hopefully you can trust me now.

> Love,
> Your Son/Daughter

And my little angels in training aren't the only ones who know the rules. The teens responding to the *Seventeen Magazine* online survey also know the rules about staying safe online.

When we asked the teenagers we surveyed for *Seventeen Magazine* online to give us tips they would give to a friend who hadn't been online before, here's what they said:

- "NEVER give out personal information such as your name, address, phone number, e-mail address, password, school name etc. to ANYONE online."

- "If someone is making you feel uncomfortable don't talk to them. Someone may try to take advantage of you."

- "Don't meet someone you met online unless you go with a friend or parent or someone like that. If you don't and the person you are meeting turns out to be bad there won't be anyone there to help you."

- "Be careful. Be careful. Be careful. . . . You may never know who is on the other side."

- "Granted there are a lot of nice people online but there are a lot of weirdos too. Why take chances? If you play with fire sooner or later you will probably get burned—at any age but especially if you are a teenage girl."

- "Don't do what you are not supposed to."

- "People aren't always what they seem to be."

- "DON'T take everything people say seriously; they could be anyone."

- "Never open any e-mail unless you are certain you know who it's from."

- "I would tell them never to agree to meet someone somewhere (in person), and if they feel pressured, threatened, or uneasy by something someone is saying/typing (online) to them, then to stop talking to that person, and if they need to disconnect the Internet for a little while. (Until the person is most likely offline.) If that person still bothers them, then they should block them. (Some Internet providers can do that for you.) I would tell them those things so that they are safe, and don't get kidnapped or something like that, or get hurt in any way if somebody they met online finds out where they live and is a stalker or something."

- "Never give anyone your address because you don't know for sure if the person you are talking to is really that dreamy 18 year old you're picturing in your head or if he's a serial rapist looking for his next victim."

- "Don't be afraid to put people on your ignore list or not respond to their e-mails."

- "Be careful about what you say, because it can be traced back to you."

- "Do not send pictures of yourself to anyone because they can easily send them anywhere or to anyone."

- "Don't fight with people, because they can find you and you will be sorry."

- "Don't give out any information that you wouldn't want published in a national newspaper."

- "Make sure you know what you're talking about when you're talking to a person you have never met."

- "Don't let people online manipulate you, after all you don't even know them."

- "Don't give out too much information. It's amazing how easily someone can find you."

- "Delete offensive e-mails."

- "Have fun and don't take anything seriously unless it's a threat and you think the person is capable of carrying it out."

- "I would tell them that if people start getting weird to block them, do not tell people too much of their personal information, and to read what a website is about before it is entered. I would do this because I care for my friends and I don't want anything to happen to them."

- "Download to a disk, NEVER to your computer, unless you are certain the information is secure and doesn't contain viruses."

- "Be wary of going to sites and getting things that may cost money, read fine print, don't agree to anything unless you know the facts. Some websites require fees to use them so check!"

- "Don't ever meet anyone!! My best friend did and it broke her and her mom's trust and she snuck him into her room and he had drugs and stolen stuff on him!!"

- "Steer clear of people with alcohol names in their name and drugs cause they usually do that stuff and I'm not into it."

- "Don't go into chat rooms at all cause you never know what will happen. It's really flattering having a guy tell you he likes you online, but he doesn't even know you and most of the time all they want to do is have cyber sex."

- "Don't download off anything and don't open strange e-mail messages from people you don't know."

- "Don't open any mail with 'attachments' because it could be a virus, pornography, or other. . . ."

- "Never talk to someone on the Internet that makes you feel uncomfortable because it's dumb and it does count as harassment even though it's online."

- "I would show them how to block IM's in case they get one that upsets them, show them how to report people, and tell them certain sites not to go to if I had been there and knew the reputation of the site."

- "Have fun but don't get obsessed."

- "DON'T ASK FOR TROUBLE!"

See? I told you they could write this book for me!

"Dear Mr. President"

A short time after the Littleton tragedy, I spent several days speaking with inner-city high school students from the Norman Thomas High School in Manhattan as part of a joint program between Cyberangels and the Vanderbilt YMCA. Few of the students attending the sessions used the Internet, and having a computer with Internet access at home was very rare among these students.

The groups ranged from ten students to more than 150 at a time. I estimate that I spoke with approximately six hundred students, from fifteen to eighteen years old. They were a very diverse group, including most ethnic and minority groups, and roughly half boys and half girls. Some were more articulate than others, while some were more reluctant to share their thoughts. But most of them opened up and told me what they thought—about Littleton, about the media, and about solutions and taking responsibility for your actions.

I was very impressed with how well thought out their comments were. Many of their responses, especially the ones about building bombs, were surprising, as were the ones about filtering content and enforcing the movie ratings. I was very impressed with what they had to say and how well they said it. Our future is in good hands. This is what they wanted to share with President Clinton concerning the summit on teen violence he held in Littleton's wake. Although this is obviously written in my words, the opinions and positions are theirs.

We believe that there is no one person or thing to blame for what happened in Littleton, Colorado. Better communication, attentive and caring parenting, more understanding and tolerance by classmates, and less easily accessible information about bomb building might have made this less likely, but we believe that no one is to blame. The shooters, ultimately, are the ones who are responsible for their own actions.

We worry that the attention given to school violence will be short lived. Following well-publicized tragedies in schools, everyone focuses on school safety and violence-prevention programs. Yet, a few months later, it's business as usual. We want to make sure that the attention remains focused on this issue and no other children have to die before we find solutions. We should keep trying various strategies until we find one that works.

It is sad that so many people focus on inner-city youth when talking about violence in schools. Our schools are equipped with metal detectors and armed guards. Yet the tragedies and mass killings in schools have come not from the inner cities, but from the suburbs and rural areas of this country. We believe that we should examine why youths who are in danger may not be the subject of scrutiny, given their more affluent suburban locations, while we are. But hindsight is always twenty-twenty. We think that this kind of thing happens more often in rural or suburban environments, and wouldn't happen in the inner city because we are too busy doing other things. These plots are staged when teenagers have too much idle time on their hands.

We believe that all schools should be equipped with metal detectors and armed security guards. Although not a guarantee against violence in schools, these can deter armed students. But helping students handle anger and find alternatives to violence should be the main thrust of any violence-prevention campaign. Students should be taught that guidance counselors are here to listen, and can be a significant help to troubled and hurt children. More money should be spent in developing counseling programs that not only receive children in need but reach out to them.

We think we understand who in our school is likely to act out violently more than even our school officials do. But even we cannot sort out empty threats from credible ones. While many of us believe that setting up a hot line might be helpful, most of us believe that we wouldn't use it. Most of us would turn to our school or law-enforcement representatives to report threats, not to our parents. However, we are concerned about confidentiality and are willing to report potential violence and threats only if given anonymity. We are seriously concerned about retribution. But we also fear our tips will not be taken seriously. While not all of us are afraid, many of us are.

Some of us use the Internet, most of us play computer games (many of us play Doom, and have for many years), and all of us go to movies and watch TV. We think that bomb-building websites should be outlawed. We don't think that there is any reason that this information should be readily available. Many of us think that if we could access this information easily, we would try to build a bomb just to see if we could. While we appreciate that this information is also available in libraries, we don't think that books teaching this should be banned. We also doubt that many teenagers would go to the bother of researching this information at the library. Its ready availability is the problem. Some of us are concerned about our younger brothers and sisters accessing adult sexual sites. Some also believe that adult sites should be password-protected. Those of us who don't believe that bomb-building sites should be banned believe that access to those sites should be restricted to adults, and also password-protected. Although we appreciate free speech, we believe that certain things should be controlled.

We believe that content selection should be made at the parent or school level, not the government level, and are willing to have our parents install parental controls or filtering software programs. We are uncomfortable, however, with monitoring software that would allow us access to all of the Internet but report our surfing activities to our parents. That feels too much like an invasion of our privacy. But we recognize that with younger children, monitoring software might be useful.

We play video games for fun. The fact that the target is a person means nothing. Any target would be the same. We don't believe that it desensitizes us from killing other human beings. We do not believe that video games or computer games can promote violence in older kids or teenagers. Many of us (especially many of the girls) think that younger children, however, can learn violent and harmful behavior by being exposed to these games. Many fear that parents just don't care about which games their children play, and that violent games purchased for older teens might be used by their younger siblings without restriction. We think that there should be age-appropriate guidance on violent games. Some of us even believe that parents and students should be compelled to sign an acknowledgment of the fact that the games they purchase contain substantial violence and should be restricted to teenagers over sixteen or eighteen years of age.

We don't believe that movies promote violent behavior. But we are happy that movies are rated, and believe that violent movies should be restricted to those over sixteen or eighteen. But apparently the ratings aren't seriously enforced. Rarely are any of us asked to prove that we are old enough to purchase tickets for an R-rated movie. We believe that the age-appropriate ratings should be strictly enforced. It is interesting to note that those of us who went to see the movie *Matrix* since the Littleton tragedy were all required to show identification proving our age, no matter which movie theater we attended. Perhaps this is a good sign. We don't think that TV is too violent.

We think that children are receiving far too little guidance from their parents. Parents too often want to be their child's friend, not their parent. We respect, need, and want guidance from our parents, and are willing to accept restrictions on our activities as long as they are consistently imposed all along. It's too late to wait until we are sixteen and older.

Some of us have been fortunate enough to receive lots of love from our parent, or parents. We receive "stress" from them too, but that is how we learn from them. Our parents should be teaching us right from wrong. But those of us who have not had a good relationship with our parent(s) cannot find any basis for blaming our parent(s) for our inappropriate activities.

We can get very angry, but we have learned to control our anger in many cases. We get help from our friends, listen to music, take showers and baths, cry, exercise, and sometimes take our anger out on our friends. While some of us act out violently sometimes, we would never dream of shooting down classmates. Many times we recognize that we have the capacity for serious anger, but have turned away from serious violence because it wasn't in our "hearts." We would like more programs that can help us control our anger, communicate better, and find alternatives to violence.

We think that there should be better gun controls. We also think that adults should listen to us more often and listen more closely to what we have to say.

Last, but not least, a few of us couldn't understand how suburban teenagers who drive BMWs and have everything they could ever want to own could be so unhappy with their lives. We are beginning to see that perhaps money and privilege aren't the root of all happiness.

We know you are busy, but hoped that you would take a few minutes to listen to what we have to say. If you ask us, we might be able to forge solutions together.

Signed,
The Teens

The Teenangels

Teenangels was born as a result of a TV special I did in April 1999 with ABC News, in New York. The special was about teen girl safety, and I was asked to be the Internet safety guru for the special. Part of the special involved me speaking to teenaged girls at a school in New Jersey. When the computer connection predictably broke down, the girls just lined up at microphones and fired off questions. That was when I first realized that teenagers were concerned about their younger siblings, cousins, young neighbors, and kids they baby-sit for when it came to online safety.

I was also thrilled to be teaching online safety pointers to people who really understood the risks, and how to tell the real dangers from the merely annoying things online.

Five of these girls were selected by their school to work with me in developing the first teenager online safety ambassador program for the Wired Kids project. The girls range in age from fifteen to seventeen and named themselves Teenangels after a program started by Cyberangels.

Then they began training. Over their summer vacation, giving up hot days at the beach and summer jobs to devote their time to this mission, they worked closely with me to learn about online safety. Sitting in my conference room, they had online safety drilled into them, and gave me the challenge of my career—questioning why things were dangerous, and wanting to know how dangerous they were. The teens were solution-based and very concerned about making sure that all children have access to the computer. When asked why they are devoting so much volunteer time to this effort, they unanimously respond that it's so parents aren't afraid to allow their children online. One of the Teenangels said that having access to the Internet used to be a benefit, but now if a child doesn't have access, he or she is at a *serious* disadvantage.

They have met and worked with the FBI's Innocent Images Unit operatives, a New Jersey State Police Cybercrime Task Force detective who was instrumental in finding the person charged as the Melissa virus creator and Net Nanny creator, Gordon Ross. They will be training with other key experts in this area, as well, like Net Nanny's creator, Gordon Ross, the National Center for Missing & Exploited Children, U.S. Attorney Lynne Battaglia (District of Maryland), the Department of Justice, the Federal Trade Commission, the U.S. Customs Cybersmuggling Unit, the New York Attorney General's office, top local cyber–law enforcement agents, like Leanne Shirey at the Seattle Police Vice Squad, executives of the American Library Association, and B. Keith Fulton, Director of Technology Policy of the National Urban League, among others.

Following their initial training they wrote several safety tip lists on their own, one for kids ten and under, one for teens, and one for parents. I would grill them and encourage them to think about things, but the tips were their own. And every time they learned more, the tips were refined. Finally, the Teenangels had a list of tips that they were happy with, and I agreed.

The Teenangels tip lists will become the first of many offline projects designed to teach parents, teens, and younger children about the benefits and risks of the Internet, and how to manage those risks, and will be printed and distributed to schools and sponsored events, as well as be made available at computer retailers and children's retailers, at no charge.

Their second project will be a video, produced by the FBI at their Quantico television studios, where we will teach other kids and teens about online safety and how to avoid the real dangers (cyberpredators) in cyberspace.

They take their show "on the road" by teaching other teenagers how to teach others about online risks. As online safety ambassadors, these girls will help other local school online safety guides build a huge network of cyber-savvy kids who will, in turn, teach others. They will also develop an online program, where children and teenagers who want to join them in the Wired Kids online safety initiative can take an online safety class right from the site, using streaming video and entertaining media interactions. We'll encourage schools across the country to join forces by developing online safety programs and websites. Like the Energizer Bunny, we hope this program will keep going . . . and going . . . and going!

The girls can be reached through me.

From the Mouths of Teens (the Real Experts) . . . Teenangels' Tips for Parents, Teens, and Kids

Teenangels' Tips for Parents

1. Make sure that your child does not spend an excessive amount of time online/on the computer. Use your own discretion when setting guidelines. It is impossible to provide an exact time limit for use of the Internet. Based on school days vs. weekends, age of child, and use for the Internet, time limits will vary. An average of one to two hours per day is probably most appropriate. However, there are always exceptions. Use your judgment in deciding what is best for your child.

2. People, not computers, should be your child's best friends and companions. Help them find a balance between computing and other activities.

3. Keep the computer in the family room, kitchen, or living room, not in your child's bedroom. Check the screen from time to time to make sure that they are viewing appropriate material. However, you should try building trust with your

child, hoping that they have the good judgment to know right from wrong.

4. Learn enough about computers so that you can enjoy them together with your kids. (Your children may be the most affordable computer specialist you can persuade to do house calls.) Don't be afraid to learn something from your kids. However, you are the parent and you must also teach your child. It is a two-way street. Know your child's experience with the computer, and exactly how extensive their knowledge of the Internet is. You'd be surprised at how much they know and how much they can teach you.

5. Be aware of the sites your children visit, and the chatrooms they go into. As they get older, trust should build. Encourage discussions between you and your child about what they enjoy online. Always be open. Take time and visit some of these sites that they enjoy (if the children are younger).

6. Make sure that your children feel comfortable coming to you with questions. When things go wrong, don't overreact. Let them know that it's not their fault. Educate yourself on what to do when things do go wrong.

7. IRC, or Internet Relay Chat, is a chat program that is very different from America Online. IRC has no terms of services like AOL, so people can talk about whatever they want and are generally not restricted. This is good and bad. It is good because its users can speak freely about whatever they want. It is bad because your children are not protected from obscenity and pedophiles. An AOL user could have their membership suspended or terminated for using obscene language, flaming, or stalking, but an IRC user could not. Some channels on IRC have channel rules, but this is the exception. That's why it is not recommended that parents let their children use IRC unless they are directly supervised.

8. Remember to monitor your children's compliance with your rules, especially when it comes to the amount of time your children spend on the computer. Be clear about your rules. Once you have discussed them with your children, you may want to post them on the computer or in another place near the computer where they can read them while they surf. It will help them remember.

9. Get to know your child's "online friends" just as you get to know all of their other friends. Ask about who is on their buddy list and whom they talk to most frequently. This way you get a feel for whom they are talking to.

10. Warn your children that people are not always what they seem to be. Discuss this with them and be open. Parents and children can both be teachers. By having open discussions about safety, dangers, advantages, and disadvantages, you and your child can learn from each other.

11. Teach your children to exercise good judgment in cyberspace, just as they do offline. It is just like taking your child to their first day of school. You can't always be there with them. But you can hold their hand along the way. The same applies on-line. "Hold their hand" by becoming educated, being open, building trust, and, most important, learning to let go.

12. Don't deprive your child of the Internet. Acknowledge the benefits of the Internet and review these advantages with your child. It used to be that a child with a computer and the Internet had a great advantage over those without these tools. However, as technology has become dominant, those without are now at a disadvantage.

13. To prevent your computer's hard drive from getting damaged, you should purchase or download antivirus programs frequently. Viruses come out practically every day, so we recommend you update your antivirus programs as often as possible. Some good programs are McAfee and Norton.

Remember that a parent is not a bad parent because they do not know everything about computers, but they can become a better parent by keeping the lines of communication open, and sometimes this involves learning from their child.

Teenangels' Tips for Teens

1. Never give your password out. If someone gains access to your password they can read your mail, buy stuff with your credit card information, and obtain personal and identifiable information. They can change your profile, play pranks using your name, and possibly get you kicked off your service. They can also change your password and lock you out of your account. Choose a password that is easy for you to remember

but cannot be easily guessed. You may want to change your password frequently, at least once a month (but make sure you write it down so you don't forget). Be careful if someone is watching you enter your password—they may look over your shoulder and steal it. He/she who controls the password controls everything.

2. Never give out any information that will allow someone to find you offline. Information such as the school you attend, the teams you are on, the place where you work, your address, your telephone number, or your detailed description when linked with other information can help someone find you if they are looking very hard. Be careful where else you put information that is publicly accessible, such as school and personal websites, friends' websites, profiles, and ICQ registries. Don't use your full name online (first and last). You may even want to be careful before you use your real first name. Your name, when linked with other information, can allow someone to find you.

3. When choosing a screen name, you should consider not using your whole or part of your real name. Don't choose one that is provocative (flirtatious, vulgar, etc.). You should choose a screen name that is easy to remember.

4. Make sure that you have an antivirus program. Your program is only as good as how frequently you update it, since new viruses are spread around every day. You should also have a utility or first-aid program that checks all your files for defects and viruses. Be careful not to delete any programs or files that you need.

5. Never meet people in real life whom you meet on the Internet. If you insist on breaking this rule, make sure that you tell someone you trust whom you are meeting and any information that you know about this person. If you don't feel comfortable telling someone this person's personal information, you might want to seal the information in an envelope and tell someone to open it only if you are not home by a specific time. Tell someone you trust where you are going and when. Before you go, talk to this person on the phone, and maybe have your parents speak to their parents. When you call, make sure that you block your phone number from caller ID (by dialing *67) or call from a pay phone. Talk

to a friend and have them look at some of your conversations to see if they pick up on anything misleading that you missed. Make sure that you meet in a very public place. Bring along someone that you trust (preferably an adult) and keep your first couple of meetings to a minimum. When you leave, don't go straight home; go to another public place and make sure that you are not being followed. Don't be afraid or embarrassed to say no.

6. Never open e-mail with an attachment from an address that you don't know. It may contain a virus or worm that can destroy your computer. Never download anything from someone you don't know or an unreliable source. If you receive an attachment from someone you do know, make sure you run it through an antivirus program. If you get a regular e-mail from someone you don't know, just delete it; don't reply to it, because it could be from a hacker. Delete chain letters and spam. Do not forward chains or "tracked" letters, because they are fake.

7. Be smart; apply common sense and good judgment. Don't let down your guard and become infatuated with people you meet online. Don't break the rules for someone. If someone seems too good to be true, they usually are. Always remain in control of the situation.

8. If you think that you are being harassed or stalked, never reply to the harasser. Make sure you let an adult know what's going on. And if you're really afraid, report it to the police.

9. Just because someone gives you their personal information or sends you an e-mail, it doesn't mean that you have to send one back, or give them your information. You are always in charge. If someone is bothering you, just sign off. You don't have to tell anyone anything that you don't want to.

10. It's easy to become addicted to or obsessed with the computer and Internet by spending too much time online. Try to maintain a healthy balance between cyberland and the real world. Remember, the Internet is a great place for learning and talking to people, but as a teen your social life shouldn't revolve around the Internet.

11. Follow chat rules. Know about the chatroom before entering

(is it moderated? what's the topic? what are the terms of service?). Before you start using the chat service, find out where you should report abuses. If you are using IRC, make sure that it's a safe server with safe topics, and know the rules. Know and follow proper Netiquette. Don't use offensive, vulgar, or provocative language. Don't get involved in flame matches. If something makes you uncomfortable, leave the room. If someone is doing something wrong, save the text, print it out, and report it to TOS (the people who enforce the rules). If you break the rules, be prepared to face the consequences: You risk getting a raised warning level, and/or having your service terminated.

12. Use common sense and trust your instincts. If you hear threatening remarks, threats made about bombs and guns, ALWAYS print the screen and make sure that you tell someone right away. If someone is threatening your school or your town, notify your school and/or local law enforcement. If your school doesn't have a report system, volunteer to set one up.

13. If you know a person who is dangerous to themselves, you, or someone else, tell someone. Everyone needs someone that they can go to. Even if you're not comfortable going to a college admissions–type counselor, you should talk to someone you trust who can help. While you may want to talk to them and help them yourself, you should be aware that you are just a teenager and cannot handle the weight of someone else's problems by yourself.

14. Don't believe everything that you read, hear, or see online. Advertisements may be misleading. You never know whom you are talking to or if they are telling the truth. Always remember that you just see a name on the screen. You don't know the person behind the computer on the other end. Just as people may not be honest in real life, they may not be honest online either. Websites can say anything, even if it is not true, and it can be very difficult to tell the difference. Websites may even dispense invalid or prejudiced information. Use your common sense while on the Internet. It is your best tool in recognizing wrong information from right information.

15. If you are threatened by a hacker, turn the computer off and

wait before going online again. Be careful whom you befriend online. If you are friends with a hacker, be extra careful, because they can really mess up your computer if you ever get mad at one another. Make sure you never trust anyone too much with your personal information, especially your password, because people you call friends can use it against you.

16. Be a smart consumer online. Though buying and trading online may seem like the easiest means of shopping available, you must take caution when using a credit card online. Make sure that the source is truthful and valid. Don't be foolish with your credit card or your parents' credit card (if they choose to let you use it). Never give your credit card information to any site that is not secure or where your information can be obtained by an unwanted third party. If possible, buy or trade with a well-known vendor.

Teenangels' Tips for Kids (10 and Under)

1. You've heard your parents say, "Don't talk to strangers." The same rule should be used when you are chatting online. Don't talk to people you don't know online unless you know them offline. Remember, people online are not your friends, just people you chat with. Here are some kid-safe chatrooms:

   a) Freezone.com

   b) Headbone.com

   c) KidsCom.com

   d) Surf Monkey chatrooms (available from the Surf Monkey Web browser)

   e) Noodles.com

   f) Cyberspacekids.com

2. Just as your parents tell you not to spend too much time in front of the TV, you shouldn't spend a lot of time on the computer. To grow up healthy and strong, kids need lots of exercise. Make sure that you spend time exercising, going outside to play, and being with your friends. Make sure you don't spend so much time online that it interferes with your other activities (homework, friends, clubs, sports teams, etc.).

You should see real clouds rather than those on the Windows desktop.

3. If a stranger walked up to you on the street and asked for your personal information, you wouldn't give it to them. The same rule applies online. Don't reveal any information about who you are, or anything that can identify you. We don't recommend filling out profiles, either! Don't tell anyone online your name, where you live, what your phone number is, what school you go to, the name of your school's team, et cetera. Remember, it only takes a little information to find out a whole lot about you. When you fill out a profile, make sure you keep it simple and don't reveal too much information about yourself. Strangers can easily access these, too.

4. You don't have to talk or respond to everyone who e-mails you or sends you an instant message. Don't think it is rude or impolite to ignore them. If you receive something that makes you uncomfortable, tell someone, and if you're in a chatroom, leave immediately. If you receive a disturbing e-mail or IM, print it out and/or save a copy and tell your parents or a teacher. Remember that it's not your fault and that you didn't do anything wrong to receive the bad messages.

5. Just as you have manners at the dinner table and in everyday life, you should be polite online. Being polite in cyberspace is learning and acting out the rules of Netiquette. Know the rules of whatever area you are in and try to follow them. Don't be rude to other members or people who are new to the Internet, don't type in all caps (it's online shouting), don't spam (send the same message over and over), don't ever get involved in or provoke flaming (online fights). Know good Netiquette. You should always respect other people. Don't do or say anything online that you wouldn't in real life. Don't take flaming personally—people are going to say stuff that isn't very nice, so just ignore it.

6. Do you open mail that is not addressed to you or that is from someone you don't know? Even if mail from an unknown source is addressed to you, the person sending it probably doesn't know your age or who you are. They may be sending you junk mail that you don't need or want. Likewise, don't open any e-mail or download anything from people you don't know, because it may contain viruses. Viruses can destroy

your computer and are a pain to deal with. Check with your parents before you download anything. Don't ever reply to mail from an unknown source. You don't talk to strangers in real life, so why would you read mail from them online?

7. Don't ever reveal your password to *anyone* (except your parents), not even to your best friend. Whoever has your password can change your profile, your account, your password, et cetera. People can then access your private information, such as your full name, address, phone number, or credit card information.

8. You may trade baseball cards or clothes with a friend. You may go to the store with your parents and buy something to eat. However, you don't usually trade things with people you've never met, and you probably don't buy things without your parents' permission. Likewise, kids should not be trading or buying things over the Internet no matter how good the offer may seem or the product may look—you never know if the other person is for real, if they are telling the truth, or if they really have the thing you want to buy. Don't do anything or click on anything that may cost money without your parents' permission and supervision. Never give out your parents' credit card information.

9. If I told you that the sky was green, that money grew on trees, or that I was Elvis, would you believe me? Chances are, you'd be smart enough to know that I was lying and you'd probably ignore me. Sometimes, however, it's not as easy to tell whether or not someone is lying. Therefore, don't believe everything you hear, read, or see on the Internet. Advertisements may not be true. Websites are easily made to fool you—they can be misleading and contain information that is wrong or prejudicial. You don't know whom you are talking to or if they are telling the truth. Remember, you just see a name on the screen—you don't know the person behind the computer on the other end. Just as people may not be honest in real life, they may not be honest online either.

10. I'm sure you've heard about the Colorado shooting and the Oklahoma City bombing. Though you may think this can never happen to you, it can. In fact, it is possible that you will receive scary threats of bombs, guns, or suicide. Never take these as a joke. They are very serious! If you EVER find

anyone sending or making threats, threatening to commit suicide, or talking about bombs or guns, make sure you tell your parents or teacher immediately. You could save everyone!

11. You shouldn't be joining mailing lists or subscribing to anything without your parents' permission and supervision. If you do join a list, and you are asked for your phone number or address, make one up. There's no reason for them to know your personal information if everything they send you is over the Internet. If they need to contact you, they can send you an e-mail.

12. When you are mad at your parents, not happy at home, mad about school, feel like complaining, or you have had a fight with your friends, you should go to an older sibling, a family member, a friend, or a teacher. The Internet may not be the best place to vent your feelings. There are also helplines that you can call to talk to someone about serious problems.

13. If someone asks for your picture, just tell them that you don't have a scanner or you don't have a picture. You shouldn't be sending your picture over the Internet.

In Conclusion

I thought I'd let the Teenangels close the discussion. Here's what they want you and your teens and younger children to know:

Parents . . .
Don't be afraid of the Internet. It's an extremely useful tool and can't be dismissed because it is new and sometimes confusing. The Internet can be an excellent way for you and your children to bond and share a common interest. Be open with your kids and get involved. Most of all, learn all that you can about being safe, keeping your child safe, and taking advantage of the Internet's myriad uses. Tell your children not to be afraid to come to you with problems of any kind.

Teenagers . . .
Although the Internet is a great way to meet new people, do research, and chat with friends, there are dangers. Be aware of these dangers. Always use common sense. Although you may think that

bad things won't happen to you, they most certainly can. Be open with your parents about what you do online. Don't shut out the real people in your life, while letting those of cyberspace in. Don't spend all of your time on the Internet. Go outside and enjoy life beyond cyberspace.

Kids . . .

While it's great to chat with people in kid-safe chatrooms online, you should spend time with friends in real life. School, family, and friends should always come before the Internet. Always tell your parents about what you do online. Let them sit with you, and teach them about the Internet. When they do sit with you, don't get mad at them. Just know they care about you and don't want to see you hurt in any way. Always remember that people online don't always tell the truth. Don't give out a lot of information about yourself. If anything bad ever happens to you on the Internet, always tell your parents or someone you trust. Always remember that it's never your fault.

Amen!

Baltimore County
Public Schools
Telecommunications
Acceptable-Use Policy
for Students

Series 6166, Form A

Baltimore County Public Schools

Telecommunications Acceptable Use Policy for Students

Purpose of Telecommunications

Telecommunications extend the classroom beyond the school building by providing access to information resources on local, state, national, and international electronic networks such as the Internet. For students, telecommunications use in the Baltimore County Public Schools is for educational purposes, such as accessing curriculum-related information, sharing resources, and promoting innovation in learning. Learning how to use this wealth of information and how to communicate electronically are information literacy skills which support student achievement and success in the 21st century.

Information Available

- Government publications and databases
- Museums and art galleries
- Maps and other geographic resources
- Encyclopedias and dictionaries
- Magazines and newspapers
- Library catalogs and community directories

Telecommunications Safety

Precautions will be taken to attempt to ensure that the Internet is a safe learning environment. Students will be supervised while using the Internet and will be instructed in the appropriate and safe use, selection, and evaluation of information. Also, software which attempts to block access to objectionable material will be accessible on computer networks used by students.

Terms and Conditions

Students shall:

√ **Use telecommunications for educational purposes only.**

√ **Communicate with others in a courteous and respectful manner.**

√ **Maintain the privacy of personal name, address, phone number, password, and respect the same privacy of others.**

√ **Use only telecommunication accounts and passwords provided by the school.**

√ **Report any incident of harassment to the supervising employee.**

√ **Comply with copyright laws and intellectual property rights of others.**

Students shall not:

X **Knowingly enter unauthorized computer networks to tamper or destroy data.**

X **Access or distribute abusive, harassing libelous, obscene, offensive, profane, pornographic, threatening, sexually explicit, or illegal material.**

X **Install personal software on computers.**

X **Use telecommunications for commercial, purchasing, or illegal purposes.**

Disclaimer

The accuracy and quality of the information cannot be guaranteed. No warranties for telecommunications access are expressed or implied; BCPS will not be responsible for any information that may be lost, damaged, or unavailable due to technical or other difficulties.

Penalities

Violations of the Telecommunications Acceptable Use Policy may be a violation of law, civil regulations, or Board Policies 5550, 5570, or 5660. Suspension of telecommunications privileges, school disciplinary action, and/or legal action may result from infringement of this policy.

BCPS 1997   **Student and parent/guardian please sign on the reverse side.**

Dear Parent/Guardian:

We are requesting consent for your child to use telecommunications in school. This policy is intended to inform you and your child about the *Telecommunications Acceptable Use Policy* , as well as document your reply. Please read the information on the reverse side before signing this document. We encourage you to discuss with your child all of the information, especially the terms and conditions for acceptable and safe use and the penalties for misuse of telecommunications.

Please read, sign, and return this document to the school. Consent is required before your child will be permitted to use telecommunications in school.

Student User Agreement

Must be signed by all students.

I hereby agree to abide by the Baltimore County Public Schools Telecommunications Acceptable Use Policy. I further understand that any violation of the policy may be a violation of law, civil regulations, or Board of Education Policy 5550 - Disruptive Behavior, 5570 - Student Sexual Harassment, or 5600 - Students' Rights and Responsibilities. Should I violate the policy, my access privileges may be suspended, school disciplinary action may be taken, and/or appropriate legal action may result.

_____   _____

Student Signature   Date

Parent/Guardian Reply (Check only one .)

Must be completed if your child is under 18 years of age.

_____   I have read and understand the Baltimore County Public Schools
            Telecommunications Acceptable Use Policy. As the parent/guardian of
            the student signing above, **I grant consent for my child to have supervised
            access to telecommunications.**

_____   I have read and understand the Baltimore County Public Schools
            Telecommunications Acceptable Use Policy. **I have decided that my child
            will not participate in the use of the telecommunications.** My child will
            complete school assignments using other information resources.

_____   _____

Parent/Guardian Signature   Date

Questions regarding the Telecommunications Acceptable Use Policy should be directed to the
Deputy Superintendent, Baltimore County Public Schools

APPENDIX 2

Trevor Day School's Acceptable-Use Policy
Trevor Net

Revised 9/4/97

Policies and Guidelines for Use by All Members of the School Community

Introduction

Trevor Day School provides a data and communication network, TrevorNet, to facilitate communication within the School community and between that community and the global community. Ready access to information resources both in the school and outside the school provides academic support and promotes innovation. Resource sharing and communication both within the School and also with other educational institutions broadens and enriches the learning environment for students and faculty.

Network Resources

TrevorNet provides the same applications as are on each student's or faculty laptop: Microsoft Office, including Word, Access, PowerPoint, a scheduler program, etc. TrevorNet also provides reference databases such as the library catalog, electronic mail, word processing, multi-tool software, spreadsheet, database, etc. In addition, through TrevorNet, students, faculty and staff have access to the Internet.

The Internet

Several million computers worldwide are connected via the digital superhighway called the Internet. Every person using these connected computers can communicate and share information. Over the past 20 years the Internet has become a common repository for text based data, audio, still images, and video. The World Wide Web, a tool for finding information on the Internet, has made use of the Internet easier and more desirable. The Web has also made the Internet a new medium for publishing. Anyone with a computer, the appropriate software, and access to the Web can publish any information for world wide consumption.

Guidelines for Using TrevorNet and the Internet

TrevorNet is provided for the benefit of faculty, staff and students for academic purposes. The following guidelines have been established so that it can be used freely, safely, and efficiently.

Sharing Network Resources

The same respect for each other and responsibility for the consequences of one's actions apply on TrevorNet as anywhere else in the school. Like any other school resource, computer resources are shared, so priority should always be given to school assignments; and arrangements for sharing time on equipment should be negotiated fairly. Do not interfere with other people's work. Do not waste shared resources. Do not use language that is not appropriate in the school community.

Because school computers interact with TrevorNet in invisible but carefully designed ways, it is possible to make destructive changes without realizing it. No alterations should be made to the hard drives of any school computers: don't change settings, add or delete programs; and don't run programs from disks without permission of the Technology Department. It is improper and illegal to copy programs, to tamper with hardware, to alter files, or to enter certain areas of TrevorNet without authorization.

TrevorNet, both within and beyond the school, is a rich forum for debate. Its value lies in the meeting of many different minds. Harsh disagreement and personal attacks are not an acceptable use of TrevorNet at any time.

Passwords

Respect the confidentiality of passwords. Do not attempt to sign on as anyone else. Don't share your password with anyone, or ask for anyone else's password. Change your password when you think someone else may know it, and notify the Technology Department if you suspect passwords are being abused.

E-Mail

The same rules of civility for speaking or writing apply to e-mail. Language inappropriate in the school community is not permitted on TrevorNet. Before you send an e-mail message read it over to be sure it communicates the content and tone you want the receiver to read. Do not send unnecessary mail that wastes the receiver's time, and do not use up paper printing out your messages unless you need them for a class assignment.

Privacy

Privacy is valued and respected in the Trevor Day School community. However, TrevorNet storage areas are like school lockers in that the school has the right to examine the contents of the file server and any e-mail to maintain system integrity and ensure responsible use of the system. In order to foster independent thought, creativity, and intellectual development, the school will only examine files when there is reason to suspect any activity or material that violates the school's code of conduct or the law. This includes criminal activity, material that is obscene, material that is violent or actively encourages violent behavior, plagiarism or violation of intellectual rights or copyright laws, activity that endangers, demeans, threatens, or libels a person or persons, and material that denigrates people based on gender, race, ethnicity, disability, religious beliefs, or sexual identity.

Copyright and Plagiarism

Responsible users of information always acknowledge their sources, both in formal and in informal communications. Use information from the Internet in the same way you use information from any other public, published source: tell where the information came from to show that it's reliable. E-mail messages are private, and may not be quoted or sent on to anyone else without the permission of the original sender. Plagiarism—using someone else's words or ideas as if they are your own—is never acceptable and can be illegal.

Internet Access

Trevor Day School provides access to the resources on TrevorNet and on the Internet as an educational service. When used wisely these resources can significantly enrich and transform learning experiences. Freedom of access to the wealth of resources available on the Internet outweighs the risks of accessing material that is questionable or offensive. Each user of the Internet must recognize his or her responsibility in accepting this freedom of access.

Safety

Communication on the Internet can reach far beyond the communities in which Trevor Day School students and community members normally find themselves. Do not share your last name, photo, address, or phone number with anyone on the Internet. Notify a teacher or administrator if someone you only know from the Internet requests personal information from you or proposes to meet you.

Disclaimer Notice

Parents, students, faculty, staff and administration should be aware that:

Trevor Day School has no control over the content of the information residing on other computers connected with the Internet, or control over the identity of individuals having access to the Internet. Parents, students, and the adult community are therefore advised that connected computers may contain material that is illegal, defamatory, obscene, profane, inaccurate, abusive or threatening, racial or ethnically offensive, or otherwise objectionable. The administration and faculty of Trevor Day School do not condone or permit the use or viewing of such material, and persons are prohibited from bringing such material into the school environment.

_____

Faculty/Staff signature   Date

Student and Parent/Guardian Responsibilities
All students using TrevorNet or accessing the Internet through TrevorNet must indicate that they and their parent or guardian understand the responsibilities of exercising this access.

I have read the Trevor Day School Guidelines for Using TrevorNet and the Internet, and I understand the failure to follow them may result in loss of my network privileges and possible further disciplinary action.

_____

Student's signature   Date

I have also read these guidelines and understand the consequences for my child of his or her failure to follow them.

_____

Parent's signature (if student is under 18)   Date

This policy is based on policies provided by The Convent of the Sacred Heart, New York City; Friends Academy, Locust Valley, New York; and Bellingham Public Schools, Bellingham, Washington.

The Safe-Surfing Contract

My Agreement About Using the Internet

I want to use our computer and the Internet. I know that there are certain rules about what I should do online. I agree to follow these rules and my parents agree to help me follow these rules:

1. I will not give my name, address, telephone number, school, or my parents' names, addresses, or telephone numbers, or anything else that would help anyone find me offline (like the name of my sports team) to anyone I meet on the computer.

2. I understand that some people online pretend to be someone else. Sometimes they pretend to be kids, when they're really grown-ups. I will tell my parents about people I meet online. I will also tell my parents before I answer any e-mails I get from, or send e-mail to, new people I meet online.

3. I will not buy or order anything online or give out any credit card information without asking my parents.

4. I will not fill out any form online that asks me for any information about myself or my family without asking my parents first. This includes forms for contests or registering at a site. I'll also check to see if the sites have a privacy policy and if they promise to keep my private information private. If they don't promise to keep my private information private, I won't give them any private information.

5. I will not get into arguments or fights online. If someone tries to start an argument or fight with me, I won't answer him or her and will tell my parents.

6. If I see something I do not like or that makes me uncomfortable or that I know my parents don't want me to see, I will click on the "Back" button or log off.

7. If I see people doing things or saying things to other kids online I know they're not supposed to do or say, I'll tell my parents.

8. I won't keep online secrets from my parents.

9. If someone sends me any pictures, links to sites I know I shouldn't be going to, or any e-mail using bad language, I will tell my parents.

10. If someone asks me to do something I am not supposed to do, I will tell my parents.

11. I will not call anyone I met online unless my parents say it's okay.

12. I will never meet in person anyone I met online, unless my parents say it's okay and they are with me.

13. I will never send anything to anyone I met online, unless my parents say it's okay.

14. If anyone I met online sends me anything, I will tell my parents.

15. I will not use something I found online and pretend it's mine.

16. I won't say bad things about people online, and I will practice good Netiquette.

17. I won't use bad language online or threaten anyone, even if I'm only kidding.

18. I know that my parents want to make sure I'm safe online, and I will listen to them when they ask me not to do something.

19. I will help teach my parents more about computers and the Internet.

20. I will practice safe computing, and check for viruses whenever I borrow a disk from someone or download something from the Internet.

21. I will tell my parents when something bad happens online, because they promise not to overreact if something bad happens online.

I promise to follow these rules.
(signed by child / teen)

I promise to help my child follow these rules and not to overreact if my child tells me about bad things that happen in cyberspace.
(signed by parent)

APPENDIX 4

AOL's Parental Controls

As of the date of printing, AOL offered the following description of its parental controls (AOL keyword: parental controls):

Parental Controls Categories

Parents of children ages 12 and under, for example, should assign the KIDS ONLY category to their children's accounts. This restricts young children to the Kids Only channel. A Kids Only account cannot send or receive Instant Message(tm) notes (private real-time communications), cannot enter member-created chatrooms, cannot use premium services, and can only send and receive text-only electronic mail (no file attachments OR embedded pictures allowed).

Parents of teenagers might want to select YOUNG TEEN (ages 13–15) or MATURE TEEN (16–17). These provide more freedom, while still preventing access to certain features. Young Teens may visit some chatrooms, but not member-created rooms or private rooms. Both groups are restricted to web sites appropriate for their age categories. They are also blocked from Internet newsgroups that allow file attachments and they cannot use premium services.

Finally, the 18+ designation provides unrestricted access to all features on AOL and the Internet.

Note: These Parental Controls categories block e-mail attachments for some age groups but do not affect who your children can receive mail from. To control who can and cannot send e-mail to your children, click on Fine-tune with Custom Controls.

These age groups are guidelines. Since maturity levels of children vary, Parental Controls give you the flexibility to choose the right level of access for your child. For example, some parents may consider their 15 year old a "mature teen," while others may wish to maintain the "young teen" setting. It's up to you.

Custom Controls

After setting a control level, you can fine-tune the settings by using CUSTOM CONTROLS. This allows you to adjust specific activities, depending on the needs of your child, such as chat, the Web, e-mail, newsgroups, and file downloads. Remember that you may change the categories at any time, so you can adjust your children's access to best accommodate their maturity level or special needs.

Parental Controls Work by Screen Name

For Parental Controls to work, each child must have his or her own screen name. Your AOL account allows you to create up to five screen names. When you create a screen name, AOL automatically asks you to set a Parental Control level for that name. To create a screen name, sign on to AOL using a master screen name. (Master screen names are the first screen name you created when you joined AOL and any other screen names that have been designated as master screen names using Parental Controls.) Then click on the Create a New Screen Name button to the right.

If your children already have screen names, click on Set Parental Controls Now below.

Note: If your children use AOL immediately after you do, please sign off AOL, then close and reopen the AOL software before your children sign on with their own screen name. This ensures that all Parental Control settings will be in effect for that screen name.

Discussing Parental Controls

Parents can discuss their questions and share their online experiences regarding child safety on AOL and the Internet in our Message Boards.

Directory of Certain ISPs, Online Services, and Products Mentioned in the Book

America Online (AOL)
22000 AOL Way
Dulles, VA 20166
Tel: (800) 827-6364 (to order software)
    (800) 827-3338 (technical support)
Website: www.aol.com

AT&T (WorldNet Service)
55 Corporate Way
Bridgewater, NJ 08807
Tel: (800) WORLDNET
Website: www.att.com/worldnet

Bess (N2H2, Inc.)
1301 5th Ave., Suite 1501
Seattle, WA 98101
Tel: (800) 971-2622 (sales)
    (206) 971-1400 (technical support, Mon.–Fri., 8 A.M.–6 P.M., PST)
E-mail: techsupport@n2h2.com (technical support)
Website: www.n2h2.com

Cyber Patrol (Microsystems Software, Inc.)
600 Worcester Rd.
Framingham, MA 01701
Tel: (800) 828-2608 (to order software)
    (508) 416-1000 (technical support, Mon.–Fri., 8:15–5:45 P.M., EST)
    (508) 416-1050 (technical support, Mon.–Fri., 5:45 P.M.–11:45 P.M., EST)
E-mail: cybersup@microsys.com (technical support)
Website: www.cyberpatrol.com

CYBERsitter (Solid Oak Software, Inc.)
P.O. Box 6826
Santa Barbara, CA 93160
Tel: (800) 388-2761 or (805) 967-9853 (to order software)
    (805) 884-8204 (technical support, 9 A.M.–5 P.M., PST)
E-mail: support@solidoak.com (technical support)
Website: www.solidoak.com

INTERNET Explorer
One Microsoft Way
Redmond, WA 90852
Tel: (800) 360-7561 (sales)
    (425) 635-7123 (technical support)

Microsoft Network
One Microsoft Way
Redmond, WA 98052
Tel: (800) 386-5550 (general information)
    (813) 557-0613 (customer service)
    (206) 635-7019 (technical support)
Website: www.msn.com

Mindspring
1430 W. Peachtree St., NW, Suite 100
Atlanta, GA 30309
Tel: (800) 719-4332
Website: www.mindspring.com

Net Nanny
525 Seymour St., Suite 108
Vancouver, BC
Canada V6B 3H7
Tel: (800) 340-7177 (to order software)
 (604) 662-8522 (technical support, Mon.–Fri., 8 A.M.–5 P.M., PST)
E-mail: Nnsupport@netnanny.com (technical support)
Website: www.netnanny.com

Netscape
Tel: (415) 937-3777 (sales)
 (800) 639-0939 (technical support)
E-mail: personal@netscape.com
Website: home.netscape.com

Prodigy
455 Hamilton Ave.
White Plains, NY 10601
Tel: (800) PRODIGY (customer service & technical support)
Website: www.prodigy.com

Sprint (Sprint Internet Passport)
8140 Ward Parkway
Kansas City, MO 64114
Tel: (800) 747-9428
Website: www.sprint.com/fornet

SurfWatch (Spyglass, Inc.)
175 S. San Antonio Rd., Suite 102
Los Altos, CA 94022
Tel: (888) 6-SPYGLASS (technical support, Mon.–Fri., 7:30 A.M.–
 5:30 P.M., PST
E-mail: surfwatch_support@surfwatch.com (technical support)
Website: www.surfwatch.com

WebTV (Sony Electronics Inc.)
1 Sony Drive
Park Ridge, NJ 07656
Tel: (888) 772-SONY (sales)
Website: www.webtv.net/pc/wtvnet.html

Glossary

Applet: A small Java program that exists inside a Web page.

Bandwidth: The rate at which information can travel through the wire into your computer. Usually measured in bits per second. A full page of English text is about 16,000 bits. A fast modem can move about 30,000 bits in one second.

Baud Rate: How many bits can be sent or received per second.

Bps (bits per second): A measurement of how fast data is moved from one place to another. A 28.8 modem can move 28,800 bits per second.

Blocking Software: Special program that allows parents to "block" access to certain sites and information on the Internet.

Bookmark: A URL saved in your browser.

Bookmarking: The process of saving a URL in your browser that allows it to be recalled instantly in the future.

Browser: A program, such as Netscape Navigator or Microsoft's Internet Explorer, that enables one to surf the Web and view Web pages.

BBS (bulletin board system): A computerized "meeting" and announcement system that allows people to carry on discussions, upload and download files, and make announcements without being connected to the computer at the same time.

Byte: A set of bits that represent a single character. Generally there are eight or ten bits to a byte, depending on how the measurement is being made.

Cache: A device, usually RAM, used to temporarily store data. It is a timesaving feature that can be especially helpful on the Web, allowing the cache file in your computer to store sites that you have recently visited, so that you can get back to them quickly.

CD-ROM (compact disk-read only memory): Optical disks that can only be read (i.e., the data cannot be changed or deleted).

Chatroom: A virtual room where users can "talk" with each other by typing.

Client: The computer browser that "asks" for information. One computer can be a client and a host at the same time (see Host).

Cookies: A piece of information sent by a Web server to a Web browser that the browser software saves and uses to send back information to the server in the future.

CPU (central processing unit): The main internal component of a computer where executions of instructions are carried out and calculations are performed.

Cyberspace: Coined by author William Gibson in his novel *Neuromancer*, the word is currently used to describe the whole range of information resources available through computer networks.

Daemons: Small programs that perform specific tasks. For example, a program that "wakes up" to deliver a message upon arrival.

Disk Drive: The device that holds a disk, retrieves information from it, and stores information on it.

Domain: The last part of an Internet address—tells the type of general category.

Dot: The period character. For brevity people say "dot."

Download: To copy a file from a multiuser system (such as WWW or AOL) to your computer.

Emoticons: Computerspeak for "emotion icons" that describe tone, body language, or feelings [e.g., :-)].

E-mail (electronic mail): Messages, usually text, sent from one person to another via computer.

Ethernet: A very common method of connecting computers into a network.

FAQs (frequently asked questions): Documents that list and answer the most common questions on a particular subject.

File: A collection of information stored on a computer as a unit.

FTP (file transfer protocol): A way to copy or transfer files from one FTP site on the Internet to another. Files may contain documents or programs.

Flaming: Directing insulting or derogatory comments at someone through e-mail, newsgroups, or chatrooms.

Floppy Disk: A disk made of plastic that stores computer data.

Gateway: In general, any mechanism that provides access to another system-e.g., AOL might be called a gateway to the Internet.

Gopher: A method of making menus of material available over the Internet. Although Gopher spread rapidly across the globe in only a couple of years, it has been largely supplanted by the WWW (World Wide Web).

Home Page: Usually the first page of a World Wide Web site. From there you interactively explore that site.

Host: Any computer on a network that sends information to other computers on the network. It is quite common to have one host machine provide several services, such as WWW and Usenet. (See Client)

Hyperlink: The images or words on the Web that are linked to another url and give you access to new information with the click of a mouse. Textual hyperlinks are distinguished by their different color font.

Hypertext: The text that is a link to other documents.

HTML (hypertext markup language): The coding language used to create all Web pages.

HTTP (hypertext transport protocol): The protocol (set of instructions) for moving hypertext files across the Internet. HTTP is the most important protocol used in the World Wide Web (WWW).

Internet (uppercase I): The vast collection of interconnected networks that all use the TCP/IP protocols and that evolved from ARPANET in the late 1960s and early '70s.

internet (lowercase): Anytime you connect two or more networks together, you have an internet.

IRC (internet relay chat): A huge multiuser live-chat facility.

ISDN (integrated services digital network): A way to more data over digital phone lines. It can provide speeds of up to 128,000 bits per second over regular phone lines.

ISP (internet service provider): Any commercial institution that provides access to the Internet for a fee.

Java: A programming language that allows programs to be downloaded through the Internet and run immediately.

Keyword: On the Web, the words that you input into search engines to find information on a particular topic. On AOL, they are a single-word "shortcut" to get to a particular area.

Kilobyte: 1,024 bytes.

Link: Allows a viewer to click on a highlighted item on a WWW page and immediately link to whatever the HTML programmer wants them to see (hyperlink).

Login: The name used to gain access to a computer system (not a password); or the act of entering into a computer system (e.g., "Login to AOL").

Macintosh: A line of computers manufactured by Apple Computer.

Megahertz: 1,000 hertz. Often used to measure CPU speed (ex: 133MHz).

Megabyte: Approximately one million bytes (or one thousand kilobytes).

Modem: Abbreviation for modulator-demodulator. A modem is the device that enables a computer or terminal to communicate over a telephone line to another computer or computer network.

Newbie: Somebody new to the Net.

Netiquette: The etiquette of the Internet.

Netizen: A "citizen" of the Internet.

Network: Anytime you connect two or more computers together so that they can share resources.

Newsgroups: The name for discussion groups on Usenet.

Operating System: The program that boots up your computer and tracks and controls files, disks, memory, etc.

PICS (Platform for Internet Content Selection): PICS is a standardized format for rating systems. PICS is not a rating system itself. You use PICS to rate the content of a website for violence, nudity, and sexual content.

Plug-in: A small "program" that adds a feature to a bigger, more complicated program. Plug-ins usually cannot be used by themselves.

POPs (points of presence): The local access telephone numbers that an ISP has.

Processor: A chip that takes data, performs calculations, and returns the results.

Program: A set of instructions that can be executed to perform one or more tasks.

Protocol: The rules the browser uses to locate and retrieve files.

Posting: A single message entered into a network communications system; or the process of entering that message.

Rating Services: Services that rate websites. Most use a PICS standard for labeling.

RAM (random access memory): The memory that is used to keep programs open and run them.

Search Engine: A software program that allows a user to search databases by entering keywords. A search engine or vehicle quickly finds any item pertaining to those keywords.

Server: A computer, or a software package, that provides a specific kind of service to client software running on other computers. (E.g., "Our mail server is down today—that's why e-mail isn't getting out.")

Snail Mail: Traditional methods, such as the United States Postal Service, for sending a message.

Spamming: Inappropriate use of a mailing list by sending the same unsolicited message to a large number of people. The term probably comes from a famous Monty Python skit that featured the word "spam" repeated over and over.

URL (uniform resource locator): The address that tells the browser how to locate a Web page.

Web Page: A special file on the Web that uses hyperlinks to access text, images, animation, and sound, using a browser.

Website: A group of interlinked Web pages.

WWW (World Wide Web): The multimedia portion of the Internet, consisting of documents viewed using a browser.

Index

Page numbers of illustrations appear in italics.

A

About.com (website evaluators), 70
Acceptable use policies, 156, 172–174, 179
Accessories, child-size, 220
Adoptive parents online, 17
Advertisers online
    Ad Bug logo, 107–108
    alcohol and tobacco, 18, 75–76
    child-focused, 106–108
    click-through, 101–102
    cookies and, 101–103
    databases collected by, 98–100
    self-regulation, 108
    website revenue and, 23
Aftab, Parry
    acceptable use policies and, 181
    address of, 258
    case of Shannon/Tiffany, 195–199
    Danielle (niece) and computer literacy, 219–221
    e-mail address, 41
    internet website, 3
    loss of AOL account, 91–92

Aftab, Parry *(Cont.)*
    meeting with students, 261
    Norman Thomas High School sessions, 273
    rules for correct Internet behavior, 216–217
    safety chat with Mr. Toad, 229
    Seventeen Magazine survey, 261–263
    Wired Kids (kids' online project), 69, 108, 137, 151, 181, 259, 277–278
Age
    computer use, 219–221, 224–225
    e-mail requirements for use, recommended, 43–44
    IRC, 38
    and online use, 219–221, 224–225
Alcohol
    advertising, 18, 75–76
    sales online, 18, 61, 76, 142–144
Aliases online and lying, 190–191, 200–202
    Seventeen Magazine survey on, 264–266
Allen, Ernie, 148
AltaVista, 21
    Family Filter, 229–230
American Library Association (ALA), 278

American Library Association *(Cont.)*
Cool Sites for Kids, 230
Internet for Teens, 230
KidsConnect, 177
recommended sites for children, 26, 70
700+ Great Sites, 229, 230
website, 177
Anarchists' Cookbook, 73
Annenberg Public Policy Center,
University of Pennsylvania, survey,
223–225
Anti-Defamation League, 67
Anti-spamming sites, 32
Anti-virus software, 82–83
AOL (America Online)
approved vendors, 111
buddy lists, 47–48
buying and payment of items through,
209
chatrooms, 34
e-mail, 40, 41
instant messages, 44–47, 54
IP address, 146–147
mail control filters, 32–33
NetFind Kids Only, 228, 250
parental controls, 29, 46, 226, 251
privacy policies and law enforcement,
118–119
proprietary filtering products, 241, 248
"terms of service" (TOS) and loss of
account, 91–92
Ask Jeeves for Kids, 23, 228
AT&T, 45, 46, 241, 248
Auction sites, 109, 111–112
Auction Universe, 116
Avery KidsSite, 108

B

Baltimore Country, Maryland
PTA survey, 262
School System, PIE program, 177–178
Battaglia, Lynne, 145, 278
Beatty, Kelley, 85, 120

Bell Atlantic school Internet project,
156–157
Berson, Michael and Ilene, 262–263
Bess (filter), 250
Best Fares, 16
Better Business Bureau, checking online
vendors and, 111
Bickel, Bill, 78–79
Big Book of Mischief, The, 72
Blocking sites. *See* Filtering and blocking
software.
Bomb-building sites, 18, 61, 72–74, 166,
263
Bonus (kids' website), 15, 233
Bookmarks, 26–27
Bridge pages, 165
Brown, Jr., Paul, 126–127
Buddy lists, 47–48
Buying goods online
auction sites, 109, 111–112
brand names and online catalogs, 112
checking on vendors, 111–112
how to pay for items, 109–111
iCanBuy.com, 110, 111, 112–113
privacy policy of site, 112
teen spending, 109
where kids can buy safely, 112–113

C

Campaign to Stop Junk E-mail, 32
Carnegie Mellon, Software Engineering
Institute's CERT Coordination Center,
72
Chain-letters, 43
Chatrooms and chatting, 20, 34–39, 35
abuses, 37–38
acronyms, 36, 38
chat cops, 37
"cyber" (cybersex discussions), 35,
119–120, 201, 264–265
flaming and threats, 268–269
how they work, 35–36, *35*
IRC, 34, 35, 36, 38, 55–57

Chatrooms and chatting *(Cont.)*
　logging, 39
　lurkers, 34–35
　monitors, 37, 38
　parental supervision of use by preteens
　　and teens, 38–39, 210
　pedophile and sexually explicit, 35, 36
　secret codes (by kids), 38
　Seventeen Magazine survey on, 263,
　　268–269
　software blocking and other parental
　　control programs, 39
　types of, 34
Chevron Kids, 233
Children's Advertising Review Unit
　(CARU), Council of Better Business
　Bureaus, 108, 233
Children's Online Privacy Protection Act,
　43, 104–105
Children's Partnership, The, 70, 231
　Parents Online: Things You Can Do
　　with Your Children and Teens, 231
Children's Television Workshop, 232
ClickChoice myFilter, 253
Clinton, Bill, Norman Thomas High
　School, New York, letter to, 273–277
Coalition Against Unsolicited Commercial
　Email, 32
College application and financial aid in-
　formation, 15–16
Columbia University, Go Ask Alice, 258
Communication, parent-child
　cyberpredators and, 50
Computer crimes, 86–87
　financial loss from, 87
Condrey, Susan M., 157–159
Continental Airlines, 16
Cookies, 99–103
Copyright infringement, 18. *See also*
　Intellectual property and pirating
　software.
Crayon Crawler, 236, 254
Credit card use and information
　buying goods online with, 109–111

Credit card use and information *(Cont.)*
　checking on purchases, 76, 110–111
　dangers of, 11
　defensive parenting and, 208–209
　password protection for, 110, 207–208
　privacy issues, 18
　secure servers and transmissions,
　　110–111
　unauthorized use by children, 18, 92
　unauthorized use and fraud, 18
Curtis, Della, 177
Cyber hoaxes, rumors, urban legends,
　70–72
　checking on, sites to access, 72
　virus rumors, 71–72
Cyber Patrol, 239, 240, 243, 251, 254, 255,
　256, 258, *258*, 259
Cyber Snoop, 39, 249, 254
Cyberangels
　approved filtering product list, 259
　CyberMoms, 37, 230–231
　CyberMoms Approved Sites List
　　(CAST), 70, 231
　Cyber-911 project, 148
　cyberpredator help, 125
　cyberstalking advice, 120–121
　cyberstalking investigations, 5, 85
　KIDList (Kids in Danger List), 142
　KIDReportline, 166, 205–206
　Maggie's advice to parents on trust and
　　snooping, 270
　Teenangels, 200, 261, 277–279
　Teenangels' safety tips, 269–273
　Teenangels' tips for children, 285–
　　288
　Teenangels' tips for parents, 279–281
　Teenangels' tips for teens, 281–285
　tipline, 5, 148
　updating of site, 169
　volunteering for, 150–151
Cyberfriends
　case of Shannon/Tiffany, 195–199
　lies and, 190–191, 264–266
　meeting offline, 189–195, 263

Cyberfriends *(Cont.)*
  stalking and, 194–195
Cyberpredators. *See* Pedophiles.
Cybersex discussions, 35, 119–120, 201
CYBERsitter, 239, 243, 254, 255, 256, 258,
  258, 259
Cyberstalkers and harassment, 18, 43, 62,
  79–80, 116–121
  case of Shannon/Tiffany, 195–199
  cyberfriends and, 194–195
  fear and, 119–120, 267–268
  kids as, 83–85
  laws pertaining to, 141–142
  online stalking that moves offline, 119
  safety rules, 121
  teens and, 120
  three types of, 117
  typical victim, 118
  what parents can do, 121

D

Death threats/bomb threats, 84–86, 118,
  165–166, 203. *See also* Cyberstalking
  and harassment.
Deja News, 55
Directory websites and reverse searches,
  53–55
Discovery Channel for Kids, 232
Disk Tracy, 39, 249, 254
Disney, 232, 235–236, 251
  Blast Pad, 45, 46, 235–236
  Club Blast, 235–236
  Dig (search engine), 229
  Go (search engine), 21
  safety chat with Mr. Toad, 229
Domain names, 21
  site to check on, 24–25
  zone abbreviations, 25–26
DoughNET (e-commerce site), 112
Drugs
  illegal, 144
  sales, 76, 142–144
  websites, 18

Dundalk Middle School, 157

E

eBay, 109, 114, 115, 116
E-cash, 109
Edmark's KidDesk, 240, 252
Educating children for safe Internet use,
  226–227
  accountability, 200, 203–204
  aliases, and lying, 190–191, 200–202,
    209, 264–266
  community groups for, 151
  credibility of information, 69–70, 72
  credibility of online friends, 128
  credibility of websites, critical thinking
    and media literacy skills, 167–170
  general rules (list), 185
  good touch/bad touch information,
    188–189
  hurtful and hateful things, 66–67
  learning to listen, 183–184, 205
  meeting online friends offline, 189–195
  Netiquette, Ms. Parry's rules, 216–217
  personal information, not sharing,
    187–188, 195–202
  pornography, 63–65
  practicing online conversations, 189
  role models, 204
  safety rules for avoiding cyberstalkers,
    121, 210
  stranger danger online, 185–186
  Teenangels' safety tips, 269–273
  Teenangels' tips for children, 285–288
  Teenangels' tips for teens, 281–285
  tattling and tiplines, 205–206
  violence and gore, 68
  volunteering for online safety groups,
    150–151
Effective Readiness Plan (ERP), missing
  children response, 151–152
E-mail, 39–44. *See also* Spam.
  abuses and risks, 41, 42–44
  address components, 41

E-mail *(Cont.)*
    age requirements for use, recom-
        mended, 43–44
    AOL, 17, 29, 40, 41
    benefits of, 17
    bombs, 42, 86–87
    chain letters, 43
    children's read-out-loud software, 40
    configuring, 40
    dual accounts, 32, 50
    employer right to monitor, 92–93
    filters, 31–33, 249
    flaming, 42
    free accounts, 30, 41–42, 44, 54
    hoaxes, 70–72
    links, 43
    listings online, 42
    members' directory, 54
    parental controls, 44
    passwords, 41
    pornographic, 12, 28–29
    screening younger child's, 210
    spam, 12, 27–33, 42
    threats via, 85–86, 263, 268
    Trojan horses, 43, 82
    viruses, 42
    Web-based systems, 41–42
Emoticons (smileys), 37, 218
Employers, online computer use, and risk
    of job loss, 92
Ethical Hackers Against Pedophilia
    (EHAP), 5, 88–89, 149
eToys, 112
Exceptional children, parent contacts
    online, 17
Excite, 21, 41

F

Family Guidebook
    bad site lists, 150
    checking cache or history files, 147
    free speech information, 139
    information literacy program, 170

Family Guidebook *(Cont.)*
    instant messaging chart, 46
    password for, 3
    tiplines, 147
    website, 3
    website directory, 17
Family PC magazine, 6
Fantasies
    aliases, 200–202
    violent, online, 84–85, 205
FBI, 5
    arrest rate, 6
    computer crime financial losses, 87
    Innocent Images Unit, 5, 126, 144–146,
        148, 278
Federal Trade Commission (FTC), 43,
    104–105, 144, 146
    television ads for children, 107
    website, 146, 149
Filtering and blocking software, 236–237.
    See also Monitoring software.
    adding sites to, 25
    alerts, 247
    blocked sites and child's requests,
        184
    blocking versus filtering, 240
    bomb-building sites, 74–75, *258*
    controversy over, 238–240
    cost, 13–14
    drugs, alcohol, tobacco, guns, poisons,
        75–76, *258*
    effectiveness against tampering, 238
    e-mail products and spam filters,
        32–33, 44, 238
    feature overview, 240–241, 247–249
    graphics, 247
    hate sites, 67, *258*
    instant messaging and newsgroup sites,
        56
    levels of application, 237, 248–249,
        259–260
    percentage of parents using, 223
    pornography and sexually explicit sites,
        11, *258*

Filtering and blocking software *(Cont.)*
  problems with inadvertent blocking,
      242–243, 246, 258
  products and product review, 234–235,
      243, 244–245, 249–260, *258*
  proprietary software (works with
      certain online service), 248
  satanic and cult sites, 258
  server-level blocking, 249–250
  updating of, 243–244
  violence and gore, 68
  web browsers, child-safe, 43, 44
First Amendment (free speech) rights, 74,
    138–139, 140, 206, 210, 238
Flaming, 42, 52, 62, 78–79, 91
  cyberstalkers and, 119–120
  newsgroups, 55–56
  parental rules and, 186–187
Fleet Kids, 232–233
Fortune magazine, 86–87
Franklin, Ray, 66
Fraud, 18, 62, 114–115
  securities, 149
Freezone (website for preteens), 234
  chatrooms, 34
Friends online. *See* Cyberfriends.
FTP (file transfer protocol), 55–56
Fulton, B. Keith, 278

G

Gambling online, 61, 77
Game sites, 15
GAP clothes website, 16, 112
Good Times virus, 72
Gory websites, 18
  kids' interest in, 11
Gun purchases online, 18, 61, 142–144

H

Hackers, 18, 82–83
  e-mail and, 33
  kids as, 86–87

Hackers *(Cont.)*
  parental control of, 88–89
  Seventeen Magazine survey on, 267
Harvesting (information), 12, 29–30
Hatch, Charles, 129–133
Hate Directory, 66
Hate Filter, 67
Hatred, intolerance, bigotry online, 18,
    65–67
  Seventeen Magazine survey on, 263, 264
Headbone, 234
  bridge pages, 165
  chatrooms, 34
  instant messaging, 45
  website address, 46
Heaven's Gate cult, 6–7
Hot Bot, 22
Hotmail, 41, 44, 50, 115

I

IBM hype alerts, 72
iCanBuy.com, 110, 111, 112–113
ICQ (I seek you), 29, 44–47, 53, 54
Information and resources online
  college application and financial aid in-
      formation, 15–16
  current events, 14
  entertainment directories, 16
  games, 15
  global thinking, 16
  international pen pals, 16–17, 49–50
  movies and movie ratings, 16
  shopping, 16, 109, 111–114
  size of Internet as resource, 10
  special families, special kids online
      communities, 17
  sports information, scores, and sporting
      events, 15
  travel, 16
  24/7 access, 17
  writing skills and research, 16–17
Infoseek, 22
Instant messaging, 20, 44–47. *See also* ICQ.

Instant messaging *(Cont.)*
   abuses and risks, 45–48
   how they work, 45
   number daily, 44
   Seventeen Magazine survey on, 264
   what they are, 44–45
Intellectual property and pirating
   software, 89–90
   "fair use," 187
   rules about, 187
Internet. *See also specific topics.*
   benefits for families and kids, 13–17
   blaming, 6–7
   egalitarian environment, 65
   global nature of, worldwide standards
      and laws, 135–136
   kid-friendly content, 227–236
   importance of internet literacy, 1–2,
      11–12
   lowered inhibitions online, 120,
      264–265
   percentage of cyberspace dangers, 4
   percentage/number of children online,
      1, 13
   percentage, schools on line, 1
   questions most-asked on safety of,
      10–14
   risks for families and kids, summary, 18
   safe use in schools, 170–179
   trusting kids and, 3
   world's biggest billboard, 50–54
Internet Fraud Watch, 115, 116
Internet Scam Busters, 111
IP (Internet Protocol) number, 146–147,
   202
IRC (Internet relay chats), 20, 38
   chatrooms (channels), 34, 36, 56
   off-limits to children and pre-teens, 38
   parental control of, 56
   sexually explicit and pornographic
      channels, 35
ISP (Internet service provider). *See also*
   AOL (America Online).
   blocking or filtering, 249–250

ISP *(Cont.)*
   dislike of spam, 30
   e-mail filters, 32–33
   free filtering software, 241
   popular service choices, 30
   proprietary filtering products, 241, 248
   reporting harassment, cyberstalking,
      and hacking to, 149
   reporting sexual predators to, 149–150
   security departments, 81

J

Junk E-mail Resource Page, 31–32
Junkbusters, 31
Junior Net, 235
Juno, 41
Jupiter Communications, 59, 109

K

Kaplan Educational Centers website, 16
Keeping Kids Safe Online: Tips & Tools for
   Parents (Lipper & Lazarus), 231
KIDList (Kids in Danger List), 142
KIDReportline, 166, 205–206
KidsClick, 229
KidsCom website, 49, 234
   advertising on, 107
   chatrooms, 34
   ParentTalk, 234
   pen pal program, 49–50
KidsConnect (ALA site), 177
Kid-Space, 220
Kids Cam, 254
Kids of the Web, 246
Klaas, Polly, 161

L

Landsend, 16
Lap surfing, 220
Law enforcement agencies, 144–146
   cyber, 4

Law enforcement agencies *(Cont.)*
  cyberstalking and, 118–119
  FBI, 5, 6, 144–146
  finding and tracking people online,
      146–147, 202–033
  FTC, 43, 104–105, 144, 146, 149
  state and local cybercops, 5, 145, 278
  U.S. Customs Cybersmuggling Unit, 5,
      6, 144–146
Laws and legal issues, 12–13, 62. *See also*
    Hacking.
  child pornography, 136, 139–140
  criminal acts and, 137–138
  cyberstalking, 141–142
  cybertorts, 92
  First Amendment (free speech) rights,
      74, 138–139, 140, 206, 210, 238
  global nature of the Internet and,
      135–136
  intellectual property and pirating,
      89–90
  libel, 89
  off-school websites and
      harassment/libel issues, 164–165
  reporting crimes (tiplines), 147–149,
      205–206
  sales of drugs, alcohol, guns, tobacco,
      142–144
  schools and liability, 171, 175, 180
  schools and restricting non-curriculum
      speech, 167
  sexual predators in cyberspace,
      140–141
Lazarus, Wendy, 231
Links
  bridge pages, 165
  in e-mail, 249
  pornography sites, 28–29, 42, 43, 140
  website evaluation and, 169–170
Lipper, Laurie, 231
Littleton, Colorado, tragedy, 7, 204
  death threats/bomb threats and,
      165–166, 203
  hate sites and, 65, 67

Littleton, Colorado, tragedy *(Cont.)*
  school violence and, 273–277
  student websites and, 154
  Trenchcoat Mafia websites, 7
Lycos, 22, 23, 70
  Directory of Internet Kids' Sites, 231
  SearchGuard, 230
Lycos Zone, 234

M

Mahoney, Debbie, 148–149
Mamamedia, 234
Martinez, Jorge, 145–146
Mayberry U.S.A., 250
McAfee Anti-Virus, 82
MCI
  Smart Surfing panel, 26
  Worldcom, 241
Melissa virus, 42, 83, 87, 278
Metatags, 22–23
Microsoft (MSN), 45
  child protection, 251
Mindspring, 241, 248
Misinformation and hype, 18, 68–70
Monitoring software, 241–242, 247–248,
    248–249, 254
Movies and movie ratings, 16

N

National Center for Missing & Exploited
    Children, 4–5, 148, 152, 278
National Geographic for Kids, 232
National PTA, 67
Net Nanny, 32, 142, 225, 239, 240, 242,
    243, 254, *255*, 256, 258, *258*, 259
Netiquette, 187, 215–216
  acronyms, 36
  bad, 217
  cyberstalkers and, 79
  emoticon (smileys), 37, 218
  Ms. Parry's rules, 216–217
  newbies and stalkers, 118, 119

Netizens Against Gratuitous Spamming, 31
Netscape Kids' Directory, 232
Newbies, 118, 119
Newsgroups, 20, 55–56
Nickelodeon, 232
Noodles (kids' and preteens' community), 235
Norman Thomas High School, New York, letter to President Clinton, 273–277
Norton AntiVirus. *See* Symantec.

O

O'Leary, Bob, 145
Onsale online auction, 109, 111, 113–114, 114
Orange County, California, Single Gender research project (Fountain Valley School), 157–159

P

Parental controls. *See also* Filtering software; Parenting, defensive.
   age of child and use, 43–44, 219–220, 224–225
   Annenberg survey of parental rules and Internet use, 224–225
   avoiding witch hunts, 204–205
   bomb-building and other dangerous sites, 61, 72–74
   buddy lists, 47
   child-safe web browser, 43
   credit card statements, checking, 76, 77
   cyberpredators, 80–81, 128, 149–151
   cyberstalking, 79–80
   e-mail, 43–44
   filters, *see* Filtering and blocking software,
   flaming, 78–79
   gambling, 77
   hacking by kids, 87–88
   hate, bigotry, and intolerance, 66–67

Parental controls *(Cont.)*
   instant messaging, 46–47
   intellectual property rights, 89–90
   IRC, FTP, Usenet, newsgroups, 56
   levels of (list), 248–249
   location of computer, 88, 209
   long-distance phone bills, reviewing, 128
   Maggie's advice to parents on trust and snooping, 270
   monitoring online friendships, 128, 191–195
   monitoring software, 241–242, 247–249, 254
   online safety rules, 121
   pen pal programs, 49–50
   personal profiles and information online, 52, 54
   Polaroid camera, as gift from cyber-predators, 124–125, 129
   pornography, 63–65, *258*
   safe-surfing contract, 213–215
   school Internet use and, 169–174, 175–177
   surfing time limits, 186, 219–220, *see also* Monitoring software;
   surfing with your child, 184
   violence and gore, 68
   volunteering for online safety groups, 150–151
Parenting, defensive, 207. *See also* Parental controls.
   active involvement with child online, 211
   basic rules, 211–212
   checking hard drive and floppies for .jpg and .gif files, 210
   checking history files, 210
   cover your own tracks, 210
   credit cards, 209
   backup or password protect files, 208
   computer in family room, 209
   don't rely on software to protect your child, 211

Parenting, defensive *(Cont.)*
  passwords, 41, 207–208
  protecting children outside home and
      online, 208
  quiz, "Get to Know Your Kids," 212–213
  screening e-mail and chatrooms, 210
  seeing what's on the monitor, 209–210
  teach good Netiquette, 211
  Teenangels' tips for parents, 279–281
  two most important rules to teach, 210
  warning kids about lies online, 209
Parenting magazine online, 242–243
*Parents' Guide to the Information
    Superhighway* (Lipper & Lazarus),
    231
Parents' Guide to the Internet, A (Aftab),
    129, 144, 177, 226, 242, 259
Parents Internet Education (PIE),
    177–178
Passwords
  credit card information and, 110
  defensive parenting and, 207–208
  e-mail, 41
  Family Guidebook, 3
  teaching children not to share, 52, 91
PBS (Public Broadcasting System), 232
  Kids Online, 165
Pedophiles, 5
  anatomy of a real case, Paul Brown, Jr.,
      126–128
  avoiding and deterring, 80–81
  Charles Hatch case, 129–133
  chatrooms, 35, 36
  cyberpredators, 18, 62
  Effective Readiness Plan (ERP),
      missing children response, 151–
      152
  instant messaging and, 45–46
  laws applying to, 140–141
  offline meeting of, 12–13, 186
  personal information shared with,
      123–124
  profile of a cyberpredator, 122
  reporting, 147–149

Pedophiles *(Cont.)*
  risk of, 11
  seducing and tricking by, 119–120,
      124–125
  thwarting, 125
  tiplines for, 5
  "travelers," 145
  typical victim, 128
  UNESCO "Innocence in Danger"
      project, 137
  what to do if your child is missing,
      151–154
Pen pal programs, 16–17, 20, 49–50, 167
Personal information online, 61–62
  aliases, ethics of, 200–202
  case of Shannon/Tiffany, 195–199
  chatrooms, blocking dissemination of,
      39
  contests, 62
  directories, 53, 54
  filling out forms, 52
  parental control of, 54
  pedophiles and, 122–124
  photos, 195, 263
  profiles, 20, 51–54, *51*
  rules about, 187
  schools and children's pictures and
      personal information, 161–163
  Seventeen Magazine survey results,
      263, 265
  websites, personal, 20, 53
Photographs, sent or receiving online,
    161–163, 195, 263
Platform for Internet Content Selection
    (PICS)-compliant websites, 150, 245
Poisons online, 61, 144
Pornography, 61, 63–65
  arrests, 5
  child, 4, 5, 136, 139–140
  e-mail and, 12, 42, 43
  hard-core content, 11
  inadvertent exposure to, 11
  legality of, 13, 136, 139–140
  links, 43

parental controls, 64–65, *258*
Pornography *(Cont.)*
    preventing access (filters), 11, *258*
    proof of age requirements, 11, 13
    spams, 28–29
    typo-scams and, 24, 25
Pranks online, 91
Priceline, 16, 114
Princeton Review, 16
    Homeroom.com, 14
Privacy issues, 95–106. *See also* Credit
    cards.
    Children's Online Privacy Protection
        Act, 43, 104–105
    collecting and selling of private infor-
        mation, 18, 96–100
    directory websites and reverse
        searches, 53–55
    giveaways and, 100
    parents' concerns, statistics on, 97
    personal profiles and, 51–54, 53
    precautions to follow, 96
    registering for instant messaging, 46
    schools and children's pictures or
        personal information, 161–163
    tracking preferences, and cookies, 98,
        99–103
    website privacy policies, 105, 112
Prodigy, parental controls and kids online
    area, 251

Q

Quiz, "Get to Know Your Kids," 212–213

R

Ramapo Catskill Library System, New
    York, 229
Raskin, Robin ("Internet Mom"), 6–7, 68
Rating websites
    services, 245
    system (PICS), 150, 245
Registering information online

instant messaging, 46
Registering information online *(Cont.)*
    websites, 20
Reverse search services, 54
    online friends, contacting and, 192–193
    seller check-out, online auctions,
        115–116
    telephone numbers, 54
Risks. *See also* Bomb building sites; Cyber
        hoaxes, rumors, urban legends;
        Hatred, intolerance, bigotry;
        Misinformation and hype;
        Pornography; Violence and gore.
    kids' exposure to online, 63–83
    kids pose to others, and you, 83–93
    types of, 60–62
Rocketcash e-commerce site, 112
Ross, Gordon, 278
RSACi, 245, 251

S

Safe harbors (closed or semi-closed
        environments), 226, 233–235
Safe Surf, 245
Safe-surfing contract, 213–15
Safety tips, Alyssa's, Lauren's, Maggie's
        Seventeen Magazine survey partici-
        pants, 270–273
    Teenangels', 269–273
Satanic and cult sites, 6–7, *258*
Schools
    acceptable use policies, 156, 172–174,
        179
    cats in India Internet lesson, 159–160
    children's creative works, 163
    children's pictures and personal infor-
        mation, 161–162
    classroom computers, 156
    critical thinking and media literacy
        skills, 167–170
    death threats/bomb threats, 165–166,
        203
    filtering policies, 156, 173–176

Schools *(Cont.)*
  indemnification from parents, 175–
    177
  Internet access of, 1, 155
  issues confronting, 155–156, 161–163
  legal liability, 171, 175, 180
  library use of computers, 156
  linking to off-school sites, 165, 173
  off-school websites and, 164–165
  parental information about (notice and
    informed consent), 162, 171–172
  parental involvement, 177–178
  pen pal programs, 49–50, 167
  plagiarism (and term paper buying),
    163
  reportlines, 166
  restricting noncurriculum speech, 167
  sharing information between schools,
    166
  student websites, provocative, 166
  teaching troubled kids and Internet,
    157–159
  team-building for, 178–179
  Wired Kids cyberschool program, 151,
    181
Schumer, Senator Charles, 143
Search engines, 21–22
  award-winning, 70
  kid-friendly (filtered), 21, 23–24, 69–70,
    227–230
  most popular, 21–22
  problems with indexing titles, 22–23
  searches, 20
  site traffic and advertising, 23
  spiders or bots, 22, 53
Securities and Exchange Commission,
  149
Sellier, Homayra, 137
Seventeen Magazine survey, 261–263
  actions online that survey subjects
    wouldn't have done offline, 264–
    266
  frightening online situations, 267–269
  general results on safety, 263–264

Seventeen Magazine survey *(Cont.)*
  pretending to be someone else online,
    266
Sexual conduct and flirtation online, 35,
  119–120, 201, 264–265
Sexually explicit chatrooms, 35
Sexually explicit websites
  KIDList (Kids in Danger List), 142
  kids' interest in, 10–11
  filters for, 23, 254–259, *258*
  links to, 28–29, 140
  NASA.com, 25, 250
  search engines and, 23, 250
Shirey, Leanne, 145, 278
Shopping sites, 16, 109, 111–116
Simon Wiesenthal Center, 67
Single parents online, 17
Sliwa, Curtis, 148
Snap (NBC's search engine), 22
SOC-UM's (Safeguarding Our
  Children–United Mothers), 5, 142,
  148–149, 154
  Effective Readiness Plan (ERP),
    missing children response, 151–
    152
  volunteering for, 150–151
  website, 5
Spam, 12, 27–33
  harvesting, 12, 29–30
  how it works, 29–30
  ISPs dislike of, 30
  lack of legal restriction of, 31
  limiting, what you can do, 31–33
  name origin, 27–28
  sexually explicit links, 28–29, 140
  website to check anti-spam legislation,
    31
Spam Exterminator, 32
Spam Recycling Center, 31
Spiegel website, 16
Sports Illustrated online, 15
Sports Illustrated for Kids online, 15, 232
Stranger danger
  cyberpredators and, 81, 124–125

Stranger danger *(Cont.)*
  instant messaging, 46
  offline, 34, 186
  online, 33–34, 185, 210
Supervision by parents. *See* Parental
  controls; Parenting, defensive.
Surf Monkey, 40, 43, 44, 231, 235, 240,
  252–253
SurfWatch, 239, 243, 254, 255, 256, 258,
  258, 259
Symantec, 72, 82–83

T

Talk City, 34
Teenangels. *See* Cyberangels
Telephone numbers, reverse searches,
  54
Ticketmaster website, 15
Time for Kids, 232
Time limits and computer use, 186,
  219–220
Tobacco sales online, 61, 76, 142–144
Toys 'R' Us website, 16, 112
Travel websites, 16
Travelocity, 16
Trojan horses, 43, 82
Turow, Joseph, 224
Twain, Mark, 66
Typo-scams, 24, 25

U

United Nations (UN) child online safety
  effort, 137, 149
  U.S. National Action Committee, 177
  Wired Kids (UNESCO kids' online
    project), 69, 108, 137, 151, 181, 259,
    277–278
U.S. Customs
  Cybersmuggling Unit, 5, 6, 144–145, 278
  hotline, 147
U.S. Department of Energy's Computer
  Incident Advisory Capability page, 72

Usenet, 55

V

Violence and gore online, 67–68
  fantasy enactment, 84, 205
  Norman Thomas High School, New
    York, letter to President Clinton,
    273–277
  Seventeen Magazine survey on, 263
  websites, 18
Viruses, 18, 82–83. *See also specific*
  viruses.
  anti-virus software, 82–83
  e-mail, 33, 42, 71

W

Weather Channel online, 14
Web browsers
  bookmarks, 27
  cache or history files, 147, 210
  child-safe, 43
  rejecting cookies and, 103
Webcrawler, 22
  Kids & Family Channel, 232
Websites. *See also* Sexually explicit sites.
  About.com (website evaluators), 70
  approved site lists, 230–231
  bad-site lists, 150, 242–243
  child-safe sites, 69–70, 231–233
  club or destination sites, 235–236
  country codes, 26
  directories of, 53–54
  evaluating credibility of, 167–170
  "last updated," 169
  number of sites added per month,
    242
  parental permission to collection data
    from children and, 104–105
  personal, 20, 53, 162
  PICS-compliant sites, 150, 245
  privacy policies posted, 105, 112
  rating services, 245

Websites *(Cont.)*
  registering at, 20
  safe harbors, 226, 233–236
  safe-site lists, 26
  secure server code, 110
  student, provocative or controversial,
      166
  typo-scams, 24, 25
  zone abbreviations, 25–26
White Pages, 53–54
Wired Kids (kids' online project), 69, 108,
    137, 151, 259

Y

Yahoo!, 22, 23, 70
    free e-mail accounts, 41
    instant messaging, 45
Yahooligans!, 23, 229, 231

Z

Zeeks, 234–235
ZeekSafe, 235, 253
Zone abbreviations, 25–26